PARTNERS OF FIRST RESORT

PARTNERS
OF
FIRST RESORT

America, Europe,
and the
Future of the West

David McKean
Bart M. J. Szewczyk

BROOKINGS INSTITUTION PRESS
Washington, D.C.

The Brookings Institution is a private nonprofit organization devoted to research, education, and publication on important issues of domestic and foreign policy. Its principal purpose is to bring the highest quality independent research and analysis to bear on current and emerging policy problems. Interpretations or conclusions in Brookings publications should be understood to be solely those of the authors.

Library of Congress Control Number: 2021932885

ISBN 9780815738510 (pbk)
ISBN 9780815738527 (ebook)

9 8 7 6 5 4 3 2 1

Typeset in Adobe Garamond Pro

Composition by Elliott Beard

For my family
—David

For Carole and Chloé,
my partners of first resort
—Bart

Contents

Preface

A struggle is currently being waged for the soul of the West: to determine whether America and Europe can recover instincts for joint action or if they are doomed to pursue divergent paths. The election of Joe Biden as president of the United States augurs well for the prospect of potentially the most transatlanticist administration in decades. Yet, reinvigorating and reimagining the transatlantic relationship will be an uphill battle amid a plethora of competing priorities. Never has so much damage been inflicted to so many areas of American foreign policy by so few as during the past four years.

During an era of global disruption, the Western alliance itself has fractured and corroded. The dangers from this strategic drift have been particularly evident during the COVID-19 crisis: an earlier exchange of information and better coordination between the United States and Europe almost certainly would have saved countless lives and livelihoods instead of both regions becoming epicenters of the global pandemic. President Donald Trump's verbal assaults against NATO as "obsolete" and the European Union as a "foe" meant that the traditional spirit of transatlantic solidarity and cooperation was glaringly absent when the coronavirus crisis broke out in early 2020. In Europe, some leaders responded to Trump's rhetoric by calling for a break with the United States and a rebalancing with other great powers. Meanwhile, illiberal states such as China and Russia exploited these tensions within the West to proffer a new alternative for global success based around authoritarianism and state capitalism. Perhaps most worrying is the apparent normalization of a divided alliance—attributed to previously unseen long-term trends or reversion to historic norms—which risks becoming a self-fulfilling prophecy.

With the West seemingly poised at the edge of a cliff, some scholars recommended taking a great leap forward by recognizing the current divisions and formalizing an alliance of like-minded democracies (excluding the United States, at least for the duration of the Trump administration) to defend liberal values and multilateralism. Others counseled greater conservatism and scaling back ambitious goals for the liberal order. Still others sought to exploit the rift, seeking a post-liberal world. All these paths are blind alleys.

Instead, there is a smarter path toward the same liberal objectives that have animated the West and built a more peaceful, prosperous, and politically inclusive world order. What is needed is a "transatlantic renaissance": U.S. and European leaders need to come together to discuss and debate the future of the alliance with the goal of writing a new Atlantic Charter over the next few years. America and Europe still need each other as partners of first resort, out of strategic necessity and commonality of interests. Moreover, the world needs a vibrant and energetic West to protect its fundamental values from illiberal forces. Modernizing the institutional links will help better address common challenges.

We seek to offer a uniquely transatlantic perspective on current foreign policy debates, both in the United States and in Europe. We both have had the privilege of serving at the State Department in the Obama-Biden administration: David as director of the Policy Planning Staff and Bart as member of the staff responsible for Europe and Eurasia. Founded in 1947 by Secretary of State George C. Marshall, the Policy Planning Staff has a long tradition as one of the offices within the U.S. government responsible for strategic thinking and policy innovation. Portraits of former directors, such as George Kennan and Paul Nitze, that hang in the seventh-floor Policy Planning offices, reminded us of our unique responsibility and opportunity to link "thought with action," as Zbigniew Brzezinski (another Policy Planning alumnus) once argued.

We served during a time of increasing crises in the West—Russia's aggression, terrorism, and China's assertiveness—and sought to recalibrate U.S. policy accordingly. Through policy planning talks with our counterparts around the world, we were able to exchange views on basic philosophy toward foreign policy and general strategic approaches, as well as specific policies the U.S. government was pursuing or evaluating, whether in Ukraine, Syria, or China. Invariably, we recognized what President Obama called "an enduring truth of American foreign policy"—that "our relationship with our European allies and partners is the cornerstone of our engagement with the world, and a catalyst for global cooperation."[1]

Although it is now fashionable to focus on the decline of the transatlantic alliance, the West still commands half of global GDP and military spending, just as it did after World War II. It is also important to recognize that relations between Europe and the United States were much more an equitable partnership during the Obama-Biden administration than during any of the preceding decades.

Over the past four years, as senior fellows at the German Marshall Fund, we have observed a drastic deterioration of the transatlantic relationship. From our respective locations in Washington, DC, and Brussels, Belgium, we conducted numerous interviews with former and current senior American and European officials, seeking to develop a better strategy for the United States and Europe as pillars of the wider liberal order. The resultant book, *Partners of First Resort*, is certainly longer than any policy planning memo but follows the same basic analytical framework: assess the state of play; identify core interests and objectives; develop policy options; and recommend courses of action. At the very least, we hope to resurrect the not-so-distant memory of transatlantic partnership under the Obama-Biden administration that we experienced firsthand; though flawed in certain respects, it can serve as a sound basis for thinking creatively about an even better relationship in the years to come. Since the modern institutional foundations of the West were established, the intellectual task has never been more urgent. However, we firmly believe that as heirs to seven decades of peace and prosperity, American and European leaders have the responsibility to update the current architecture to meet the challenges of our time. Having served as informal advisers to the Biden campaign, we are confident that the new Biden-Harris team will help seize this once-in-a-generation opportunity.

Acknowledgments

I served in government for twenty-five years, including five years at the Department of State, where I was fortunate to work for one of our nation's greatest public servants, Secretary of State John Kerry, as his Director of Policy Planning. At Policy Planning, known in the Department by its acronym S/P, I was also fortunate to have assembled a staff that included some of the smartest and most capable strategic thinkers in Washington, DC.

Just as he did when we served at Policy Planning together, Bart has brought his intelligence, creativity, and hard work to this book. I could not have asked for a better co-author. I also want to especially thank two other former members of Policy Planning: Andrew Imbrie and Michael Kimmage, both of whom provided critical insight as well as helpful edits and comments. Since leaving S/P, both Andrew and Michael have written first-rate books on foreign policy.

I would also like to thank Michael O'Hanlon, Director of Research in Foreign Policy at Brookings and a long-time friend, for his support and encouragement. Bill Finan, director of the Brookings Institution Press, does herculean work in overseeing Brookings' publications. We would like to thank Bill for recognizing the importance and timeliness of our book, and for his consistent and expert help in guiding the publishing process. We also would like to thank Cecilia González and Elliott Beard for shepherding this project under the unusual conditions surrounding COVID-19.

Finally, I want to thank my wife Kathleen for her unwavering support. I also want to thank my daughter Kaye, who read portions of the manuscript. Kaye is a second-year student at the Fletcher School of Law and Diplomacy and perhaps one day will be a policy planner herself.

—David

In 2014, David brought me onto his Policy Planning Staff at the State Department, where he assembled the most talented group of people I ever had the honor of working with. Over the years, he has become not only a great boss, but also a wonderful mentor, colleague, and friend. I could not imagine a better coauthor and am confident this partnership will endure. He and his wife Kathleen were kind enough to travel to southern France to attend my wedding. And writing this book with David has been a true privilege.

Public service at the State Department, as well as at the U.S. Mission to the United Nations, was an unparalleled experience. The ethos, morale, and dedication far exceeded any other place in which I have served. The work was also profoundly meaningful and often incredibly fun. There were too many wonderful colleagues to list everyone, but special thanks go to my other two bosses in government, Jon Finer and Samantha Power, who epitomize the best in public service.

My wife Carole and baby daughter Chloé were boundless sources of support, joy, and inspiration during this process, for which I am eternally grateful. Home daycare amid a pandemic is not necessarily as conducive to research and writing as a library or office. But it is infinitely more enjoyable, as any writer's block is quickly diffused by laughter or new games. Time constraints also help focus the mind, making the two or three hours during naps remarkably productive. It is commonplace to say, but no less true, that periods of crisis clarify what is truly important, such as love and health. I could not be luckier than to have Carole and Chloé by my side. It is to them that the book is dedicated.

—Bart

PARTNERS OF FIRST RESORT

Turning and turning in the widening gyre
The falcon cannot hear the falconer;
Things fall apart; the centre cannot hold;
Mere anarchy is loosed upon the world,
The blood-dimmed tide is loosed, and everywhere
The ceremony of innocence is drowned;
The best lack all conviction, while the worst
Are full of passionate intensity.

—*W. B. Yeats,*
The Second Coming (1919)

It can sometimes seem like the order
that we've created is fragile,
maybe even crumbling;
maybe the center cannot hold.

—*Barack Obama,*
remarks in England (2016)[1]

Introduction

June 4, 1989, Warsaw, Poland: Gary Cooper is featured in campaign posters in a sheriff's uniform with *Solidarność* (Solidarity) at his back and a voting ballot in his hand. As much as anything, this iconic image (sometimes replaced with Ronald Reagan's photo) embodied the spirit of 1989—a sense of optimism, confidence, openness, and the seeming success of liberal democracy and market capitalism—that permeated the West. In the first free elections in the Soviet bloc, this poster, adapted from the popular Western film *High Noon*, captured the imagination throughout the streets of Poland. As Poles voted overwhelmingly in favor of the anticommunist Solidarity party, the world knew that the battle for freedom was won and the Cold War was nearly over. A few months later, the Berlin Wall fell, and in two years, the Soviet Union itself disintegrated.

With the collapse of communism, President George H. W. Bush called for a "new world order" characterized by "the rule of law rather than the resort to force, the cooperative settlement of disputes rather than anarchy and bloodshed, and an unstinting belief in human rights."[1] In the 1990s and early 2000s, the golden age for liberalism, institutions such as NATO and the EU rapidly expanded, and China was welcomed to the WTO to help support its political and economic liberalization.

September 15, 2008, New York, NY: The collapse of the investment bank Lehman Brothers shook the foundations of the international financial system and wiped out a staggering $10 trillion in market capitalization from global equity markets over the following months—the largest decline on record at the time. The subprime mortgage crisis—whereby U.S. homeowners were extended unsustainable levels of debt at rates that did not reflect the underlying default risk—spread like wildfire across the world, forcing systemic restructuring of U.S. financial markets and the car industry through a $700 billion bailout fund. The S&P 500 stock market index would eventually bottom out in March 2009 at half of its peak the previous year. The U.S. unemployment rate doubled to nearly 10 percent, and housing prices—the main asset for many Americans—decreased by over 30 percent, more than during the Great Depression of 1929. Millions of Americans lost their homes, livelihoods, wealth, and hopes for the future. According to one economic historian, U.S. household wealth losses reached close to "$21–22 trillion—$7 trillion from real estate, $11 trillion in the stock market and $3.4–4 trillion in retirement savings." Overall, median household wealth "halved from $107,000 to $57,800."[2] In Europe, the financial crisis erupted the following year, with negative effects continuing to reverberate for several years as austerity measures required by the public bailouts entailed significant cuts in government spending, which, in turn, precluded faster recovery. Depending on the country, household wealth declined between 10 and 50 percent.

On both sides of the Atlantic, liberalism became associated with deregulation, irresponsibility, and recklessness. Even worse, the liberal order appeared to many to be rigged: it delivered prosperity for the global elite but stagnating wages for the middle class.[3] Moreover, economic globalization helped countries such as China and Russia increase their wealth but without effectuating political reform; in fact, both grew more authoritarian as they became richer.

The story of the West is a struggle between the hopes of 1989—a year that celebrated the success and enlargement of the liberal order—and the fears of 2008—a year remembered for its internal challenges and external threats from illiberal actors. The main question for the current moment in time is whether leaders will live up to their best aspirations or succumb to panic and doubt.

———

For our purposes, the West is interchangeable with the liberal order, and the transatlantic partnership is its core engine. It is less a geographic description than a reflection of a set of political and economic ideas that originated in Western Europe and North America during the Enlightenment.[4] More succinct and more resonant than other monikers, such as the "liberal international order" or the "rules-based global order," the "West" developed a crisp identity during the Cold War in juxtaposition to the Soviet bloc, and now includes a broad geographic scope, including countries such as Australia, Japan, and South Korea. In the United States, it also seems to have greater bipartisan resonance, making it a more viable strategic concept.[5]

"Order" refers to any set of institutions, rules, and norms created to govern state and nonstate behavior, through international law as well as political norms generated through state practice.[6] Its primary objective is to minimize violence and provide stability, and it can be liberal or illiberal (for example, the Soviet bloc). And its opposite is "disorder," characterized by war, conflict, and uncertainty.

"Liberal" connotes a specific set of institutions, rules, and norms— democracy, human rights, rule of law, market economy, and free trade— designed to promote political and economic freedom. These values, universal in aspiration, are, nonetheless, partial in reality.[7] In contrast, an "illiberal" order is characterized by authoritarianism, arbitrariness, and nonmarket economies.

Any order (international or domestic) is best envisioned as a complex quilt, with layers and threads incorporated over time and with varying degrees of coverage and protection. The liberal order—often referred to historically as the "free world"—was a new vision to organize international politics and governance after the devastation of World War II.[8] It sought to transcend balance of power politics and eschew concepts of spheres of influence, though its underlying theory was based more on hope than experience.

As John Ikenberry has written, new international orders historically tend to arise in the aftermath of great power conflict.[9] After World War II, the liberal order was established with the overarching objective of achieving and sustaining a lasting *peace*. Both the European Communities (EC) and NATO were constructed as peace projects to prevent conflict from within and deter aggression from the outside. An integrally related interest was the creation of *prosperity,* not only to raise the standard of living but also to help sustain peace. Economic stability reduced the potential causes of conflict and provided the liberal order with the material resources necessary to protect it from external threats. Over time, economic security became synonymous with national security. The final core interest was *political inclusion,* through democratic processes, rule of law, and protection of human rights. Whereas other orders could provide peace (as, for example, the bipolar balance of power during the Cold War), and perhaps even prosperity (as, for example, in China), only the liberal order considered the individual as the central actor with inalienable rights. Like prosperity, liberal democracy was an end in itself, but also served the wider cause of peace; democracies were viewed as less likely to go to war with one another and more likely to sustain peace than prior balance of power models.[10]

Since the end of World War II, the liberal order's phenomenal growth and overall attractiveness has obscured periodic critiques of the order. With an accumulation of challenges over the past decade—Russian aggression; China's assertiveness; economic crises; terrorist attacks throughout Europe and the United States; large-scale flows of refugees and migrants into Europe; Russian interference in European and American elections; Brexit; and the rise of illiberal populist movements—the transatlantic alliance has been overwhelmed and now faces an existential crisis, with broader consequences for the liberal order and global stability.

In addition to the many political and economic challenges, Donald Trump's election as president of the United States in 2016 shook the foundations that undergirded the liberal order for the past seven decades and exacerbated a preexisting feeling among many on both sides of the Atlantic that the transatlantic alliance was unraveling.[11] The COVID-19 pandemic and its global political and economic consequences further upended basic assumptions. Yet, more important than any particular challenge is the psychological loss of a common lodestar and joint "sense of purpose," as argued by former U.S. Deputy Secretary of State Bill Burns.[12] The damage left in the wake of the Trump administration requires addressing several fundamental choices, but the recent election of Joe Biden as president offers hope that America and Europe can develop a new set of organizing principles to guide their decisionmaking.

There is currently both the need and the opportunity to make institutional adjustments and, more importantly, to reaffirm the values of the liberal order, while acknowledging geographic limitations. This will not be easy given that the global environment is less permissive than the twenty-year interlude between 1989 and 2008, when the United States reigned as the only global superpower and liberal democracy served as the benchmark for global success. The late Zbigniew Brzezinski likely reflected the ethos of the Cold War and zeitgeist of the Barack Obama–Joe Biden administration in assuming the necessity of the West without making an affirmative case for it.[13] For instance, he argued that the United States should be a promoter and guarantor of the West and a balancer of the East.[14] However, in the current and near-term geopolitical context, there is no integrated East as a strategic power, and Western unity is also open to question. With the rise of China and the disruptive role adopted by Russia, the geographic scope of the liberal order no longer aspires to be global.[15]

The struggle between democracy and autocracy, and the attendant global challenges, demand new joint transatlantic strategies and an innovative framework for global implementation. For instance, the Paris Call for Trust and Security in Cyberspace, signed by fifty-four countries (including all twenty-seven EU member states) and hundreds of companies and organizations, is likely to be ineffective without U.S. support. Conversely, a U.S. confrontation with China over intellectual property rights and technology is, undoubtedly, weakened if European countries ultimately embrace Huawei, join the Belt and Road Initiative, or provide support to China in the World Trade Organization (WTO). Another example of mutual transatlantic dependence was the standoff during the past four years over the Iran nuclear deal (the Joint Comprehensive Plan of Action, JCPOA) crafted by the United States and its European partners in 2015; notwithstanding its "maximal pressure" campaign of economic sanctions on Iran, the Trump administration was unable to overturn that agreement. Finally, there have been more than 100 vaccines being worked on around the world to confront COVID-19, most of them based in Europe and the United States, but the Trump administration failed to even show up at an EU-led global fund-raising summit to help support these research efforts. Now that a couple of vaccines have proven effective, to ensure efficient and fair distribution across the globe, the United States and Europe must collaborate. To paraphrase Franklin Roosevelt, the pandemic has shown that if your neighbor is sick, you are in danger—and with globalization, everyone is a neighbor.[16]

European leaders, in contrast to Donald Trump, generally recognized there was no realistic alternative to working with the United States in addressing their foreign policy concerns. For instance, Dutch Prime Minister Mark Rutte stressed this strategic necessity when he delivered the Churchill Lecture in February 2019:

> Our transatlantic bond may change, [but] it will never become weak or obsolete. There's too much at stake on both sides of the Atlantic. Europe and the US share many values and interests. We are the bedrock of freedom, democracy and the rule of law. We are the world's biggest trading partners. And together, we form the world's most powerful military alliance. The simple truth is this: if Europe succeeds, America benefits, and vice versa.[17]

The European Commission's former Secretary-General Martin Selmayr put it more succinctly in a speech at Brookings in March 2019: "we have to work together."[18] And former President Jean-Claude Juncker noted in *Politico* in June 2019 that any U.S. president deserves Europe's respect by sheer virtue of the position and its importance to Europe's security.

Given declining relative shares of global GDP and an assertive China, which increasingly has the material resources and political will to shape a world order on its illiberal terms, neither America nor Europe will be able to address their challenges alone. But together—by pooling nearly half of the world's material resources and defense spending—they are stronger than any single competitor or coalition of adversaries and can succeed in protecting their strategic interests.[19] For Washington, the road to success in foreign policy—whether confronting Beijing, Tehran, or Moscow—leads through synergies with Brussels and other European capitals, and vice versa for Europe.

This strategic necessity should compel transatlantic cooperation, and, generally, the history of transatlantic relations since 1945 offers a sound foundation for a common future. Despite this logic, Europe and the United States risk drifting apart. Though we believe President Trump's foreign policy represented an aberration rather than the culmination of previously unseen trends or the reversion to prior historical norms, self-fulfilling misperceptions of prior transatlantic disunity may lead to discord beyond his presidency. America and Europe risk losing each other as partners of first resort due to the bad blood and acrimony generated by Trump.

For its part, Europe has spent the last four years focused almost exclusively on Brexit negotiations and what Britain's withdrawal will mean for the future of the European Union. The EU published numerous White Papers and scheduled a series of summits on various issues internal to Europe, such as migration, jobs, and security. French President Emmanuel Macron called for a "European renaissance" ahead of elections in May 2019 for the European Parliament, which German leaders also embraced. In 2020, the EU-27 launched a two-year process on the "Future of Europe" that called for civic debates in town halls, boardrooms, and living rooms across the European continent. But in our view, this question cannot be addressed without discussing the transatlantic relationship.

In fact, there is not much dialogue, let alone vision for the future of the West. For example, Germany, which has for decades been a leading supporter of the transatlantic alliance, released in 2018 a new strategy toward the United States, calling for realignment in U.S.-European relations, balancing with other great powers, and for greater European strategic autonomy. Most foreign policy experts in Europe focus on issues such as European defense or European sovereignty, but without significant analysis as to what any of it means for the health and future of the transatlantic community.[20] At the Munich Security Conference on "Westlessness," in 2020, German President Frank-Walter Steinmeier concluded, the "we of the West that was [previously] taken as given is something that can no longer be taken for granted."[21] President Macron also noted the current "weakening of the West" but did not offer any ideas to address it, instead focusing solely on European strategy and "sovereignty."[22] In so doing, Macron framed Europe's choice as between transatlantic cooperation and strategic autonomy: whether European countries will prioritize relations with the United States (as preferred by Poland or the United Kingdom) or prioritize action at the European level (as preferred by France). Germany and many other EU member states tend to oscillate between the two views depending on the issue and the interlocutor.

Europeans have also weakened the alliance with unhelpful remarks, though their rhetoric is hardly on a par with Trump's. For instance, in 2019, French President Macron preceded the NATO leaders meeting in London by calling the institution brain dead, questioning the guarantee of Article 5, and arguing for Europe as a "balancing power."[23] Though German Chancellor Merkel and British Foreign Secretary Rabb immediately repudiated his statements, the French president exposed a deep rift among the Europeans that has been building for years.[24]

———

As calls for separation grow louder on both sides of the Atlantic, there are currently a number of critics offering a variety of alternatives to the transatlantic alliance. For instance, some dismiss the prospect of maintaining the transatlantic partnership—even with a Biden administration—as a "common but delusional hope" due to the decoupling of interests resulting from power asymmetry.[25] Instead of seeking cooperation, they argue that the United States should embrace Europe's strategic autonomy, even if the two sides eventually clash on policies. In a variation on the theme, other skeptics proposed an alliance of like-minded democracies in Europe and Asia, excluding the United States for the duration of the Trump administration, in a so-called G9 to defend the liberal order.[26]

However, we believe the rationale for a strong transatlantic partnership remains as compelling as ever, and the alternative proposals are seriously flawed. For instance, the G9 proposal would have only accelerated the divisions within the alliance and make them more difficult to overcome in the future. In any event, the idea had little support within the G9 countries themselves. Moreover, since World War II, national interests have frequently pulled American and European decisionmakers in separate directions. The art of effective statecraft requires overcoming these challenges through better default instincts and institutional structures for cooperation that help define a common interest.

There are other scholars who doubt the long-term viability of the West but acknowledge its importance and recommend refocusing the liberal order's sights onto more limited horizons. They argue for the need to conserve what has been attained rather than expand it further.[27] This approach, which might seem attractive in theory, is a cul-de-sac in practice. For instance, Jennifer Lind and William Wohlforth criticize NATO for offering membership to North Macedonia but understate the importance of NATO's open-door policy and its right to choose its allies. NATO has succeeded precisely because it has maintained its ability to change with the times, and given the variety of new challenges, it must continue to do so.

Last, some have argued that the debate about the West is somewhat outdated, claiming that the world has moved to a post-Western conception of international order, given the perceived decline of the West and the relative rise of the rest of the world. Fareed Zakaria views this as a positive development and argues that the global economy grows when more nations participate—"more consumers and producers, investors and inventors"— which inures to the benefit of the United States.[28] In contrast, Charles Kupchan argues that the norms of liberal democracy, industrial capitalism, and secular nationalism were a product of social and economic conditions unique to Europe and America, and, thereby, not necessarily transferable to other parts of the world. With the rise of other emerging powers, such as China, Russia, India, Turkey, and Brazil, he maintains that the world eventually will be organized into multiple orders with multiple models of modernity and standards for global success.[29] Kupchan recommends that the United States and Europe accommodate this transition and seek a new consensus on legitimacy, sovereignty, and global governance.

Whereas Kupchan contends that the future world order will be no one's, but, rather, organized around various models of legitimacy and governance, Parag Khanna predicts that the future will be centered on an Asian system.[30] Given the shift of global economic activity to Asia and emerging commercial and diplomatic links among Asian countries, he claims that the Asian model will be the global standard.

The approaches by Zakaria, Kupchan, and Khanna strike us as either too optimistic, too passive, or too defeatist. It is certainly possible that illiberal global trends will prevail over democratic forces and develop new sources of political legitimacy that the current international system will need to embrace. It is also possible that, in the future, China's sheer economic scale will translate into commensurate political influence and ability to reshape the world in its image. Fortunately, however, the balance of material resources still lies in the West's favor. It is equally possible, and certainly preferable in our view, that globalization will return to a Western model with the transatlantic alliance providing global leadership.[31]

———

We believe the presidential election of 2020 was critical to the future of the West, as it offered a basic choice between two competing visions of foreign policy: the transatlantic partnership as the core engine of the wider liberal order versus an ethno-nationalist and illiberal West.

The Obama-Biden administration came into office with global aspirations for the liberal order. It elevated the promotion of a "just and sustainable international order" as one of four enduring U.S. national interests (in addition to security, prosperity, and values).[32] It stressed the centrality of international institutions such as NATO and the UN to the success of the international order, and considered the relationship with Europe to be "the cornerstone for U.S. engagement with the world, and a catalyst for international action."[33] In 2015, in the aftermath of Russia's aggression in Ukraine, the administration doubled down on its commitment to the international order, arguing it had "an opportunity—and obligation—to lead the way in reinforcing, shaping, and where appropriate, creating the rules, norms, and institutions that are the foundation for peace, security, prosperity, and the protection of human rights in the 21st century."[34] It stressed the need for "a rules-based international order that promotes global security and prosperity as well as the dignity and human rights of all peoples."[35] Yet, universalist aims for the liberal order have generated backlash from illiberal powers such as China and Russia, with destabilizing effects both for the West and the world.

The Trump administration's 2017 National Security Strategy eschewed any mention of the "rules-based international order," let alone a liberal order, focusing its analysis, instead, on great power competition, putting "America first" and seeking "national greatness."[36] At the G7 summit in Canada in 2018, the United States sought to delete any references to the rules-based international order, and Trump withdrew his consent to the final communiqué purportedly based on this issue. Trump had little lasting foreign policy impact, reportedly subordinating all decisions to his reelection goals. Yet, his administration sowed the seeds for an even darker scenario: transforming the West into a vehicle for illiberalism, autocracy, and state capitalism.[37]

Any realistic future strategy will need to acknowledge that Russia and China are unlikely to democratize and, instead, will seek to promote their own versions of illiberal order. In limiting its geographic ambitions, the United States will need to focus on building up strength within the liberal order. Indeed, near the end of his administration, President Obama noted that "there appears to be a growing contest between authoritarianism and liberalism right now," and that he was "not neutral in that contest," aiming merely for any order that is based on rules. Instead, he emphasized, the United States should lead a "liberal political order: an order built not just through elections and representative government, but also through respect for human rights and civil society and independent judiciaries and the rule of law."[38] On the eve of leaving office, President Obama emphasized the "great responsibility" that comes with the "leadership of the free world"[39]— echoing the Cold War language and signaling that the West must prepare for a struggle pitting liberal democracy against illiberal autocracy.[40]

———

As the United States and Europe enter the eighth decade since the end of World War II, we believe a liberal, open, and enlightened concept of "West," with the transatlantic partnership as its core engine, continues to be an idea worth preserving. To better understand our view of the West and its potential, it is necessary to briefly review where it has been and how we have arrived at this moment.

As we recount in chapter 1, in the aftermath of World War II, the United States and its European allies created a new world order through a series of economic and political institutions. Though the order has been extraordinarily successful, especially for the West, strains in the transatlantic relationship have occurred at various times, and the alliance's history is replete with examples of leaders who miscalculated or disrupted accepted norms. In chapter 2, we describe how, during the Obama-Biden administration, the United States and Europe each provided global leadership, yet it was often unclear to what extent they remained the indispensable partners that had worked so closely together during the Cold War and its aftermath. In chapter 3, we chronicle the damage that President Trump has inflicted on the transatlantic relationship and provide an assessment of the current state of the relationship. After providing a historical perspective, we lay out a strategic vision to reinvigorate the transatlantic alliance, with a series of practical steps that begins with the need for a new Atlantic Charter.[41]

Thomas Jefferson once noted that each generation of leaders and citizens inevitably determines its own political norms and priorities in light of historical experience and with a view to the future. Due to the broad, deep, and historic commitment to common values shared across societies and governments in Europe and the United States, a vast amount of good will and trust built up over the decades has, thus far, preserved the relationship even as it has hit rock bottom. Indeed, given the assaults it has faced during the past four years and the erosion of trust, the transatlantic relationship's resilience has been nothing short of remarkable, though it will require substantial repair. Reinvigorating the transatlantic partnership will be not only crucial for the wider West but also for global order. Thus, the affirmative case for the continued necessity of a vibrant and strong alliance—a "transatlantic renaissance"—needs to be made anew.[42]

1

Establishment and Expansion of the Liberal Order (1941–2008)

> One of the great contributions of statesmanship at the end of the Second World War was the creation of the Atlantic partnership because it reflected the reality that neither Europe nor the United States would by themselves be able to bring about a solution of the chaos that had been created.
> —*Henry Kissinger, remarks at Davos (2017)*

The West was not built in a day. With remarkable foresight, even as they were still immersed in the fog of World War II, transatlantic leaders set out the organizing principles for a postwar world. Following the Allied victory, they created a number of multilateral institutions—the United Nations, NATO, and, later, the European Communities among them—that, together, became the foundation for the contemporary liberal order. In hindsight, the path may appear to have been self-evident, but the choices were not always clear, and the decisions often were contested.

At each juncture, both U.S. and European leaders ultimately determined that their strategic interests were intertwined and that they were better off working together. The liberal order, which generations of policymakers constructed, would eventually mature into a real partnership in the Barack Obama and Joe Biden administration.

ATLANTIC CHARTER

President Franklin Roosevelt first met Winston Churchill in 1918, when Roosevelt served as assistant secretary of the Navy and Churchill was minister of Munitions. Their encounter had not gone well, with Roosevelt recalling that Churchill was "a stinker." For his part, Churchill did not even remember meeting the much younger Roosevelt.[1]

Roosevelt was elected America's thirty-second president in a landslide victory in 1932, in the depths of the Great Depression. Churchill became Britain's prime minister in May 1940, only hours after Germany invaded France but months after Neville Chamberlain, his predecessor, naively proclaimed in the wake of the 1938 Munich Agreement with Chancellor Hitler that he had secured "peace in our time." Upon hearing the news that Churchill had replaced Chamberlain, Roosevelt declared, "He is the best man for the job."

In August 1941, with war raging in Europe and before the United States entered the fight, President Roosevelt met with British Prime Minister Churchill aboard the HMS *Prince of Wales* off the coast of Newfoundland, Canada. It was the first time they had seen each other in twenty-three years. Both leaders had sought the meeting, which had been facilitated by Roosevelt's respected aide Harry Hopkins. At the president's direction, Hopkins had spent six weeks in Britain in early 1941 and gained the trust of Prime Minister Churchill; Hopkins facilitated the eventual delivery of "Lend-Lease," U.S. military and economic assistance to Great Britain.

Now, three years after the Munich Agreement, as war destroyed much of Europe, Roosevelt and Churchill committed to defeating Hitler's Germany and rebuilding the future. At home, facing opposition from an isolationist public and a recalcitrant Congress, President Roosevelt had, nonetheless, successfully rammed the Lend-Lease program through the U.S. Congress to provide war materiel to Great Britain as well as later to the Soviet Union. Though the United States had not created a formal alliance with either country, Lend-Lease represented a fledging partnership with both nations in the fight against Hitler's Third Reich.

In their meeting off the Newfoundland coast, Roosevelt and Churchill discussed war strategy, but more important, they laid out their common vision for a postwar world in a joint statement later known as the Atlantic Charter. The charter set out eight common principles that not only cemented their alliance but, in many ways, laid the foundation for a new international order.

Roosevelt, though not an intellectual, was well acquainted with European history; he rejected the two previous historical pillars of European order: the first being the balance of power between nations—the foundation of the 1648 Peace of Westphalia—and the second being the restoration of empire based on nationalistic objectives—the overriding principle that emerged from the Congress of Vienna in 1814.[2] Balance of power and nationalism had at various points in its history been at the heart of British international relations, but Churchill recognized that Britain, though still a formidable empire, had suffered extraordinary losses in both blood and treasure, and would need to assume—at least until victory was at hand—the role of junior partner to the United States.

In the interests of transatlantic unity, the Atlantic Charter papered over profound differences in the way President Roosevelt and Prime Minister Churchill viewed the world. The charter called for the restoration of self-government to those deprived of it. While this principle was most clearly directed to those nations occupied by Hitler's army, such as France, Poland, and Czechoslovakia, it also included, as both leaders undoubtedly understood, such valuable British colonial possessions as India, Australia, and South Africa. Likewise, the charter made clear that there should be no territorial changes against the wishes of people belonging to a sovereign nation—again, an area where the United States and imperialist Britain had starkly different histories and, therefore, different perspectives.[3] To be sure, the United States had its own imperialist episodes at the turn of the twentieth century, with Puerto Rico, Cuba, and the Philippines, and its troubled history of land seizure from Native Americans. By World War II, however, those impulses had faded, and the United States conceived of its global role in liberal terms to make the world safe for democracy.

Roosevelt had long believed that free trade promoted economic prosperity, and on this matter, he and Churchill were in complete agreement. They also issued the somewhat vague call for "global cooperation to secure better economic and social conditions for all." Other areas of agreement between the two leaders included the need in the future "for freedom on the seas, abandonment of the use of force, and the disarmament of aggressor nations." Since assuming the office of president in 1933, Roosevelt had been pushing for a global disarmament conference and agreement but had encountered British resistance, which he found deeply annoying and detrimental to the goal of peaceful coexistence. By specifying in the Charter that only "aggressor nations" should be disarmed—an obvious reference in Europe to Germany and Italy—the president and the prime minister made clear that only Western-style democracies would retain military power. Of course, Roosevelt was fully aware that Great Britain in 1941 was essentially bankrupt, and would, along with the rest of Europe, need to rebuild its economy. President Roosevelt did not foreclose the potential for Great Britain and France to rearm, but at least for the foreseeable future, the United States would control the agenda. Of course, both Great Britain and France did eventually become nuclear powers, but only the United States would claim the mantle of superpower.

Perhaps the most aspirational component of the Atlantic Charter was the goal that nations should work together to achieve "freedom from fear and want," a goal that echoed Roosevelt's "Four Freedoms" speech delivered seven months earlier, and one that resonated with the "New Deal," his domestic program for economic relief and recovery from the Great Depression.

The president acknowledged that the Atlantic Charter did "not provide rules of easy application." However, he insisted that "it was a good thing to have principles" so that humanity has something to aim for. He hoped the Charter would take its place beside other historically important declarations, such as the Magna Carta, "as a step toward a better life of the people of the world."[4]

Although Roosevelt would not live to see the end of World War II, the Atlantic Charter inspired many of the postwar institutions that comprised the liberal order. The United Nations, NATO, and the General Agreement on Tariffs and Trade (GATT) are all, to some extent rooted, in the vision that Roosevelt and Churchill laid out on a ship off Newfoundland in 1941.

Preparing to rebuild the international economic system while World War II was still raging, 730 delegates from all forty-four Allied nations gathered at the Mount Washington Hotel in Bretton Woods, New Hampshire, in July 1944, to attend the United Nations Monetary and Financial Conference, also known as the Bretton Woods Conference. Believing the Great Depression had been exacerbated by a tendency for nations to look inward, to act independently, and to make shortsighted economic and financial decisions, delegates chose to create an economic community—undergirded by multilateral institutions—to rebuild the global economy.[5]

The delegates deliberated for three weeks, eventually signing the Bretton Woods agreement on July 22. Setting up a system of rules, institutions, and procedures to regulate the international monetary system, these accords established the International Monetary Fund (IMF) and the International Bank for Reconstruction and Development (IBRD), which today is part of the World Bank Group.

Although a majority of the delegates adopted the agreement, the deal had been primarily negotiated between the United States and the United Kingdom. The final draft reflected the impending postwar economic dominance of the United States, which controlled two-thirds of the world's gold. U.S. negotiators insisted that the Bretton Woods system rest on both gold, which had replaced sterling as the international reserve currency, and on the U.S. dollar.[6]

Soviet representatives attended the conference but later declined to ratify the final agreements, claiming the United States manipulated the conference to create institutions that were "branches of Wall Street." This was an early sign of a clash between ideologies that would devolve into the Cold War. Nevertheless, after ratification of the Bretton Woods agreement in late 1945, a new international economic infrastructure became operational the following year. A half-century later, Bowman Cutter, a former deputy chair of the National Economic Council under President Clinton, described the agreement as "perhaps the most successful and sustained effort to create a community of cooperating nations in the history of the world." According to Cutter, "it produced a rapid postwar reconstruction in Europe and the subsequent flourishing economies of the West. It was sufficiently flexible to include recent World War II enemies, Germany and Japan." Most important, as Cutter notes, "It made vast improvements in the lives of hundreds of millions of all these nations. And it played a crucial role in strengthening the Western democracies, enabling them to sustain successfully a fifty-year confrontation with the Soviet Union."[7]

UNITED NATIONS

The European Allied nations, as well as the Soviet Union, had recognized the importance of unity when confronting the Axis powers, but in 1945, they had very different visions for the postwar order. The economies of Europe were in desperate shape. The United States emerged from World

War II not only with the strongest military but with the strongest economy, as well. As Henry Kissinger wrote, "American idealism and exceptionalism were the driving forces behind the building of a new international order."[8] The responsibility for that world order and the indispensability of American power fell to President Harry Truman, a man with virtually no experience in international relations. Truman's first test would be to realize a critical component of the Atlantic Charter's vision by establishing the United Nations.

On April 25, 1945, representatives of fifty governments from around the world met in San Francisco for a conference convened to draft the Charter of the United Nations. Adopted in June, the organization's objectives closely tracked a number of the principles laid out by Roosevelt and Churchill four years earlier in the Atlantic Charter, including maintaining international peace and security, protecting human rights, and upholding international law. At its founding, the United Nations had fifty-one member states, but from the beginning, its mission to preserve world peace was complicated by competing visions of international order by the Europeans, the United States, and the Soviet Union.

The Soviet Union, decimated by war, had lost 25 million people, but its leader, Joseph Stalin, was determined that the American vision of a new international order—with the United States at its center—should not go unchallenged. As Kissinger has written, Marxist ideology challenged the legitimacy of Western institutions, rejecting them "as forms of illegitimate exploitation."[9]

In the end, the United Nations adopted a dual mechanism for decisionmaking that provided member nations an open and transparent forum for discussing differences and potentially finding common ground but also hampered both the efficiency and the effectiveness of the institution. Delegates agreed that the UN General Assembly would be universal in membership and based on the doctrine of "one state, one vote." However, the real power within the organization—most notably authorizing the use of force outside of each country's inherent right to self-defense—would be vested in the UN Security Council, consisting of the five major powers: the United States, Britain, France, the USSR, and China, along with a rotating group of additional countries (currently ten nonpermanent members). The "permanent members," as they are known, would have veto power over any resolution adopted by the Security Council.

However, the compromises made to ensure maximum participation in the United Nations turned out to be incompatible with the emerging reality of existential conflict between the West and the Soviet bloc. Instead of allowing free and fair elections in the Central and Eastern European countries it controlled, and thereby abiding by the UN Charter's principle of noninterference in domestic affairs, the Soviet Union installed puppet regimes and imposed its will across the region. Fault lines emerged between the liberal order of the West and the illiberal order of the Soviet Union as spheres of influence became the new balance of power. The liberal vision of the Atlantic Charter as embodied through the UN would be put on hold until nearly a half-century later. Instead, its global ambition became more geographically delimited through regional programs and institutions, such as the Marshall Plan and NATO.

MARSHALL PLAN

During World War II, the Nazis destroyed most of Europe's great cities, including some of the continent's leading industrial, financial, and cultural centers. By 1945, General George Marshall received reports indicating that entire regions of Europe were on the brink of famine because the fighting had disrupted agricultural production and halted food distribution. In addition, both Allied and Axis bombing had destroyed the region's transportation infrastructure; railways, roads, bridges, and ports had all suffered extensive damage and would need to be rebuilt. Moreover, the shipping fleets of many countries had been incapacitated and, in some cases, decimated.

Planning the postwar occupation of Germany—as well as rebuilding the rest of Europe—turned out to be a chaotic, cumbersome, and often contentious process involving a number of governments and their respective bureaucracies. The democracies of Europe were organized differently, and the level of expertise within their governments varied greatly. Even when there was agreement among governments on policy and organizational issues, as Kenneth Weisbrode has pointed out, "There was never a system in place for implementing a single set of recommendations at wartime conferences."[10]

In February 1946, the deputy chief of mission at the U.S. Embassy in Moscow, George Kennan, opened his so-called "Long Telegram" by stressing that the "USSR still lives in antagonistic 'capitalist encirclement' with which in the long run there can be no permanent peaceful coexistence."[11]

The following month, Winston Churchill argued that an "iron curtain" descended across the continent threatening the return of the "dark ages."[12]

Although Churchill pointed to a special relationship between the United States and the United Kingdom as the necessary condition to resist Soviet expansion, the British Empire was running out of resources and could not sustain its global commitments. In particular, the British government stated in February 1947 that it would terminate all of its economic and military aid to Turkey and Greece, exposing them to Soviet influence and domination. To forestall this turn of events, President Truman announced the following month a significant aid program to both countries, totaling over $4 billion dollars in current terms.

In a speech at Harvard in June 1947, U.S. Secretary of State George C. Marshall pointed to the dire economic situation in Europe and the need for U.S. resources over several years to sustain it. Shortly thereafter, Kennan captured the emerging strategic thinking within the U.S. government, arguing that "the main element of any United States policy toward the Soviet Union must be that of a long-term, patient but firm and vigilant containment of Russian expansive tendencies."[13]

In this strategic context, the Marshall Plan, also known as the European Recovery Program, was developed to provide much-needed aid to Western Europe. Enacted by the U.S. Congress in 1948, the Department of State disbursed more than $15 billion (over $150 billion in current terms) over a four-year period to help finance rebuilding efforts on the continent, including the reconstruction of cities, industries, and infrastructure that had been heavily damaged during the war. The plan was the brainchild of Marshall and his aides, but as Kissinger has pointed out, it was President Truman who had made a "strategic choice fundamental for American history and the evolution of the international order."[14]

It could be argued that the Marshall Plan reflected a certain strain of Eurocentrism in post–World War II U.S. foreign policy: as Dean Acheson, the secretary of state who succeeded Marshall, stated, "Europe, we had always believed, was the world."[15] Yet, the emphasis on Europe was not an end in itself, but rather part and parcel of the U.S. interest in shaping a wider liberal order that would ensure peace, prosperity, and political inclusion at home.

The Marshall Plan also envisioned the removal of trade barriers between the nations of Europe—as well as between Europe and the United States. As price controls and other trade restrictions were lifted and currencies were stabilized, Western European countries began to expand to markets abroad and to greatly expand intra-regional trade. West Germany led the way with exports increasing by an average of 16 percent per year between 1948 and 1962.[16]

As the economies of Western Europe improved, the Soviet Union was locking in territorial gains in Eastern Europe. The United States was not especially worried about Soviet military aggression directed at some of the poorer countries of Central and Eastern Europe but, rather, focused on Soviet exploitation of social upheaval and political disarray facing the continent.[17] In addition to economic redevelopment, one of the stated goals of the Marshall Plan was to halt the spread of communism on the European continent.

America's role as the leader of a new global order was hardly undisputed. Many in Europe, devastated by six years of war, accepted America as a "European power," but even within Europe, there were competing visions. Jean Monnet, a former cognac merchant turned politician, pushed for a united Europe—one allied with the United States but, nevertheless, distinctly European.[18] Secretary of State Acheson and the U.S. Department of State were strongly supportive of a transatlantic alliance but had reservations about both the feasibility and advisability of a united Europe. Given its long history of war and nationalism, Acheson argued there was no guarantee that a united Europe would remain allied or even friendly with the United States. New mechanisms were necessary to facilitate transatlantic cooperation.

NATO

The Atlantic Charter's commitment to disarm aggressor nations addressed only the immediate security needs of Europe; the Charter omitted any language charging the democratic nations of the world to ensure lasting peace and provide long-term security. In the spring of 1947, British Foreign Secretary Ernest Bevin, concerned about Soviet ambition, encouraged newly appointed Secretary of State George Marshall to convene a conference of like-minded allies to establish a transatlantic defense treaty. Bevin's concept ran contrary to America's long-standing position, dating back to President George Washington, of avoiding, as Washington put it, "entangling alliances."

Chip Bohlen and George Kennan, two rising diplomatic stars in the

Truman administration, argued that Bevin's concept would backfire because Congress would never sign on to a peacetime military alliance. Additionally, Kennan argued that "non-Atlantic" countries, such as Italy, Greece, or Turkey, should not be included in the proposed North Atlantic alliance; otherwise, Kennan claimed, no geographic limits could be drawn, as countries around the world would seek protection against the Soviet Union and the United States would overextend itself. Nevertheless, Bevin continued to press the issue at every international gathering, and offered language to an early draft committing all signatories to respond together in case of attack. In addition to the United States and Canada, only European states would be able to join. Bevin's plan would evolve into Article 5 of the North Atlantic Treaty: if one member of NATO was attacked, the other member nations would come to its defense. This notion of collective defense appealed to Secretary of State Marshall.[19]

After months of negotiation, in April 1949, representatives from Belgium, Canada, Denmark, France, Iceland, Italy, Luxembourg, the Netherlands, Norway, Portugal, the United Kingdom, and the United States gathered in Washington, DC, to establish the North Atlantic Treaty Organization (NATO). President Truman participated in the ceremony and delivered a six-minute speech that, in many respects, echoed President Roosevelt's call for Lend-Lease nearly a decade earlier. Truman maintained that the national representatives of twelve nations had come together in the interest of preserving the peace, like "a group of householders in the same locality." He viewed the treaty as a bookend to the Marshall Plan, emphasizing the need for "a cooperative economic effort." However, the Senate still needed to ratify the treaty, and Truman knew that isolationism still ran through the veins of many senators. As historian Derek Leebaert has noted, "the treaty's name—the North Atlantic Treaty was . . . necessary to emphasize the security of defending ocean, the Atlantic, and not of the sinful continent, Europe."[20] The NATO proponents in the Truman administration were fervent Atlanticists who successfully persuaded members of the Senate that, to check the Soviet Union, an alliance with Europe would be in the national interest. The treaty was ratified on April 12, 1949. In 1952, Greece and Turkey became members of the alliance, joined later by Germany in 1955 and Spain in 1982.

THE GERMAN QUESTION

West Germany—a political entity created by the United States—was not originally included in NATO, a decision consistent with the original promise of the Atlantic Charter that World War II aggressor nations should disarm. Even more important, by 1949, Germany had emerged as a flashpoint in Europe between the Western democracies and the Soviet Union.

At the conclusion of World War II, the Allies divided Germany into four zones, with the United States, Britain, France, and the Soviet Union each controlling a zone. In 1946, reparation agreements broke down between the Soviet Union and the Western zones after France, Great Britain, and the United States merged their zones in 1947.

By combining the three Western zones into one area, the West hoped to revive the battered German economy. However, the Soviet Union feared the combined zone would threaten it politically by potentially subsuming its area. On June 24, 1948, one day after the Western powers introduced a uniform currency into the Western zones to facilitate trade with the rest of Europe, the Soviet Union imposed the Berlin Blockade to block Western assistance to West Berlin. The blockade ultimately failed, but it signaled the start of the Cold War and the West's determination to halt Soviet expansionism in Europe

Aligned with the democracies of Europe and with the United States, West Germany eventually became a member of NATO in 1955, but it was not without substantial controversy and opposition, both from within Germany and from its neighbors, especially France, which had serious reservations about permitting its former adversary to rebuild its military.[21] Indeed, French foreign minister Robert Schuman—one of the founding fathers of European integration—vigorously opposed German rearmament.

Nevertheless, President Dwight D. Eisenhower and Secretary of State John Foster Dulles prevailed. They had a clear set of objectives for Germany. First, they wanted Germany integrated into the Western community of nations, as Secretary of State Dulles put it, "to diminish danger [of] resurgent German nationalism." Second, they wanted to contain the Soviet Union, which by 1953 had become a nuclear power. And third, they wanted to solidify the United States' leading role in Western Europe.[22]

Spurred on by the creation of the Council of Europe in 1947, many countries in Western Europe experienced a convergence of national interests during the 1950s. Britain and France, once mighty empires, began to shed their global colonial possessions. Consistent with its commitment to the Atlantic Charter, but with extreme controversy and difficulty, Britain navigated the emergence of Pakistan as it separated from India in 1947. Three years later, India gained its full independence. France, which had not been a party to the Atlantic Charter, became mired in a military quagmire in Algeria, which, after a protracted, bloody war, gained independence in 1962.

However, for the most part, the rapidity with which Britain, France, and other European nations separated from their former colonies during the decade of the 1950s was stunning: Britain from nearly twenty former colonies and France from fifteen. Though decolonization denied Britain, France, and other European nations the imperial status they had once enjoyed, it had little negative effect on their growing national economies. One of the most significant components of the Atlantic Charter had been successfully realized, but the question still remained: How could Europe come together so that war would never again divide it?

EUROPEAN COMMUNITY

Besides serving as an important transatlantic security pact, NATO represented the first step toward European unity. West German Chancellor Konrad Adenauer stated to President Eisenhower: "there is a saying that the Americans are the best Europeans, and there is much truth to that."[23] Not long after the creation of NATO, the French offered an economic proposal for cooperation with the Germans, the Schuman Plan, in the area of coal and steel, key industries on the continent. Four other countries joined the Schuman Plan—Belgium, the Netherlands, Luxembourg, and Italy—creating an incipient common European economic system. Trade among the six countries expanded, with steel production rising over 40 percent over the next few years. In 1957, the six nations established a formal structure under the European Economic Community (EEC) with the goal of eliminating tariffs and abolishing customs barriers. By 1963, the EEC had emerged as the leading exporter and importer of raw materials and a global powerhouse in steel production. Perhaps most significant, EEC countries collectively boasted a population of 165 million consumers.

Great Britain had pegged international trade initially to the Commonwealth and their relationship with the United States. However, as Europe prospered, Britain saw its trade and economy as comparatively uncompetitive with the nations of the EEC. In 1961, Britain began talks to join the EEC, but French President Charles de Gaulle vetoed their application for membership in both 1963 and 1967. De Gaulle claimed that "a number of aspects of Britain's economy, from working practices to agriculture" had "made Britain incompatible with Europe," and that Britain harbored a "deep-seated hostility" to any pan-European project. In 1973, after de Gaulle had left the stage, Britain's application was finally approved.[24] Great Britain's participation in the EEC not only benefited its economy but, as the EEC evolved eventually into the European Union, London served as a kind of portal for the United States into Europe, greatly strengthening the transatlantic relationship in the process.

To meet the needs of the growing economy, Europe welcomed an influx of immigrants. In 1961, the foreign-born population in Great Britain totaled approximately 2.5 million. Belgium and Switzerland had an even higher proportion of immigrants, though most were from other parts of Europe and not from overseas. In France, the number of Algerians who immigrated doubled over the course of the decade to approximately 700,000.[25] Notwithstanding these high levels of immigration, the countries of Europe never relinquished a strong sense of their national identity. Unlike the "melting pot" of the United States, Europeans remained more homogenous and less welcoming to "outsiders." Issues surrounding immigration have been debated for decades in Europe, but would not reach their apex until 2015.

While Western Europe enjoyed unparalleled economic growth during this period, it also became increasingly ensnared in the nuclear arms race conducted by the United States and the Soviet Union. In 1950, the United States had fewer than 300 nuclear weapons, but by 1962 it had more than 27,000. Although the Soviet Union had nowhere near the capacity of the United States, it rapidly expanded its arsenal of nuclear weapons. The Soviets shocked the world in April 1957 when they successfully tested the first intercontinental ballistic missile, and then five months later, using the same missile, launched the first space satellite, known as Sputnik. Europe, divided into West and East, became the epicenter of a Cold War between the United States and the Soviet Union.

In sum, the decade of the 1950s saw the emergence of Western Europe as a political entity.[26] NATO provided collective military security; the Marshall Plan provided economic stimulus and greater opportunities for trade; and a number of national leaders championed a postwar political commitment to democracy and the rule of law as the best alternative to the repression and ideological rigidity of Soviet-style communism. Western Europe experienced a period of unparalleled growth and prosperity. Germany, remarkably, led the charge, as European economic output climbed 30 to 35 percent higher than it had been before World War II. Inflation barely registered, and employment reached record levels. While the United States and individual countries in Western Europe certainly had disagreements—most notably the Suez Crisis of 1956 in which Britain and France invaded Egypt over the objections of the United States—the transatlantic relationship was generally positive.

EVOLUTION OF NATO'S MILITARY STRUCTURES

Henry Kissinger describes President John Kennedy as delivering the most "articulate of American principles—a new endeavor," by which JFK meant, "not a balance of power but a new world of law." It would be a "grand and global alliance" against "the "common enemies of mankind." It was, according to Kissinger, "a specific blueprint for global action."[27] This was especially true in the area of nuclear weapons. However, the Soviet Union had little interest in abandoning balance of power politics for a new world of law. And, while Kennedy and subsequent presidents achieved historic nuclear agreements with the Soviet Union, within Europe, France proved to be an outlier to the global alliance.

General de Gaulle returned to the presidency of France in 1958, two years before Kennedy's election. De Gaulle did not believe a natural alliance existed between the United States, Britain, and France, especially in opposition to the Soviet Union. Instead, he felt that France, along with the rest of Europe, was caught in the middle of superpower ambitions, most clearly evidenced in the nuclear arms race. In the long run, he questioned America's commitment to Europe. Stubborn and arrogant, but more than anything a committed nationalist, de Gaulle believed that France, because of its history, its culture, and its people, should aspire to the status of world power. For this reason, he insisted on a French nuclear deterrent even though it was unpopular, hugely expensive, and of limited military value.

De Gaulle also considered that the nations of Europe, notwithstanding their ideological differences, had more in common with one another than with either the United States or Russia. Yet, he did not envision European political unity, and initially opposed the Common Market. He saw France as participating both politically and economically in a loose confederation of sovereign states. Interestingly, however, de Gaulle believed that European security and prosperity depended on close cooperation between France and Germany—bitter enemies in two world wars.

In 1959, President de Gaulle ordered that all French naval units be removed from NATO's Mediterranean command. De Gaulle's disengagement of his navy had an insignificant impact since France's presence in the Mediterranean was small, but the French president sent a message that he would repeat over the next several years. Finally, in 1966, de Gaulle refused to integrate France's nuclear deterrent with other North Atlantic powers or to accept any collective form of control over its armed forces. By withdrawing France from the U.S.-led integrated military command, de Gaulle downgraded France's membership in NATO, although the "twenty-year rule" prevented France from completely leaving NATO altogether.[28]

De Gaulle further distanced his country from the United States by ordering the closure of U.S. military bases in France. NATO subsequently moved its headquarters from Rocquencourt, France, to Mons in Belgium. It would be another four decades before President Nicolas Sarkozy, with the support of the French Parliament, returned France to full participation in NATO's military structures.

Until this point, the United States had enjoyed a generally good relationship with the nations of Europe. America was supportive of NATO and of the European Communities,[29] and both had become pillars of the international order. The transatlantic relationship seemed to benefit both sides of the Atlantic: America continued to project power in Europe through NATO, and the EC provided an enormous market for trade. Europeans did not necessarily like having their defense policy largely dictated by the United States—but neither did they have to devote as large a percentage of their GNP to security, leaving them the capacity and flexibility in their budgets to fulfill other needs. France's decision to leave NATO's military structures and de Gaulle's open disdain for the United States represented a low point for the transatlantic relationship. It would take years to repair the damage.

Notwithstanding the tension between France and the United States during this period, the Soviet Union reminded both the United States and Western Europe on numerous occasions of its commitment to spheres of influence. In 1956, when a student protest in Hungary grew into a national revolution, a large Soviet military force invaded Budapest and other regions of the country. Over 2,500 Hungarians and 700 Soviet troops were killed in the conflict, and 200,000 Hungarians fled as refugees. Five years later, East Germany began construction on the Berlin Wall to prevent its citizens from fleeing to the West. Germany was already divided into two countries, and the wall quickly became the most potent symbol of the Cold War and the divide between the communist Soviet bloc and the Western democratic, capitalist bloc.

In 1968, students in Czechoslovakia rose up to protest authoritarian rule. As Ian Kershaw notes, "the protests blended into growing pressure from wider sections of the population for more democracy and liberalization of the system . . . Protests [in Czechoslovakia] attracted support across the social and age spectrum, largely prompted by widespread economic discontent."[30] As the demonstrations grew, the challenge to communist authority came from within the party itself. Moscow feared that if communists in Czechoslovakia were allowed to undertake radical reform, the viability of the entire Warsaw Pact could be undermined. On August 20, 1968, a half million soldiers from five Warsaw Pact countries, supported by 7,500 Soviet tanks and 1,000 planes, began their invasion of Czechoslovakia. The challenge to Soviet domination was quashed.

While the West had based its lexicon on law and values, cognizant of power realities and interest calculations, the Soviet Union, in contrast, established an illiberal order based on the Warsaw Pact and the Comecon (the Soviet counterparts to NATO and the Marshall Plan). Its institutional structures reflected naked power, protected by a secret police to enforce its edicts. Periodically, the Soviets reinforced their rule using military muscle to crush resistance, as during the Hungarian uprising, the Prague spring, and, later, in 1981, the imposition of martial law in Poland.

The two orders coexisted uneasily in the world, most notably in an awkward balance of power between freedom and oppression within the United Nations, which accommodated both liberal values and illiberal participants.[31] Paradoxically, the UN was constructed to make the world safe for democracy (through its references to human rights and political freedoms) as well as to make the world nonthreatening to authoritarians (through its protection of sovereignty and political independence).

For Western Europe, in particular, the liberal order during the Cold War provided the necessary structural conditions to establish supranational institutions of the EC, as well as to establish democratic governance in countries such as Germany, Italy, Spain, Portugal, and Greece. NATO's Article 5 guarantee—under which an attack against one ally was deemed an attack against all allies—and the presence of U.S. troops in Western Europe took the historical security concerns among the European states off the table.

According to Lord Hastings Lionel Ismay, NATO's first secretary-general, the aim was "to keep the Soviet Union out, the Americans in, and the Germans down."[32] Similarly, European political and economic integration framed the national interest for EC member states, especially for West Germany, from a European-wide perspective.

For the first post–World War II generation, the events in Eastern Europe reinforced the value of the West and the liberal order: NATO, GATT, the EC, and the UN all provided some measure of collective security, economic prosperity, and political inclusion at home. Truman, Eisenhower, Churchill, and Adenauer understood intuitively the need for transatlantic cooperation because their own survival had depended on it. Yet, this general consensus began to fray over time with the next generation of leaders.

TRANSATLANTIC TENSIONS

Beginning in the early 1970s, West Germany, led by Chancellor Willy Brandt, sought a détente with East Germany, leading many Atlanticists to fear that the transatlantic ties uniting the West against the Soviet-dominated Eastern European bloc were eroding. Yet, events outside of Europe had a much greater impact on the transatlantic relationship, especially in South Asia, where U.S. foreign policy led to increased tension.[33]

The United States had first become involved in Vietnam a decade earlier, during the administration of President Eisenhower, when Secretary of State Dulles feared that a communist insurgency might lead to a domino effect in South Asia. Dulles envisioned the use of the NATO model to contain communist-controlled North Vietnam, and he sought to employ a Marshall Plan model for the economic and political rehabilitation of democratic

South Vietnam. Eisenhower introduced American military advisers to shore up the democratically elected government of South Vietnam, and by 1968, America's commitment to the Vietnam War peaked when the number of combat troops reached a high of 550,000.

As Henry Kissinger, President Nixon's secretary of state, later described the roots of America's early involvement in Vietnam, "The Marshall Plan and NATO succeeded because a political tradition of government remained in Europe, even if impaired. Economic recovery could restore political vitality. But in much of the underdeveloped world, the political framework was fragile or new, and economic aid led to corruption as frequently as to stability."[34] Kissinger was correct about the political fragility of less developed nations, but for the United States, the war in Vietnam represented the larger struggle against global communism. Over the course of twenty years, the United States became increasingly mired in Southeast Asia, pouring tens of thousands of soldiers and billions of dollars into an unwinnable war. Vietnam represented the apex of postwar balance of power politics and, in many respects, an acknowledgment that much of the Atlantic Charter had failed on a global scale.

The Vietnam War was also deeply unpopular in Europe, and led to a souring of transatlantic relations. France, which predated the United States in conflict with South Vietnam, scorned America's involvement, while the rest of Europe simply viewed the United States as misguided and foolish for wasting its blood and treasure. Not only were there protests against the war in the United States, major demonstrations against the war took place in France, West Germany, Italy, and other parts of Europe.[35] Notably, in contrast to the Korean War, when six European countries participated, none sent troops during the Vietnam War to support the United States.

Other economic and foreign policy issues also roiled the relationship between the United States and Europe. On August 15, 1971, President Richard Nixon, concerned about rising inflation in the United States, announced without warning that he was suspending the gold convertibility of the U.S. dollar. Almost overnight, currencies that had been pegged to the price of gold were subject to sudden and wide fluctuations. Business confidence plummeted.[36] As Ian Kershaw has written, "With that move, the Bretton Woods system—the basis of the postwar economy—was dead."[37] Many European economies were suddenly adrift.

Two years later, in the wake of the Arab-Israeli War, both Europe and the United States experienced a nearly fourfold rise in the price of oil, leading to a global recession. Germany saw its economic growth dwindle to half of what it had been only years earlier, while France registered zero growth. Britain not only suffered record low growth, it experienced 16 percent inflation.[38] In 1976, Great Britain's sagging economy forced the government to seek a $3.9 billion loan from the IMF. Then, in 1979, there was another oil crisis, and the price soared to almost $50 a barrel. According to Kershaw, "The crisis marked the end of the optimism that had characterized the previous two decades."[39] It also exposed another fissure in the transatlantic relationship. The United States continued to maintain its close relationship with Israel, the Middle East's only democracy, while the EC showed increasing sympathy for the plight of the Palestinians.

Perceived American adventurism in Vietnam had left many in Europe with a dim view of the United States. Anti-Americanism was further fueled by NATO's decision to install intermediate nuclear weapons in Western Europe. By this point, Europe, theoretically, had the manpower and resources to defend itself and feared the United States might somehow involve it in a conflict with the Soviet Union. At the same time, Europe was far from united and still dependent on the United States' defense umbrella. Instead of resolving their differences, the United States and Europe coexisted in what was now an uneasy alliance, with tension over a number of issues bubbling just below the surface.

While the 1970s was a decade marked by both military and economic difficulties and disagreements in the transatlantic relationship, there were also positive developments related to both the prospect of European unity and to the future of transatlantic relations. In a speech titled the "Year of Europe," Kissinger noted that the United States and its Western European allies at that time—a period of heightened political integration in Europe with the European Political Cooperation process in 1970 and West Germany's *Ostpolitik* outreach to the Soviet Union—had entered a period of strategic "drift": no longer bound by the unity imposed by necessity in the aftermath of World War II and without a renewed sense of purpose for new common challenges and threats. This "dramatic transformation of the psychological climate in the West" required "a new era of creativity," argued Kissinger. Otherwise, the Atlantic partnership would "atrophy" or "erode through neglect, carelessness or mistrust." Kissinger emphasized that the "United States will continue to support the unification of Europe," but that

"European unity is what it has always been—not an end in itself but a means to the strengthening of the West." Most importantly, he observed that "the perception of common interests is not automatic; it requires constant redefinition."

Having just extricated the United States from the Vietnam War in January 1973, the Nixon administration sought a renewal of the transatlantic alliance. But the Watergate scandal derailed President Nixon's fledgling attempt to strengthen the alliance. The following year, Nixon resigned under threat of impeachment. Yet, even during these turbulent times, both Europe and America developed the concept of multilateral transatlantic summits, beginning in 1973 with four finance ministers and culminating in 1975, during the Gerald Ford administration, with the G7—the United States, West Germany, the United Kingdom, France, Italy, Japan, and Canada. The United States also began regular consultations with the European Communities starting in 1974. The Helsinki Final Act of 1975, brokered with the Soviet Union, in part codified the balance of power in Europe, and, in part, opened the possibility for the liberal order's expansion in 1989, with its references to democracy and human rights.

Other positive developments in Europe expanded prospects for the liberal order. In 1973, the military dictatorship in Greece was overthrown; one year later, the Portuguese dictatorship was defeated; and in 1976, after the death of Francisco Franco in 1975, Spain celebrated its first democratically elected government in over forty years.[40] These events led to several major changes during the 1980s among the countries of the EC that were to have a lasting impact.

Having been composed solely of the industrialized countries of northern Europe for many years, with the UK, Ireland, and Denmark joining in 1973, the EC opened its doors to the emerging democracies of southern Europe, with the accession of Greece in 1981 and Spain and Portugal in 1986. While creating political stability and economic development in Europe's Mediterranean region, there remained significant economic and social obstacles impeding the integration of these mainly agricultural countries into the highly industrialized EC.

Indeed, the economic disparity between northern and southern Europe highlighted the need for a common regional policy, but achieving greater integration was difficult due to a global economic downturn. During the 1980s, European unemployment reached levels that had not been seen since the Great Depression. The annual unemployment rate in the EC rose sharply in 1981, and continued rising until 1985. Protracted negotiations and lengthy transitional periods would prove necessary for the successful integration of the new member states.

In February 1986, the EC adopted the Single European Act (SEA), which set out an objective of establishing a single market by December 31, 1992. This phase of European integration included the establishment of a regional identity without internal borders. The implementation of a new migration paradigm had not only economic implications but social and political ones as well. Moreover, while previously the relatively small number of nations in the EC allowed for a relatively uncomplicated decisionmaking process—as, for example, on the creation of a common market, a common agricultural policy, and various European funds—that changed after the mid-1980s. As the EC grew larger and more complex, internal debates became more contentious, with increasingly clear contrasts between supporters and opponents of the European project.

For the second generation of policymakers after 1945, the enduring truth of transatlantic cooperation was less obvious, as there was clear disagreement over issues such as Vietnam or détente, and the global economic environment was more contentious. European leaders focused on internal economic and political integration, and Nixon's overtures to renew the West had limited impact. The main geopolitical activity occurred in places other than within the West: rapprochement with the Soviet Union, opening of diplomatic relations with China, and conflict in the Middle East. At the same time, NATO persisted; the EC expanded its membership and deepened its authority; and the G7 began to emerge as a focal point for regular consultation within the core of the liberal order, which now included Japan.

FALL OF COMMUNISM

A seminal year for advancing the liberal order was 1989. While autocrats in China crushed a fledgling pro-democracy movement at Tiananmen Square in June 1989, Polish democrats half a world away cast their ballots in the first free elections in Central and Eastern Europe since 1945. By the end of the year, Communist authoritarianism crumbled when the Berlin Wall fell.

Talks surrounding reunification of East and West Germany soon followed. While some in Europe worried that a united Germany could mean a resurgence of German nationalism and dominance over Europe, the democracies of Europe in 1989 were much stronger and much closer to one another than they had been in the 1930s. Most European leaders hailed the possibility of German reunification as signaling the beginning of a new democratic era rooted in the free flow of capital, goods, and people.

Members of President George H. W. Bush's administration also supported German reunification, and discussed the role the United States should play in the process.[41] One possibility was to simply let the two Germanys determine the process themselves, understanding that, due to agreements at the end of World War II, the Soviet Union, Britain, and France would also continue to have input into Germany's future. Second, administration officials considered allowing the thirty-five members of the Conference on Security and Cooperation in Europe to hammer out the details. However, this plan was not widely supported because of the likelihood that the process would bog down due to input from so many countries. A third suggestion was a framework that became known as "Two-plus-Four," which contemplated resolution by the two German states and the four World War II victorious powers, including the United States.

On December 4, 1989, President Bush visited NATO headquarters in Brussels and, during a press conference, made what was to become the definitive statement on German reunification. He declared that the German people should decide the future of Germany, and that a unified Germany should be free to choose its alliances.

In February 1990, the Two-plus-Four approach was formally approved. East and West Germany dealt with the internal details while the four victors of World War II worked with the two Germanys on external issues. The talks began in May and finally concluded in September 1990. An American team of negotiators headed by Secretary of State James Baker represented the United States. The principal controversy surrounding reunification was whether a united Germany would be part of NATO. The Soviets initially opposed the proposition, preferring it to be part of the Warsaw Pact or exist as a neutral, nonaligned country. In the end, the Bush administration helped broker a compromise: Germany would be part of NATO but no NATO troops would be stationed in East Germany. In addition, Soviet troops would have three to four years to withdraw from East Germany, and Germany agreed to provide economic assistance to the Soviet Union. In part, the subsequent Russian narrative included the argument that Western leaders promised Gorbachev that NATO would not expand further east beyond East Germany. However, there was no written or binding commitment to this effect by the alliance or from individual Western leaders. There may have been sporadic oral statements suggesting as much as part of the overall aspirational debate about the post-1989 European order,[42] but such foundational issues would have required codification, such as the subsequent NATO-Russia Founding Act of 1997, to signify real obligations.

By refusing to declare victory over the Soviet Union, both President Bush and Secretary Baker avoided a backlash from hardliners in Eastern Europe. Bush and Baker had not wanted to jeopardize future negotiations with the Soviet Union, and, indeed, in the same month the two Germanys reunited, President Bush attended a summit with Soviet President Gorbachev in Malta, where the two leaders discussed arms reductions and strengthening their relations. At a summit in Washington, DC, six months later, Bush and Gorbachev signed a broad arms reduction agreement in which the United States and Soviet Union consented to decreasing their nuclear arsenals.

As the year ended, Brent Scowcroft, President George Bush's national security advisor, offered an optimistic view of opportunities for the liberal order: "When those creators of the 1940's and 1950's rested, they had done much. We now have unprecedented opportunities to do more, to pick up the task where they left off, while doing what must be done to protect a handsome inheritance."[43] Scowcroft specifically envisioned a Europe that was free, democratic, and prosperous—and closely aligned with the United States.

Given the cooperation of the Soviet Union on arms control and the reunification of Germany, President Bush sensed a broader opening for renewal of the transatlantic relationship that had been slowly eroding over the previous twenty years. In 1990, at a summit meeting of the Commission on Security and Cooperation in Europe (CSCE) in Paris, President Bush, Prime Minister Giulio Andreotti of Italy, and European Commission President Jacques Delors, signed the Transatlantic Declaration. The Declaration established a framework for transatlantic discussions with language that in many respects echoed the aspirations of the Atlantic Charter nearly fifty years earlier.

The Declaration set out six common goals and described four general areas of cooperation. Perhaps most important, the Declaration contained a broad and ambitious commitment to align the United States and Europe: "To achieve their common goals, the European Community and its Member States and the United States of America will inform and consult each other on important matters of common interest, both political and economic, with a view to bringing their positions as close as possible, without prejudice to their respective independence. In appropriate international bodies, in particular, they will seek close cooperation."[44]

Though nonbinding, the Transatlantic Declaration marked an important renewal of transatlantic relations. However, the Declaration was overshadowed by events the following year in the Soviet Union.

In August 1991, Soviet President Gorbachev's opponents attempted a coup to oust him from power. Although the coup failed and Gorbachev retained his position, the Soviet Union was in evident decline. There were many contributing factors. Economic stagnation had hobbled the country for years, and the "perestroika" initiated by Gorbachev's reforms only exacerbated the problem. Mismanagement of fiscal policy made the country vulnerable to external factors; a significant decline in the price of oil plunged the Soviet economy into debt; and the government supported increases in wages by printing money, fueling an inflationary spiral. Meanwhile, Soviet military spending continued to rise, ranging between 10 and 20 percent of GDP.

In addition to budgetary matters, the decade-long war in Afghanistan was a key military factor in the breakup of the USSR. As many as a million Soviet troops participated in the ten-year occupation, and approximately 15,000 soldiers were killed, with thousands more wounded. Finally, the Soviet public was fed up with the widespread corruption endemic to the Soviet state, tired of its inefficiency and ineffectiveness, and tired of being lied to.

Throughout the fall of 1991, the Soviet Republics began to declare their independence from the Soviet Union, and in December, Russia, Ukraine, and Belarus announced a new confederation, having signed the Alma-Ata Protocol formally establishing the Commonwealth of Independent States (CIS).

On Christmas Day 1991, President Gorbachev called President Bush to tell him that he was resigning; the Soviet flag flew over the Kremlin for the last time the following day. While the Soviet Union disintegrated, Russia remained a military power, albeit devoid of its empire and hobbled by a lack of confidence for the future. It marked the beginning of a decade described by *Washington Post* columnist David Ignatius this way: "The Russians remember that time as a great national humiliation." According to Ignatius, "They talk about Boris Yeltsin," the buffoonish, former mayor of Moscow, who succeeded Gorbachev, "as a shameful symbol of their country's pathetic, drunken, feeble state at the time."[45]

For the most part, the end of the Soviet Union and disintegration of the Soviet bloc in Eastern Europe did not alter existing geographic borders as had happened after both world wars. However, the Baltic States, which Stalin's army had occupied in 1940, proved the exception and applied for membership of NATO and the EU. Estonia, Latvia, and Lithuania all became NATO members in March 2004, and joined the European Union in May 2004. To date, they remain the only former Soviet states to have joined either organization.

After the fall of communism in 1989 and the dissolution of the Soviet Union in 1991, the liberal order began to enlarge rapidly. Institutions on both sides of the transatlantic alliance recognized the utility of laying out general organizing principles to guide the expansion. NATO's periodic strategic concepts, European strategies, and U.S. national security strategies consistently focused on the importance of democracy, human rights, and market economy around the world. In short, the hopes of 1945 were validated by subsequent decades of historical experience, notwithstanding occasional setbacks and a number of contentious disagreements along the way. The fundamental commitment on both sides of the Atlantic to each other's security, prosperity, and political inclusion remained steadfast and grew stronger over time, with the prospect of expansion of the liberal order to other parts of the world.

LIBERAL ORDER AFTER THE COLD WAR

The Revolutions of 1989 in Germany and Eastern Europe, combined with the 1991 breakup of the USSR marked the end of the Cold War. However, it also removed the original rationale—the Soviet threat—for the Atlantic Alliance, and many feared that NATO would wither on the vine.

Just a few months after the collapse of the Soviet Union, on February 7, 1992, representatives of the EC convened in Maastricht, the Netherlands, and signed the treaty establishing the European Union. The treaty led to the creation of the single European currency, the euro, and greatly expanded the capacity, expertise, and power of the EC.

Perhaps the most significant change as a result of the collapse of the Cold War was what J. Bryan Hehir has called "the relativization of nuclear weapons." While both the United States and Russia retained large nuclear arsenals, Hehir claimed that "the possibility of a massive nuclear exchange" had been "radically reduced."[46]

Without the specter of the Soviet Union to confront, the question of NATO's future became a hotly debated question in both Washington and the capitals of Europe. Not surprisingly, defense spending within NATO during this period decreased as member states focused on building up their national economies. At the same time, a number of newly independent nations in Europe sought membership in NATO. The transatlantic military alliance would expand, but it had yet to be seriously tested.

In the United States, at the dawn of the new order, the administration of George H. W. Bush produced a final national security strategy that noted "an extraordinary possibility that few generations have enjoyed—to build a new international system in accordance with our own values and ideals, as old patterns and certainties crumble around us."[47] It observed that "democracy was gaining ground as were the principles of human rights and political and economic freedom."[48] And it determined that the interests of the United States "are best served in a world in which democracy and its ideals are widespread and secure."[49]

William Clinton defeated President Bush in November 1992. Though he served only one term in the presidency, George H. W. Bush had significantly reinvigorated the transatlantic relationship. As it turned out, the "inheritance" Scowcroft had predicted was far greater than he or anyone else had could have imagined. Few among President Bush's advisers had believed a unified Germany could be realized in less than a year. Even more surprising was that a united Germany became a member of NATO. And, to top it off, the Soviet Union and the Warsaw Pact had been dissolved, yet relations between the United States and Russia appeared stable with constructive dialogue. U.S. strategy shifted from containment of the Soviet bloc to enlargement of the liberal order.[50]

President Clinton and his administration elevated democracy promotion as one of the three pillars of U.S. national security strategy, noting that "all of America's strategic interests—from promoting prosperity at home to checking global threats abroad before they threaten our territory—are served by enlarging the community of democratic and free market nations."[51] It even set out as a long-term goal "a world in which each of the major powers [including Russia and China] is democratic, with many other nations joining the community of market democracies as well."[52]

However, President Clinton faced a significant international crisis during his first term when Yugoslavia broke apart. Border disputes and ethnic conflicts in the Balkans disrupted a tenuous peace among the six former republics of Yugoslavia. When Bosnia proclaimed its independence from Yugoslavia in 1992 after a national referendum, its Serbian population, led by Radovan Karadzic and backed by Slobodan Milosevic, a Serbian nationalist and former president of Yugoslavia, resisted and threatened bloodshed. The Luxembourg foreign minister Jacques Poos declared: "This is the hour of Europe—not the hour of the Americans. . . . If one problem can be solved by the Europeans, it is the Yugoslav problem. This is a European country and it is not up to the Americans. It is not up to anyone else."[53]

The Serbs wished to create a nation only for Serbians, and Milosevic deliberately created conflict between Serbians, Croatians, and Muslim Bosniaks (the three main ethnic groups in the region). Only days after members of the EC and the United States recognized Bosnia's independence, Serbian forces launched an offensive, bombing Bosnia's capital, Sarajevo. The region was suddenly mired in an ugly war, described by Kissinger as the reenactment of "century-old bloodlusts."[54] More than 150,000 combatants and civilians were killed during the decade-long conflict.

The Balkans conflict exposed important differences not only within Europe but between the United States and Europe as well. In essence, the post–Cold War relevance of NATO was being tested. Europeans were deeply divided within the twelve-member European Union. While Germany, Austria, and Italy pleaded for a confederation of sovereign states, France and Great Britain favored Milosevic's approach of a reconfigured federation (even if they did not approve of his highly centralized perspectives). While EU members dithered, failing to agree on a model of Balkan cohesion, the bloodshed and killing continued. The United States played a critical role when it spearheaded NATO's interventions in the Balkan War and succeeded in bringing the various factions to the negotiating table.[55]

At the same time, a number of newly independent nations in Europe sought membership in NATO. According to Celeste Wallender, "thanks to the internal cohesion created by its democratic values, and the incentives its standards created for aspiring new members, the alliance defied predictions."[56] Instead of becoming a relic of the Cold War, NATO reinvented itself, maintaining its status as a pillar of transatlantic security.

By safeguarding democratic gains in Europe, the United States added to the allure of the Western model predicated on human rights, free speech, and free trade. Lurking beneath America's success, however, was what Scowcroft and another former respected national security advisor, Zbigniew Brzezinski, referred to as the hubris associated with Francis Fukuyama's argument about "the end of history."[57] Brzezinski explained that the United States had adopted the view that "we could sit back and enjoy this new imperial status . . . The arrogance was we thought that we could now define the rules of the game in an international system that was still somewhat interdependent, in spite of our overwhelming power, and that these new rules would permit us to decide when to start wars, how to start wars, how to pre-empt wars and prevent them."[58] The "arrogance" described by Brzezinski would have a profound impact on the transatlantic relationship.

But hubris and overconfidence were not limited to the United States. French President Jacques Chirac told Polish foreign minister Bronislaw Geremek that Poland had to choose between Europe and America, EU or NATO: "whether Poland wanted to be part of Europe or be 'the 51st state.'"[59]

Ultimately, however, most Europeans viewed both NATO and the EU as integral to the wider liberal order. As two observers have written: Europeans "expected their model would spread naturally, whether through the enlargement of NATO, the extension of EU ties to states on the union's periphery, or the ascent of global institutions that enshrined European norms."[60] During the 1990s, the EU and NATO continued to add members; Sweden, Austria, and Finland joined the EU in 1995, and the Czech Republic, Hungary, and Poland joined NATO in 1999. In just one year, 2004, ten countries of Central and Eastern Europe joined the EU.

Indeed, there was enormous optimism among the leaders of Europe in 1999 when the European Union adopted the euro as the single currency for its members. There had been concern that a monetary union would mean countries forfeited the ability to devalue their currencies, thereby depriving them of a tool to improve their country's trade balance by increasing exports at a time when the trade deficit might have become a problem. But supporters of the single currency successfully argued that financial crises could be avoided through adherence to the Maastricht rules designed to prevent countries from accumulating too much debt. They would turn out to be terribly mistaken.

The European Union completed the transition to the euro as the single currency for its members. It was, in many respects, the capstone to the vision of European federalism, with politicians and economists alike predicting growth due to increased efficiency, and less inequality among member states. Trust in the institutions of the European Union was higher in many countries than trust in national political institutions.

However, the single currency failed to deliver the economic miracle many had hoped for. While the single currency facilitated travel and trade, each country maintained its own fiscal policy, and the budgets and economic models of each country varied greatly. This led to significant economic imbalances within the EU. In fact, only Germany significantly prospered during the ensuing decade. Most of Europe stagnated, and countries such as Greece, Spain, and Italy—countries that had accumulated extensive public and private debt—experienced credit squeezes leading to high unemployment and a reduction in state social services. The disparity of national wealth and economic prosperity led to a high degree of consternation within the EU and significant friction among member states.

Europe's malaise was exacerbated in 2000 when George W. Bush, son of the forty-first president, was elected president of the United States. While European leaders had admired and respected his father, almost immediately the forty-third American president got off on the wrong foot with U.S. allies in Europe. In June 2001, President Bush, notwithstanding intense lobbying by German Chancellor Gerhard Schröder, withdrew the United States from the 1997 Kyoto Protocol to control greenhouse gas emissions. Europeans considered the protocol an important step in combatting climate change, and given that the United States was at the time the largest emitter of greenhouse gases, Bush's decision felt like a betrayal. It was only the beginning.

The 1990s represented the golden age for the West: internal confidence, external enlargement, and a sense of convergence around a common vision for global success. Norms and institutions of the liberal order, many of which had sprung from the Atlantic Charter, had taken root and expanded around the world. The United Nations appeared to resume centrality in international politics and was the premier forum for questions of international peace and security, as well as crisis management. The General Agreement on Trade and Tariffs transformed into the World Trade Organization in 1995, and opened accession negotiations with China and Russia. Economic liberalization was not only intended to promote global prosperity but also political liberalization. In 1997, the G7 invited Russia to join its club. And in 1999, finance ministers of the top twenty economies began meeting in the G20 format, on the model of the G7 established more than a generation earlier.

The West was partly a victim of its own success, as it was less clear what, if anything, united the transatlantic allies in contrast to the rest of the international community. Soon, the whole world stood as one with the United States in the aftermath of the worst terrorist attack ever carried out on American soil.

WAR ON TERROR

On September 12, 2001, the day after Middle East terrorists flew passenger airplanes into the World Trade Center towers in New York City and into the Pentagon in Washington, DC, President Bush declared to the world: "Make no mistake—the United States will hunt down and punish those responsible for these cowardly acts." In Berlin, 200,000 Germans marched to show their solidarity with America. German Chancellor Schröder described the attacks as "a declaration of war against the entire civilized world," and the European Union immediately pledged its full support to the United States. The attack strengthened the transatlantic relationship, but also highlighted a new phenomenon: the globalization of insecurity.

The sheer scale of the devastation on 9/11—more than 3,000 innocent Americans lost their lives—convinced Europeans of the risk of terrorism at home. It also quickly became a test for institutions of the liberal order. NATO had originally been created to provide common defense for the United States and Western Europe in the face of Soviet aggression. But soon after the September 11 attacks, a meeting of NATO ministers invoked Article 5 to defend against a new threat. For the first time in NATO's history, the countries of Europe would assist the United States in fighting terrorists far away from either the United States or Europe. NATO Secretary-General George Robertson declared: "These barbaric acts constitute intolerable aggression against democracy and underlie the need for the international community and the members of the alliance to unite their forces in fighting the scourge of terrorism." In addition to invoking Article 5, the United States and the European Union drafted a UN declaration condemning in strongest terms the attacks upon the United States. On September 13, the UN Security Council passed Resolution 1368, condemning the attacks and authorizing all necessary steps to respond to them and to combat all forms of terrorism.

The United States and Europeans also signed numerous agreements to enhance cooperation in combatting terrorist activities, including the sharing of information pertaining to threat assessments. Europol headquarters hosted liaison officers from several U.S. law enforcement agencies, including US Customs and Border Protection, the FBI, ICE, the New York Police Department, and the Transportation Security Administration.

President George W. Bush demanded that the Taliban hand over Osama bin Laden and expel al-Qaeda from Afghanistan. When the Taliban declined to deliver bin Laden and ignored demands to shut down terrorist bases, the United States, supported by the United Kingdom, retaliated by launching operation "Enduring Freedom." A coalition of forty countries, including all the members of NATO, provided troops, war materiel, or logistical support for the war in Afghanistan. Within days, the United States and its allies drove the Taliban from power and began constructing military bases near major cities across the country.

The increased pressure on European jihadist networks and the participation of European states in the military campaign in Afghanistan angered the jihadists, who decided to retaliate and set their sights on Europe. Al-Qaeda, in particular, recruited European foreign fighters in the Middle East to return to the continent, form terrorist cells, and plan attacks. The 2004 Madrid bombings and the 2005 London attacks, which killed 191 and fifty-two people, respectively, were bitter fruits of this strategy.

President George W. Bush, unlike his father, had very little experience in international relations. He began his presidency by emphasizing the defense and expansion of the liberal order, noting that: "the great struggles of the twentieth century between liberty and totalitarianism ended with a decisive victory for the forces of freedom—and a single sustainable model for national success: freedom, democracy, and free enterprise."[61] He recognized the "balance of power" struggle, but maintained that it favored "human freedom: conditions in which all nations and all societies can choose for themselves the rewards and challenges of political and economic liberty."[62]

Notwithstanding Bush's soaring rhetoric and the outpouring of support for the United States in the wake of 9/11, he proved to be a difficult and unreliable ally for many Europeans. The most significant disagreement between the United States and its European allies occurred in September 2002 when President Bush argued before world leaders at the United Nations that Iraq threatened global security by stockpiling weapons of mass destruction. Five months later, Secretary of State Colin Powell amplified the president's case when he appeared at the United Nations to provide evidence—which turned out to be false—of Iraq's weapons of mass destruction. Assured of the case for military preemption, President Bush, Vice President Dick Cheney, and Secretary Powell sought to form a coalition force to topple Saddam Hussein.

Within the European Union, only British Prime Minister Tony Blair made the case for regime change in Iraq. Indeed, NATO was far from unified on the matter, with France and Germany ultimately among the most vociferous critics of the U.S. invasion.[63] At the Munich Security Conference, German foreign minister Joschka Fischer confronted U.S. Secretary of Defense Donald Rumsfeld, saying, "My generation learned you must make the case, and excuse me, I am not convinced."[64] French President Chirac scolded Central European countries that supported the U.S. position for "miss[ing] a good opportunity to keep quiet."[65] As historian John Lewis Gaddis wrote at the time, "the rush to war in Iraq, in the absence of a 'first shot' or 'smoking gun' [created] a growing sense throughout the world [that] there could be nothing worse than American hegemony if it was to be used in these ways."[66]

Europeans also began to question NATO's role in the war against Afghanistan's Taliban as well as the coalition's treatment of prisoners, deemed "terrorists" and exemplified by the U.S. Guantanamo Bay prison in Cuba. The "inheritance" Brent Scowcroft described in 1989—America's role as a benign and moral superpower, along with the world's goodwill in the aftermath of 9/11—had been squandered by the arrogance and prevarication of the George W. Bush administration. It marked a nadir in U.S.-European relations and once again called into question both the purpose and continued viability of NATO, not to mention the transatlantic alliance itself.

Nonetheless, the EU's 2003 Security Strategy—its first—proclaimed triumphantly that "Europe has never been so prosperous, so secure nor so free," with the EU's creation as "central to this development" and the

United States playing a "critical role in European integration and European security, in particular through NATO."[67] It argued that the EU's "security and prosperity" depended on an "effective multilateral system,"[68] and set out as the EU's strategic objective the "development of a stronger international society, well functioning international institutions and a rule-based international order."[69] During this period, the European Union doubled in membership and geographic size. Alongside EU enlargement, NATO expanded and considered (albeit briefly) the possibility of including Russia as a potential member.

While the 1990s represented the golden age for the West (internal confidence, external enlargement, and a sense of convergence around a common vision for global success),[70] the following decade was less optimistic, dominated by the war against terrorism. Yet, nations continued to embrace the Western model for global success. Indeed, six days after 9/11, the WTO successfully concluded negotiations with China for its entry three months later; Russia also eventually entered the WTO, in August 2012. During these two decades, the number of democracies around the world nearly doubled, and freedom was on the rise. Peace among the great powers continued and was intended to facilitate integration of China, Russia, and other states into the liberal order by adopting the same model of democracy, human rights, rule of law, and market economy.

But not everyone viewed the liberal order's expansion as a good development, perceiving it, instead, as a fig leaf for U.S. hegemony. In 2007, President Vladimir Putin criticized what he perceived as a "unipolar world," where there is "one centre of authority, one centre of force, one centre of decision-making." He argued that "one state and, of course, first and foremost the United States, has overstepped its national borders in every way."[71]

In April 2008, NATO announced that Ukraine and Georgia "will become members" of NATO, without specifying the exact timeline or process.[72] For Putin, these prospective plans, however distant, proved to be an unacceptable overreach. He told the NATO secretary-general that the alliance had crossed Russia's "red lines."[73] Four months later, Russia enforced its red line by invading Georgia and occupying two of its provinces, South Ossetia and Abkhazia—its first large-scale military intervention since Afghanistan in 1979. The twenty-year interlude post-1989 had come to an end. Within six years, Russia would also invade Ukraine.

Although the conflict with Georgia lasted less than two weeks, the

Kremlin threatened to seize Tbilisi and hang Georgian president Mikheil Saakashvili "by the balls."[74] French president Nicolas Sarkozy mediated between the two sides and brokered a cease-fire that enabled Russia to preserve its gains in the breakaway provinces of South Ossetia and Abkhazia. The George W. Bush administration extended a $1 billion aid package to Georgia and dispatched several high-level officials as a show of support. But very quickly, the West's attention became absorbed by the global financial crisis, which replaced the sense of confidence and success that had permeated the spirit of 1989 with a new sense of fear and anxiety.

2

Partners with Europe and Everyone
(2009–2016)

President Barack Obama entered office in the midst of the greatest economic crisis since the 1930s, which consumed his administration for the first two years. Obama faced a fundamental struggle within the transatlantic partnership: it was important but not urgent, essential to everything but prioritizing nothing, with a deep history but an ambivalent future. The United States continued to dominate the relationship, even when it did not especially want to; for its part, Europe strived for greater independence from the United States, even as fissures emerged within the EU.

While Obama sought to build a more equitable partnership with Europe, with numerous transatlantic summits and meetings in the first three years, the main diplomatic action and concrete achievements occurred elsewhere: reset with Russia, pivot to Asia, and new engagement with the world. The most tangible form of transatlantic cooperation—NATO's intervention in Libya in 2011—proved to be a short-lived success but a long-term cautionary lesson. During Obama's second term, the Syrian civil war further created the perception of transatlantic divisions. Yet, by 2014, Russia's aggression in Ukraine, ISIL's terrorist attacks throughout Europe, and mass irregular migration due to the Syrian conflict crystalized the need for transatlantic cooperation.

In many ways, the West had become a victim of its own success: its model of democracy, human rights, rule of law, market economy, and free trade had widespread appeal around the globe. Thus, the first post–Cold War generation, during the 1990s and 2000s, transformed the somewhat narrow strategic concept of the West into the broader liberal international order, or the more neutral-sounding rules-based global order—a trend Obama sought to continue. However, the West overextended its ambitions and gave insufficient priority to its core engine, the transatlantic alliance.

Paradoxically, what some observers viewed as Obama's benign neglect of Europe, rather than the intended building of an equitable transatlantic partnership, made the West more resilient when it would face its biggest test with the election of Donald Trump.

RISE OF THE G20

During the Obama years, a somewhat subtle, but nonetheless important, shift occurred with the emergence of the G20 as the focal forum for international economic coordination in lieu of the G8. In important ways, this institutional change marked the beginning of the new post–Western global order.

In the final months of the George W. Bush administration, it was clear that shifts in the strategic context were already underway as a result of the 2008 international economic crisis. At the UN General Assembly in late September 2008, President Bush repeated familiar arguments about fighting terrorism, but his focus seemed oddly discordant with the rest of the world. For instance, Brazilian President Lula da Silva adopted a starkly different approach and pinned the global economic crisis on "speculators," responsible for "entire peoples [now] suffering anguish in the wake of successive financial disasters that threaten the world's economy."[1] British Prime Minister Gordon Brown, likewise, argued that "living through the first financial crisis and the first resources crisis of globalization, [the] world [was] not simply in transition, but facing transformation."[2] Similarly, French President Nicolas Sarkozy stressed "the duty" for global leaders "to examine together the lessons of the most serious financial crisis the world has experienced since that of the 1930s."[3]

World leaders would come together two months later to address, specifically, the global financial crisis, for the first time in the G20 format.

Established at the end of the 1990s, the G20 included the world's largest economies, collectively accounting for over 80 percent of global GDP and 80 percent of trade. Yet for ten years, it met only at the level of finance ministers and central bank governors and was not viewed as the fulcrum of international economic decisionmaking, which still rested in the hands of the G8 (United States, Canada, Japan, United Kingdom, France, Germany, Italy, EU, and Russia). That changed in November 2008, when G20 heads of state and government met for the first time in Washington, DC.

There were several essential economic problems to manage. First, financial institutions had to be stabilized by injecting additional liquidity into the markets and reforming bank capital requirements. Political leaders viewed the financial markets not only as the engine of individual national economies but of the wider global economy, as well; the markets had to be secured first to save the overall system. Next, macroeconomic aggregate demand had to be increased to stave off an economic depression. In the short term, this required significant additional government spending. Finally, countries had to avoid "beggar-thy-neighbor" protectionist trade policies whereby increased tariffs would provide a short-term boost to domestic production and employment but with detrimental medium-term consequences for the protectionist economy and its counterparts. This dynamic had exacerbated the effects of the 1929 financial crisis and prolonged the economic downturn.

In April, the G20 leaders convened in London. Both U.S. and European policymakers preferred the G20 to the G8 as the multilateral forum necessary to address all three sets of problems because it was perceived to include the relevant actors who, together, wielded enormous economic power.[4] They committed to do "whatever is necessary" to restore economic growth, reform the financial system, promote global trade, and ensure an inclusive and sustainable recovery. Toward those ends, they agreed to fund a $1.1 trillion program for the IMF, Multilateral Development Banks, and trade finance. Moreover, the G20 also committed to fiscal expansion of approximately $5 trillion to save existing jobs and create new employment.

Notably, President Obama, in office for only two months, acknowledged the changes in relative economic power that the financial crisis exposed. He remarked how the G20 leaders had a more difficult challenge than the American and British delegates at the 1944 Bretton Woods conference: "Well, if there's just Roosevelt and Churchill sitting in a room with a brandy . . . that's an easier negotiation. But that's not the world we live in, and it shouldn't be the world that we live in."[5] He also argued that the level of international coordination was "historic," pointing out that it would have been unimaginable ten or thirty years ago to "have the leaders of Germany, France, China, Russia, Brazil, South Africa . . . United States . . . former adversaries, in some cases former mortal enemies, negotiating this swiftly on behalf of fixing the global economy."[6]

G20 leaders viewed the format as sufficiently useful to keep convening, meeting twice per year in both 2009 and 2010. The frequency of their meetings underscored the seriousness of the economic crisis, as well as the determination of the members to address it cooperatively and globally. In July, the G8 summit in Italy was expanded to include seventeen leaders on an ad hoc basis, thereby approximating the G20 and once again signaling the importance of working in a larger, international group. When asked whether the "days of the G8 are over," President Obama responded that existing international institutions needed to be "refresh[ed] and renew[ed]" and argued that it was impossible to deal with "global challenges in the absence of major powers, like China, India, and Brazil" and representation of entire continents like Latin America and Africa.

In practice, the G20 fiscal spending commitments fell short of the intended targets set out at the London summit in April 2009. According to one economic historian, fiscal expansion over three years totaled $1.8 trillion, with the United States contributing nearly 40 percent. Notably, Europe's fiscal contribution was limited, especially in comparison to China or other Asian economies.[7] On the other hand, the European Central Bank and EU regulatory authorities were important actors in stabilizing and reforming financial markets.

PARTNERS WITH EUROPE, NOT PATRONS OF

Even as the United States invested significant political capital in the G20, it continued to focus on the importance of the transatlantic alliance, but it sought more equitable cooperation with Europe: real partnership, not patronage. However, the extensive high-level political attention did not translate into concrete deliverables, and over time, better return on investment appeared elsewhere.

Following the G20 summit in London, President Obama attended the NATO summit in Strasbourg, France, marking the sixtieth anniversary of the military alliance. The alliance also celebrated France's return to its military command structures (after being absent for more than forty years) and welcomed Albania and Croatia as new members. Obama reaffirmed "the basic premise of NATO was that Europe's security was the United States' security and vice versa."[8] Describing this mutual commitment as "a pillar of American foreign policy that has been unchanging over the last 60 years," he also noted that the United States was "not looking to be the patron of Europe" but, rather, "to be partners with Europe."[9] In subsequent town hall remarks, he observed "the fundamental truth that America cannot confront the challenges of this century alone, but that Europe cannot confront them without America."[10] Obama called for renewing the transatlantic partnership, "one in which America listens and learns from our friends and allies, but where our friends and allies bear their share of the burden."[11]

After the G20 summit in London and the NATO summit in Strasbourg, the Obama team traveled the following day to Prague for a summit with the European Union, represented by European Commission President José Manuel Barroso, the Czech prime minister Mirek Topolánek in his capacity as EU Council president, and all the twenty-seven EU member state national leaders. This large and diverse group discussed a range of issues—including the economic crisis, climate change, energy security, and nuclear disarmament—but concluded with no deliverables and only a limited statement.[12] Although reflecting some weariness from the weeklong summitry with many of the same individuals, President Obama emphasized that: "when Europe and the United States act in concert, . . . we can make a difference not just on local issues but on international issues."[13] He further acknowledged that while "sometimes we may take for granted these relationships," they are "one of the key foundations for progress in the world."[14]

European leaders later echoed Obama's view. Angela Merkel, in the first address to a joint session of Congress for a German chancellor, argued "there is no better partner for Europe than America and no better partner for America than Europe."[15] She stressed that beyond "shared history" and "shared interests and the common global challenges that all regions of the world face," what makes the special partnership between Europe and America last is the "common basis of shared values."[16] In a subsequent official state visit to the United States—the first such visit for a European leader during the Obama-Biden administration—the president awarded the chancellor the Medal of Freedom; she is one of the few foreigners to ever receive this distinction.[17] In her remarks at the White House, she emphasized that the "close partnership with the United States is just as much part and parcel of Germany's *raison d'être* as is European integration. Both belong together. Both are and remain the pillars of German foreign policy."[18]

However, a sour note was sounded in Central and Eastern Europe.[19] On the seventieth anniversary of the Soviet Union's invasion of Poland, the United States—oblivious to the historical context—announced a shift in plans for its previously scheduled deployment of a missile defense shield in Europe. Leaders in Poland and the Czech Republic, where the military hardware was supposed to be installed, found out about the news from leaks to the press and apparently were neither consulted nor informed of the change beforehand. Local public outrage was somewhat paradoxical because, originally, the two countries had to be persuaded to host the shield, in part as a deterrent to Iran and in part as a favor to the United States. But over time, the shield had come to be viewed regionally as a potentially useful tool against Russia (particularly by Russia itself), so changes to the initial plans were perceived as part of a wider strategy of resetting U.S.-Russia relations and, therefore, detrimental to the interests of Central and Eastern Europe. The controversy cast a shadow over the Obama administration's foreign policy by contributing to a wider narrative that it had lost interest in Europe.

The themes of discord, neglect, and ineffectiveness built up gradually over time. Notwithstanding generally positive views expressed by both European and American leaders, the transatlantic summits did not appear to deliver much in terms of substance. In November 2009, a second EU-U.S. summit took place in Washington, DC, this time with a full communiqué. However, once again the deliverables were marginal as diplomats merely heralded the launch of a U.S.-EU Energy Council at the ministerial level.[20] Extensive time and capital had been expended at the highest levels in transatlantic formats to produce what was, in essence, yet another study group. As if searching to add some greater sense of accomplishment to the summit, President Obama remarked pointedly that he met with the Swedish prime minister "for the second day in a row"[21]—but seemingly without much return on investment.

The following year, at the NATO summit in Lisbon, Portugal, transatlantic leaders adopted a new Strategic Concept. In particular, the new strategy noted that "the Euro-Atlantic area is at peace and the threat of a conventional attack against NATO territory is low." It emphasized that NATO "poses no threat to Russia," wants a "strategic partnership" with Russia, and expects "reciprocity from Russia."[22] Indeed, after a two-year break in meetings of the NATO-Russia Council in the aftermath of the war in Georgia, Russian President Medvedev met with all twenty-eight NATO leaders and committed to a "a true strategic and modernized partnership based on the principles of reciprocal confidence, transparency, and predictability, with the aim of contributing to the creation of a common space of peace, security and stability in the Euro-Atlantic area."[23] The main agenda item for the summit was the ongoing NATO-led coalition in Afghanistan, the International Security Assistance Force, consisting of "48 nations with over 40,000 troops from allied and partner countries."[24]

On the same day the NATO summit ended, President Obama met with European Commission President Barroso, and European Council President Herman Van Rompuy. Obama noted that he "value[d] these meetings for a simple reason: America's relationship with our European allies and partners is the cornerstone of our engagement with the world, and it's a catalyst for global cooperation."[25] But, ultimately, he acknowledged that the "summit was not as exciting as other summits because we basically agree on everything."[26]

The three leaders met again the following year primarily to emphasize the same themes. Focusing on economic issues, President Van Rompuy noted that, "the EU and the United States have the strongest trade and economic relationship in the world and remain partners of first resort."[27] The main outcome from the summit was the launch of a high-level working group on jobs and growth, chaired by the U.S. Trade Representative and the European Commissioner for Trade.[28]

Within the first three years of his administration, President Obama met with his European counterparts in four EU summits (including one, initially, with all EU member states leaders), in addition to the NATO summit, three G8 summits, five G20 summits, and one summit with Central and Eastern European leaders. Moreover, he hosted or visited the leaders of the United Kingdom, France, and Germany at least once a year—a record not equaled by any other world leader during the same period. He called German Chancellor Angela Merkel one of his "closest partners"[29] and "a trusted partner throughout [his] entire Presidency—longer than any world leader."[30] Notwithstanding extensive contact and genuine good will at the highest level of U.S. and EU governments, the transatlantic relationship appeared to lack a concrete plan for the future, or even a general purpose. U.S. policy toward Europe appeared somewhat indifferent. After all, transatlantic goals had been largely accomplished: Europe was whole, free, and at peace.[31]

However, lurking below the surface of transatlantic tranquility was the issue of burden-sharing. President Obama noted briefly during his first trip to Europe that a true partnership meant "our friends and allies bear their share of the burden."[32] Obama rarely raised the issue, but Secretary of Defense Robert Gates, a veteran of transatlantic debates, emphasized it in remarks a few weeks before leaving office: "The blunt reality is that there will be dwindling appetite and patience in the U.S. Congress—and in the American body politic writ large—to expend increasingly precious funds on behalf of nations that are apparently unwilling to devote the necessary resources or make the necessary changes to be serious and capable partners in their own defense."[33] Burden-sharing would gain greater resonance under President Trump, but for the time being, American diplomacy was focused elsewhere.

RESET WITH RUSSIA

Since the Obama-Biden administration came into office only five months after the Georgia-Russia war, it may not have been a particularly apt moment to seek rapprochement with Russia. Yet, the origins of that particular conflict were sufficiently complex and murky, and the geo-economic concerns sufficiently grave, to treat it as a potential outlier event. And with Dmitry Medvedev having replaced Vladimir Putin as Russian president, it appeared that U.S.-Russian relations could be renewed.

Vice President Joe Biden set the stage at the Munich Security Conference in February 2009 when he expressed the administration's intention "to press the reset button and to revisit the many areas where [the United States] can and should be working together with Russia."[34] Secretary of State Hillary Clinton and Russian Foreign Minister Sergey Lavrov continued the discussions with an eye toward setting a meeting date and agenda for their two presidents. (Perhaps somewhat inauspiciously but presciently, Clinton gave Lavrov a big red button with "reset" misspelled in Russian as "overcharged."[35]) Then, on the margins of the G20 summit in London in

April, Obama met with Medvedev and noted a range of issues of "mutual interest" with Russia, such as nuclear reductions, nonproliferation, counterterrorism, and promoting peace and stability in the Middle East.[36] In particular, the two sides launched talks on a new START treaty to reduce and limit their respective nuclear armaments.[37]

Three months later, President Obama visited Moscow to meet with President Medvedev. The two leaders announced a wide range of new initiatives between the United States and Russia, including cooperation on Afghanistan through a new overland supply route via Russia,[38] missile defense,[39] nuclear issues,[40] and the establishment of a U.S.-Russia Bilateral Presidential Commission to "explore new opportunities for partnership."[41] The two sides also reached a preliminary agreement on the new START treaty.[42] The cordial atmosphere between Medvedev and Obama, palpable during their press conference, stood in stark contrast to the tone of the president's meeting with Putin.[43] Referencing the Rose Revolution in Georgia and the Orange Revolution in Ukraine, Putin noted that the "history of relations between Russia and the United States has very many different occasions and events of different, shall we say, color. There were periods when our relations flourished quite a bit, and there were also periods of, shall we say, grayish mood between our two countries and of stagnation."[44]

For the time being, U.S.-Russian relations were amicable, imbued with what President Obama referred to as the "spirit of Elbe," echoing the first meeting between American and Soviet troops on the Elbe River in Germany in 1945.[45] This sentiment facilitated significant achievements, including signing of the Strategic Arms Reduction Treaty and expansion of the overland supply route through Russia into Afghanistan.[46] The following year, after eighteen years of talks, Russia completed its accession negotiations with the World Trade Organization.[47]

Yet, just as the original spirit of Elbe turned out to be ephemeral and quickly supplanted by the Cold War and containment, the cordial atmosphere of the Medvedev interregnum ended abruptly when Putin announced in September 2011 that he would once again take over the Russian presidency the following year.[48] His decision was driven partly by NATO's intervention in Libya in March 2011, which, as discussed later in this chapter, had been supported by Russia in the UN Security Council. Putin ultimately concluded that the West had hoodwinked Medvedev by expanding its military operations beyond the initial mandate: Putin saw an American agenda predicated on regime change rather than civilian protection. Surprised and offended by this *volte-face* at the top, Russians turned to the streets to protest what they perceived to be false parliamentary elections in December. Secretary Clinton, at an Organization for Security and Cooperation in Europe (OSCE) ministerial meeting (with Lavrov in attendance), expressed "serious concern about the conduct of the elections" and called for a "full investigation of all reports of fraud and intimidation."[49] Putin viewed this as unacceptable interference in domestic affairs and Russian sovereignty, and as an existential threat to his regime. He claimed that Clinton had sent "a signal" to "some actors in [Russia] . . . They heard the signal and with the support of the US State Department began active work."[50] Four years later, he would exact his revenge on Clinton through his own active measures in support of her opponent, Donald Trump, in the 2016 U.S. presidential election.

In 2012 and 2013, Obama met three times with the Russian president— once with lame duck Medvedev on the margins of the G20 in Seoul, and twice with Putin at the G20, first in Los Cabos and then in Northern Ireland. In contrast to previous summits, none of the meetings produced any significant deliverables.[51] The final rupture occurred when Edward Snowden, a criminally indicted contractor for the National Security Agency, arrived in Moscow with a treasure trove of U.S. classified intelligence and the Kremlin granted him political asylum as a "humanitarian" gesture. Obama called off the forthcoming U.S.-Russia summit in Moscow and announced a "pause" in the relationship.[52] Reset reverted to reticence.

NEW ERA OF ENGAGEMENT WITH THE WORLD AND PIVOT TO ASIA

Dealing with the global economic crisis through the G20, equalizing the transatlantic partnership, and resetting relations with Russia reflected the Obama-Biden administration's overall approach of a "new era of engagement with the world"—a key feature of which would be the so-called pivot to Asia.[53]

At a reception at the White House for foreign ambassadors, the president announced that the United States would "engage on the basis of mutual interest and mutual respect, so that we can build new partnerships for progress."[54] In his first speech to the United Nations General Assembly (UNGA), he declared that "more than at any point in human history, the interests of nations and peoples are shared."[55] To be sure, countries would still pursue their national interests, but progress would be limited on many collective challenges—such as climate change, global economic growth, nuclear nonproliferation, or counterterrorism—without global cooperation.

This new approach placed diplomacy first, rather than the use of force, and emphasized new initiatives, collaboration on common interests, and the sharing of both the responsibility and the burden for collective action. For instance, the Obama-Biden administration used each UNGA high-level week to mobilize efforts on behalf of a particular global challenge, such as nonproliferation and nuclear disarmament,[56] sustainable development,[57] and open government.[58] It also meant a rebalancing of resources—away from the over-investment of troops and war materiel in the Middle East and toward greater investment of economic resources to under-prioritized parts of the world, particularly Asia.

Obama delivered his first major foreign policy speech in Cairo. The president hoped to improve relations between the United States and Muslim-majority countries by directly confronting the atmosphere of "suspicion and discord" that characterized the prior administration. He noted that the "relationship between Islam and the West includes centuries of coexistence and cooperation, but also conflict and religious wars."[59] Seeking a "new beginning," Obama returned to his foreign policy organizing principles of "mutual interest and mutual respect." He argued that "America and Islam are not exclusive and need not be in competition," and share many principles in common.[60] The United States removed combat troops from all Iraqi cities the following month, pursuant to its agreement with Baghdad, and by the end of 2011, had withdrawn all of its troops from Iraq.

As the Obama-Biden administration reduced its military presence in the Middle East, it simultaneously expanded its diplomatic and economic presence in Asia. Obama always viewed the United States as both "a Pacific nation as well as an Atlantic nation,"[61] and his administration launched a new Strategic and Economic Dialogue with China, noting that the "relationship between the United States and China will shape the 21st century."[62]

The United States combined its outreach to China with efforts to build partnerships throughout the region. On a state visit to Japan, Obama declared himself "America's first Pacific President," and promised the United States would "strengthen and sustain our leadership in this vitally important part of the world."[63] He later met with the leaders of the ten ASEAN countries,[64] seeking to strengthen relationships with each of them.[65] The president succeeded in accelerating trade negotiations with eleven countries of the Trans-Pacific Partnership (TPP),[66] and committed the United States to "the goal of shaping a regional agreement that will have broad-based membership and the high standards worthy of a 21st century trade agreement."[67] In 2011, the United States also participated for the first time in the East Asia summit, grouping the ASEAN ten countries, six others (China, Japan, South Korea, Australia, New Zealand, and India), and Russia.[68]

Notwithstanding President Obama's frequent visits to Asia and his rhetoric about a "pivot" or "rebalance" to the region, he spent as much time meeting with leaders in Europe, and clearly recognized its enduring importance to the United States. Secretary of State Hillary Clinton also argued that America's ongoing relationship with Europe should be the model for its engagement with Asia:

> By virtue of our unique geography, the United States is both an Atlantic and a Pacific power. We are proud of our European partnerships and all that they deliver. Our challenge now is to build a web of partnerships and institutions across the Pacific that is as durable and as consistent with American interests and values as the web we have built across the Atlantic. That is the touchstone of our efforts in all these areas.[69]

She later noted, "Europe is and remains America's partner of first resort."[70] Likewise, Secretary of Defense Leon Panetta described Europe as our "security partner of choice for military operations and diplomacy around the world."[71] In his 2012 State of the Union, President Obama argued that America's "oldest alliances in Europe and Asia [we]re stronger than ever."[72]

President Obama believed that for decades the United States had spent too much time, energy, and money on problems in the Middle East. He was especially concerned about America's ongoing military presence in the region. In contrast, he saw Asia as critical to the economic and political future of the United States. Instead of remaining mired in the Middle East, the president hoped to increase America's commitment to the Asia-Pacific region through diplomatic and economic "forward-deployment."[73] Ironically, however, his emphasis on Asia fed the misperception that the United States was pivoting away from Europe. Indeed, former EU Ambassador to the United States David O'Sullivan, citing the pivot to Asia, argued that,

"Obama did not see Europe as central to his preoccupations."[74] On the other hand, O'Sullivan's counterpart in Brussels, U.S. Ambassador to the EU Anthony Gardner, considered that "Europe always figured as a major part of U.S. foreign policy, including during the Obama years" notwithstanding the pivot. He added, "we just weaken ourselves when we actually do not consider each other as partners of first resort."[75]

In part, the misperception stemmed from the fact that during President Obama's first term, the administration found few opportunities to collaborate with Europe relative to extensive prospects in Asia. In the end, the president was not able to engage either region to the degree he had hoped; and as committed as he was not to be "sideline[d]" from his strategy of pivoting to Asia,[76] he could not avoid continuing to be absorbed by crises in the Middle East in the aftermath of the Arab Spring in 2011.

ARAB SPRING AND NATO'S INTERVENTION IN LIBYA

On December 17, 2010, a spark spread like wildfire across the Middle East and North Africa when a young vendor in Tunisia set himself aflame to protest the indignity he suffered when the police confiscated his cart. Obama later described his act as akin to the "defiance of those patriots in Boston who refused to pay taxes to a king or the dignity of Rosa Parks as she sat courageously in her seat."[77] Faced with a rapidly growing opposition movement later known as the Jasmine Revolution, Tunisian President Zine El Abidine Ben Ali ended his twenty-three-year rule and fled to Saudi Arabia.

Elsewhere, change occurred less smoothly. In response to peaceful protests that began on February 15, 2011, in opposition to Colonel Muammar al-Qaddafi's rule, the Libyan regime deployed military force to suppress the protests. The following week, the League of Arab States condemned the violence against civilians and suspended Libya's membership. In turn, the U.N. Security Council issued a similar condemnation, called for a cease-fire, and referred the case to the International Criminal Court to investigate the possibility of war crimes.[78]

On March 16, with his troops poised outside Benghazi, a city of over 500,000 people, Qaddafi escalated the crisis by threatening a large-scale massacre of the protesters. Using language commonly associated with prior acts of genocide and crimes against humanity, he warned: "We will come house by house, room by room. It's over. The issue has been decided. . . . We will find you in your closets. We will have no mercy and no pity."[79] The Arab League called for the imposition of a no-fly zone over Libya to protect civilians.[80]

Given the imminent risk and with the request from the Arab League, the Security Council authorized "all necessary measures . . . to protect civilians and civilian populated areas under threat of attack" in Libya, including imposing a no-fly zone and providing arms.[81] The League's resolution calling for the imposition of a no-fly zone "changed everything" by galvanizing international public opinion in support of the intervention and preventing regional resistance during the military mission.[82] After the Security Council approved the resolution, Arab League Secretary-General Amr Moussa argued, "the no-fly zone could not have been imposed were it not for the Arab League."[83] The following day, President Obama declared that Qaddafi had lost "the legitimacy to lead" and declared a U.S. interest in humanitarian intervention and regional stability.[84]

On March 19, select NATO countries (this time led by the UK and France rather than the United States) began air strikes against Libyan military targets that constituted an ongoing threat to the civilian population.[85] In what later would be derided as "leading from behind,"[86] the NATO military intervention in Libya represented a paradigm of burden-sharing in cases of collective action where America's security was not threatened directly but its interests and values were challenged. As Obama explained: "The burden of action should not be America's alone. As we have in Libya, our task is instead to mobilize the international community for collective action. Because contrary to the claims of some, American leadership is not simply a matter of going it alone and bearing all of the burden ourselves."[87]

Whereas the United States carried "the lion's share of the burden when it came to setting the stage for NATO operations" by disabling Libya's air defense systems, once NATO assumed command and control, the United States' "primary role would be a whole range of support that utilized America's unique capabilities."[88] In this manner, NATO allies conducted 90 percent of overall strike missions. Besides NATO, regional actors—such as Qatar, the United Arab Emirates, and the local rebel movement—also contributed to the operation. Obama argued, the "alliance must work in the 21st century" with "more nations bearing the burdens and costs of peace and security."[89]

Due to the international intervention, the impending humanitarian disaster in Libya was averted. Civilian casualties, estimated by the new Libyan government to be in the range of 30,000 to 50,000, were substantially lower than the potential massacre threatened by Qaddafi's forces in the city of Benghazi alone. By September 2011, the opposition movement seized control of the capital, Tripoli, along with other key cities and strategic points in Libya, and eventually captured Qaddafi. The United States' total share of the military operations in Libya was approximately $1.65 billion, or less than two weeks spent in Iraq.[90] NATO's intervention in Libya appeared to be the new benchmark for effective transatlantic cooperation.

Indeed, the spring and summer of 2011 were heady times. Long-standing autocrats in Tunisia, Egypt, Cote d'Ivoire, Yemen, and Libya fell from power. In a covert operation, U.S. Special Forces killed Osama bin Laden, who had been hiding in Pakistan for ten years.[91] The G8 announced a range of economic and political support for the changes sweeping through the region through the so-called Deauville Partnership[92] and viewed the Arab Spring as a continued expansion of the liberal order, freedom, and democracy.[93] In language reminiscent of National Security Advisor Brent Scowcroft two decades earlier, President Obama argued that "this historic moment must not be squandered."[94]

However, within twelve months, both the tenor of the Arab Spring and implications of the Libyan intervention would significantly change after a terrorist attack against the U.S. embassy in Benghazi killed several American diplomats, including Ambassador Christopher Stevens.[95] Neither NATO nor the Arab League partners provided the necessary peacekeeping forces to maintain post-conflict stability in Libya, mainly because the fledgling Libyan government did not want external troops but also because the outside powers did not want to have troops on the ground.

Rather than serving as an example of transatlantic partnership, Libya became the anti-precedent: an example of what the United States should avoid, namely being persuaded by European allies to engage in military intervention with unknowable consequences and high risk of long-term failure. This lesson came to explain much of the transatlantic tension that evolved over U.S. policy in Syria.

SYRIA

The crisis in Syria bedeviled the Obama-Biden administration and caused underlying friction between the United States and Europe. Two months after the outbreak of conflict in Libya, protesters in Damascus, like in other parts of the Arab world, rose up against the forty-year autocratic rule of the Assad family.[96] Violence escalated, and the Assad regime cracked down on protests at the same time the opposition in Libya seemed to be close to overthrowing the Qaddafi regime. By mid-August 2011, President Obama used language similar to that he had used regarding Libya, and called for Bashar al-Assad to "step aside."[97] The United States and the EU imposed economic sanctions against Syria, and the Arab League suspended Syria's membership.[98] In October, several opposition groups combined into the Syrian National Council. By the end of 2011, the conflict in Syria had claimed the lives of approximately 10,000 soldiers and civilians.

Increasing the diplomatic pressure, Obama declared, "Assad has no right to lead Syria and has lost all legitimacy with his people and the international community."[99] The United States closed its embassy, as did the Gulf Cooperation Council. In February 2012, the United States and Europe worked within the UNGA to support the Arab League's plan for Assad to step down, yielding a nonbinding resolution of 137 in favor and twelve against. Underlying the vote, many hoped the successful military intervention in Libya would reverberate with Assad.

However, the conflict continued, and the casualties accumulated. Without any political resolution, pressure built up within the United States and the wider global community for military intervention. President Obama decided against the use of force, and rejected comparisons between Libya and Syria. He pointed out that in Libya there was the "prospect of imminent massacre"[100] and a clear international mandate for action from the UN Security Council while in Syria there was extensive violence but no immediate risk of mass casualties. Moreover, Assad led a much stronger military than Qaddafi's, and confronted a significantly more diffuse local opposition, numbering in the hundreds of separate groups. Finally, due to Russian and Chinese vetoes, there was no consensus in the Security Council.

The crisis became even more complicated in the summer of 2012. In July, the Syrian regime acknowledged for the first time that it possessed chemical weapons, which it claimed it would use only against external aggression. Given long-standing U.S. vital interest against the use or prolifer-ation of weapons of mass destruction, Obama drew what became known as the "red-line": "We have communicated in no uncertain terms with every player in the region that that's a red line for us and that there would be enor-mous consequences if we start seeing movement on the chemical weapons front or the use of chemical weapons. That would change my calculations significantly."[101]

The phrase "enormous consequences" evoked the memory of the George W. Bush administration. Bush had talked of "significant consequences" in the run-up to the Iraq war, thereby justifying the use of force based on the U.S. vital interest in nonproliferation of weapons of mass destruction (WMD). In particular, the United States was concerned that WMD could be trans-ferred to a terrorist group, such as al-Qaeda, that could not be deterred from using it against civilians. Meanwhile, Syrian casualties reached 60,000, with 300,000 refugees and 2 million internally displaced persons (IDPs).

Several senior officials in the Obama-Biden administration, notably Secretary of State Clinton and CIA Director David Petraeus, urged more robust intervention, either through the imposition of a no-fly zone (as in Libya) or greater assistance to the rebels. Yet, the no-fly zone option lacked a UN mandate and faced the military obstacle of the significant Syrian air defense systems (backed by Russia). And the assistance option lacked a unified opposition to support. Moreover, by the fall of 2012, Libya hardly looked like a good precedent for intervention, given the attacks against the U.S. embassy and overall instability in the country.

In December 2012 and March 2013, international organizations on the ground in Syria reported the use of sarin gas in Homs and Aleppo on a small scale, resulting in numerous casualties. Over the next few months, a UN inspection team investigated these attacks. Then, on August 21, 2013, reports emerged of large-scale use of chemical weapons in Ghouta, on the outskirts of Damascus, with more than 1,000 casualties.

With the red line seemingly crossed, British Prime Minister David Cam-eron and French President François Hollande called for air strikes. But on August 29, the UK House of Commons voted against military intervention, eliminating British support. Only the French remained poised to launch air strikes. The following day, the United States released a government assessment expressing "high confidence" that the Syrian government had used chemical weapons. Given this determination, Obama decided that the

"United States should take military action against Syrian regime targets" to hold Assad accountable for the use of chemical weapons, deter its future use, and degrade the regime's capacity to do so.[102] However, he also decided to seek authorization from Congress for the use of force, even though he did not believe it was constitutionally required. At one point, President Obama became uncharacteristically defensive, stating that his "credibility is not on the line, the international community's credibility is on the line. And America and Congress's credibility is on the line because we give lip service to the notion that these international norms are important."[103]

The vote in Congress never occurred, and the air strikes were aborted. In response to a question at a press conference in London, Secretary of State John Kerry said that Assad could avoid an attack if he turned over all of Syria's chemical weapons within a week—also, concluding that "he isn't about to do it, and it can't be done, obviously."[104] In a surprise move, Russian Foreign Minister Sergey Lavrov proposed that Syria could turn over its chemical weapons under international control and dismantlement. The next day, Syria agreed to the Russian plan and President Obama called off the vote in Congress to pursue the diplomatic option while maintaining the threat of the use of force.[105] He declared, "if diplomacy fails, the United States remain[ed] prepared to act."[106] The deal was formalized in mid-September, and by June 2014, the Assad regime announced it had removed all of the declared chemical weapons stockpile.

Obama's decision against arming rebels in 2012 and launching air strikes to enforce the red line in 2013 came to be perceived as reflecting a retrenchment from global affairs and a reluctance to use force. There were sound reasons for each decision: a subsequent Pentagon training program in 2015 proved ineffective, and the deal to remove chemical weapons from Syria was itself made possible solely under the threat of the use of force. Particularly in the case of the red line, Russia would not have proposed the deal—and Syria would not have accepted—if the threat had not been credible. Some argued that the United States should have taken the deal *and* launched air strikes, but under that scenario, Russia and Syria would have perceived the deal as broken by the United States and would have kept the weapons in Syria. If the United States waited to launch the air strikes until after all the declared stockpiles were removed, it would have appeared as an arbitrary act of aggression rather than the enforcement of an international norm against chemical weapons.

The red line episode came to be viewed widely around the world as epitomizing the lack of U.S. resolve and consistency in foreign policy. Though Europeans broadly welcomed, in principle, Obama's reluctance to use force as a course correction for George W. Bush's reckless policies, his credibility was paradoxically diminished even in Europe. Even seven years later, for instance, French President Macron linked U.S. inaction over the red line to Russian aggression in Ukraine, where Putin was emboldened to intervene due to perceived American and European passivity in Syria.[107]

Divisions also emerged over perceived national interests. In Europe generally, and France in particular, U.S. policy on Syria came to be viewed as reflecting U.S. indifference to European interests, given that U.S. security and prosperity was less affected by events in the Middle East. In contrast, Europe's borders could be easily crossed by land via Turkey or by sea through Greece. Within a year of the red line episode, ISIL began conducting its first terrorist attacks in Europe. And the following year, the EU was in existential crisis due to the irregular migration of millions of refugees and economic migrants into the continent.

Obama defined the U.S. national interest in Syria in more limited terms. In contrast to the claim that U.S. influence in the Middle East and global credibility were at stake, Obama argued that the United States shared an interest in Syria with other international actors in eliminating chemical weapons and countering terrorism; there was, he stressed, "no Great Game to be won."[108] As he had in other conflicts, Obama concluded that the collective interest in Syria, both its humanitarian and security dimensions, required collective action rather than U.S. intervention.

Generally, Obama distinguished between core interests and non-core interests in the Middle East and North Africa. The United States was prepared to use all instruments of power, including military force, unilaterally or with like-minded partners, to secure four categories of "core interests" in the region: confronting external aggression against U.S. allies and partners; ensuring the free flow of energy from the region to the world; dismantling terrorist networks that threaten U.S. citizens; and countering the development or use of WMD.[109]

He also defined broader categories of U.S. non-core interests, such as general peace and prosperity in the Middle East and North Africa, with the promotion of democracy, human rights, and open markets. These objectives, however, were not attainable through U.S. unilateral or military action, and were served better through partnership with other international actors.

Though not widely known at the time, nor sufficiently appreciated currently, the United States had, in fact, initiated an extensive covert train-and-equip program to support the Syrian rebels.[110] The administration committed more than $1 billion over four years to the largest operation of its kind since support for the mujahedeen in Afghanistan in the 1980s. President Obama would "not comment on specifics around [U.S.] programs related to the Syrian opposition,"[111] which had the perverse consequence that the United States was criticized for not doing more to help the rebels in Syria at the same time it was, in fact, conducting a significant intervention. It is unclear to what extent European allies were briefed on the covert operations, but, apparently, it was insufficient to assuage their fears and concerns.

With an accumulation of over 70,000 casualties, 2 million refugees, and 6.5 million IDPs, 2013 became the deadliest year in Syria to date—with no end in sight.

———

During President Obama's second term, his administration found itself preoccupied with a fight against ISIL, the civil war in Syria, and other problems in the Middle East. Moreover, both the United States and the EU confronted another serious foreign policy challenge when a revanchist Russia seized Crimea and initiated a conflict in eastern Ukraine.

CONFRONTING NEW CHALLENGES: ISIL AND RUSSIA

ISIL emerged formally in 2013 amid the chaos of the civil war in Syria and instability in Iraq after the withdrawal of U.S. combat forces at the end of 2011. In January 2014, it captured Falluja and threatened the Iraqi government in Baghdad. Yet, President Obama initially viewed the group as a localized threat, comparing it to a "jayvee team" that did not have "the capacity and reach of a bin Laden and a network that is actively planning major terrorist plots against the [U.S.] homeland" but rather consisted of "jihadists who are engaged in various local power struggles and disputes."[112] By June, however, the group had captured Mosul, the second-largest city in Iraq, and proclaimed itself as the government of a caliphate, the Islamic State.

Obama initially resisted intervening militarily. In a speech at West Point, he reiterated his argument that "when issues of global concern do not pose a direct threat to the United States," it "must mobilize allies and partners to take collective action."[113] Noting that "invading every country that harbors terrorist networks is naïve and unsustainable," he stressed that the United States must, instead, "more effectively partner with countries where terrorist networks seek a foothold."[114]

The United States eventually ordered unilateral military strikes against ISIL in August 2014—not as a counterterrorism mission but, rather, to avert an impending threat of genocide against the Yazidi religious minority group, tens of thousands of whom were stranded on Mount Sinjar. Similar to the justification for the Libyan intervention, the attack was comparably swift and successful. It also paved the way for further intervention after ISIL beheaded several Americans hostages.

On September 10, Obama announced a strategy to "degrade and ultimately destroy ISIL" by leading "a broad coalition to roll back this terrorist threat."[115] The policy consisted of authorizing airstrikes, deploying U.S. Special Forces, and launching a new train-and-equip program to develop local forces. Holding back also encouraged the Iraqi government to form, after the prior one under Prime Minister Maliki collapsed amid the emerging instability.[116]

Most important, it involved mobilizing an international coalition of over forty countries to counter and destroy ISIL.[117] Notably, the Counter-ISIL Coalition (C-ISIL) included all twenty-eight NATO allies, as well as NATO and the EU as institutional partners. For the first time in its history, Germany supplied weapons to equip 4,000 Iraqi Kurds. On the other hand, the United States conducted the initial airstrikes with regional allies such as Saudi Arabia, United Arab Emirates, Jordan, Bahrain, and Qatar, but without any European participation.[118] Eventually, other countries contributed troops as well as support through other means, such as tackling terrorist financing, preventing the movement of foreign terrorist fighters, and countering ISIL's propaganda. By December, the coalition had grown to nearly sixty countries, which met at the NATO headquarters in Brussels. Yet, ISIL also had expanded to control 8 million people between Syria and Iraq, with the capital of its so-called Islamic State in Raqqa.

The following year saw steady coalition gains against ISIL amid the back-and-forth of military conflict. But the security environment became increasingly complex. In fact, two wars raged within Syria: one between Assad (backed by Iran and Russia) and the opposition groups (backed by the West and several Arab countries) and another between ISIL and the U.S.-led coalition. The United States' primary interest was in fighting Islamic terrorists, but it needed to rely on local forces, which were committed to fighting Assad. The Assad regime and Russia, in turn, wanted to conflate ISIL with all opposition groups, treating all opponents as terrorists. Some countries within the U.S.-led coalition also wanted to expand the fight against ISIL to include the Assad regime, arguing that ISIL emerged, in part, because of the violence and chaos caused by Assad—thus, both cause and consequence had to be addressed concurrently. In the fog of war, it became more and more difficult to distinguish between friend and foe and to discern the core political and military objectives.

At the G7 summit in Germany in June 2015, Obama conceded that, notwithstanding the military progress, the coalition did not "yet have a complete strategy because it requires commitments on the part of the Iraqis as well about how recruitment takes place, how that training takes place. And so the details of that are not yet worked out."[119] The crux of the problem was that the United States viewed defeating ISIL in terms of collective security rather than as a "direct threat to the homeland."[120]

Europe, however, experienced the terrorist violence firsthand: in May 2014 in Brussels against the Jewish Museum, killing four; in November 2015 in Paris at the Bataclan nightclub, killing over 130 and injuring over 400; again in Brussels in March 2016 at the airport, killing over thirty and injuring over 300; in July 2016 in Nice, killing over eighty and injuring over 400; and in Germany in December 2016, killing twelve. ISIL had both direct and indirect links to the attacks, some of which were planned in Syria and then implemented by local terrorist cells.[121] Moreover, terrorist attacks generally fluctuated with ISIL's success, which attracted new followers from around the world, whereas its setbacks led to fewer attempts.

In response, the coalition flew approximately 9,000 sorties in 2015, trained and equipped numerous local forces in Iraq and Syria, and killed tens of thousands of ISIL fighters.[122] As the fight against ISIL progressed, so did the civil war against Assad, so that by the summer of 2015, the Syrian regime was "crumbling."[123] At the UN General Assembly high-level week, the United States held a summit on countering ISIL and violent extremism, mustering a broad coalition of leaders from "more than 100 countries,

20 multilateral bodies, and 120 civil society and private sector organizations."[124] President Obama also stressed the need for "a managed transition
away from Assad and to a new leader and an inclusive Government."[125]
Both wars, against ISIL and against Assad, appeared to be progressing according to the U.S.-led coalition's preferences. And then, a day after the
U.S. C-ISIL summit and a bilateral meeting between Putin and Obama on
the margins of the UNGA, Russia surprised many observers by intervening
heavily with troops and materiel in support of the Assad regime. With this
move, Putin turned the tide in Assad's favor.

Russia tried to position its intervention so as not only to shore up its
Syrian ally but also to defeat ISIL. And as Obama readily acknowledged,
"the United States and Russia and the entire world ha[d] a common interest
in destroying ISIL."[126] But Russia did not differentiate "between ISIL and
a moderate Sunni opposition that wants to see Mr. Asad go," and, instead,
treated all these groups as terrorists.[127] The U.S. administration argued
that "a military solution alone, an attempt by Russia and Iran to prop up
Assad and try to pacify the population is just going to get them stuck in a
quagmire."[128] Over time, Russia would direct most of its firepower against
non-ISIL opposition groups, leaving most of the fight to the coalition. Notwithstanding the reality on the ground, Russia manipulated the strategic
narrative sufficiently so that some in Europe, and even in the United States,
began to view it as leading the fight against global terrorism. And due to
the need for deconfliction of military operations between Russia and the
United States in Syria, some wanted this military channel (which was a
matter of necessity) to serve as the basis for a wider U.S.-Russia dialogue
and cooperation (which was a matter of choice). Yet, Russia never expressed
any interest in joining the sixty-five-country C-ISIL coalition, preferring,
instead, its own "coalition of two" along with Iran in propping up Assad.[129]
Notwithstanding hopes to the contrary, a coalition between Russia and the
United States in Syria would never have been possible given their conflicting political and military objectives.

By the end of 2015, the U.S.-led coalition had liberated 40 percent of
the territory once held by ISIL in Iraq, as well as territory in Syria.[130] Gradually, the United States also sent Special Forces into Syria, starting with
a small unit of fifty and expanding to 300 by mid-2016 (alongside over
4,000 combat troops in Iraq).[131] European allies fielded over 6,000 troops
to Iraq and Syria to conduct training and advising missions, air combat,

and special operations.[132] By the end of the Obama-Biden administration, the coalition had grown to over seventy countries, and flown more than 16,000 airstrikes, at a cost of $10 billion over the two years—the same amount spent in one month at the peak of the war in Iraq.[133] Within a few months, the coalition and local Kurdish forces in Syria would liberate Raqqa, and ISIL's territorial control was eventually destroyed, further illustrating what the United States and Europe can accomplish together alongside like-minded partners. Yet, for many observers in the United States and Europe, these years of relatively effective transatlantic cooperation are likely to be remembered as much for the discord over the 2013 red-line episode as for the subsequent military success against ISIL.

UKRAINE

The conflict that came to epitomize Western unity—Russia's aggression in Ukraine—had a relatively benign beginning early in the Obama-Biden administration. In April 2010, President Obama met with the newly elected Ukrainian President Viktor Yanukovych to reaffirm their "strategic partnership" launched under the George W. Bush administration with the U.S.-Ukraine Charter on Strategic Partnership.[134] The bilateral meeting occurred on the margins of the Global Nuclear Security Summit amid six other bilateral meetings that day, but Ukraine did not feature prominently on the U.S. foreign policy agenda until conflict erupted later in 2014.

Meanwhile, the European Union launched negotiations on an Association Agreement (AA) and a Deep and Comprehensive Free Trade Agreement (DCFTA) to facilitate greater political and economic integration with Ukraine. In March 2012, after four years of technical negotiations, the two sides initialed the agreements with further electoral, judicial, and constitutional reforms as preconditions for a final signing planned for the next EU Eastern Partnership summit in Vilnius in November 2013. In September 2013, the Ukrainian government approved the draft AA and the Parliament expressed its intention to enact the reforms required by the EU. Ukraine, a former member of the Soviet Republic, appeared to be drifting into the orbit of the West.

Two months later, however, in the days shortly before the planned signing, the Ukrainian government reversed course and stated it would not conclude the EU agreement given opposition from Russia. The EU responded that its offer was still on the table.[135] Tens of thousands of protesters turned to the streets in Kyiv—in *Maidan Nezalezhnosti* (Independence Square), later also dubbed Euro-Maidan—to express their continued support for integration with the EU (and, implicitly, the West). Russia, in turn, offered the Ukrainian government a $15 billion loan and a subsidized gas deal, but it was clear the public wanted separation from Moscow as protests swelled to nearly a million in Kyiv alone.

In February 2014, the protests escalated into violence when Ukraine's secret services opened fire on the protesters, killing nearly 100. As a result of the massacre, Yanukovych lost all credibility. Parliament impeached him and appointed a new interim government, and the former, disgraced president fled to Russia.

During this four-month period, President Obama noticeably refrained from comment regarding the emerging conflict in Ukraine. He made an oblique reference in the January 2014 State of the Union speech about standing for "the principle that all people have the right to express themselves freely and peacefully and to have a say in their country's future."[136] Only after Yanukovych was overthrown did Obama address the situation directly. He warned Russia that there would be "costs for any military intervention" and emphasized U.S. interest in permitting the Ukrainian people to "determine their own future."[137] The president's rhetoric, like so many of his predecessors dating back to Roosevelt, was rooted in the concept of self-determination.

By then, Putin had already decided to seize Crimea, a Ukrainian peninsula on the Black Sea where Russia had a lease on a naval base in Sebastopol until 2042. Crimea had been conquered by Catherine the Great in 1783 and remained part of the Russian Empire, and had remained within Soviet Russia until 1954, when Khrushchev transferred it to Soviet Ukraine. While the formal transfer was celebrated by Ukraine, it was largely inconsequential at the time, since both Russia and Ukraine were part of the Soviet Union and controlled by the Kremlin. After the collapse of the USSR in 1991, Crimea remained within Ukraine while continuing to host the Russian Black Sea Fleet.

Russia's so-called "little green men" poured into Crimea, either covertly or under the pretext of snap military exercises. On February 27, they seized government institutions in Crimea and, within two weeks, held a referendum on Russia's annexation of Crimea. The implausible vote of 96 percent in favor on an 82 percent turnout suggested blatant rigging of the process. Two days later, Russia completed the annexation.[138]

On March 18, the day of annexation, Putin delivered a sweeping address justifying Russia's actions. Noting their "shared history and pride," he argued that, "Crimea has always been an inseparable part of Russia."[139] He then accused the West of numerous abuses: lying behind Russia's back, violating international law, expanding NATO to Russia's borders, deploying the missile defense system, and finally "cross[ing] the line" in Ukraine.[140] Though negotiations with the EU triggered the conflict in Ukraine, Putin viewed it as part and parcel of Ukraine's wider integration with the West, including NATO—his primary threat. He observed:

> We have already heard declarations from Kiev about Ukraine soon joining NATO. What would this have meant for Crimea and Sevastopol in the future? It would have meant that NATO's navy would be right there in this city of Russia's military glory, and this would create not an illusory but a perfectly real threat to the whole of southern Russia. . . . NATO remains a military alliance, and we are against having a military alliance making itself at home right in our backyard or in our historic territory.[141]

Initially, the West ejected Russia from the G8. However, over the course of the next several weeks, the United States laid out a more comprehensive series of steps that included hosting Arseniy Yatsenyuk, the new Ukrainian prime minister, at the White House, and extending $1 billion in loan guarantees. The Obama-Biden administration imposed economic sanctions against Russia and its agents in Crimea (and later in the Donbas in eastern Ukraine), but offered Russia an off-ramp through negotiations and deescalation.[142] The United States also committed to shore up NATO allies, particularly those in Central and Eastern Europe that felt vulnerable to Russian threats.

Only a week later, the G7 leaders met on the margins of the Nuclear Security Summit in The Hague, Netherlands, to reaffirm their resolve against Russia's actions in Ukraine. President Obama once again condemned the seizure of territory through the use of force, and dismissed Russia as a "regional power"[143] led by a someone who has "got that kind of slouch, looking like the bored kid in the back of the classroom."[144] He argued that "the

Ukrainians shouldn't have to choose between the West and Russia."[145] Yet, on the same trip to Europe, Obama stopped in Brussels for a summit with the leaders of the EU and observed that "the United States has long supported European integration as a force for peace and prosperity" and that "Europe's progress rest[ed] on basic principles, including respect for international law, as well as the sovereignty and territorial integrity of nations."[146]

Later in the day, Obama gave a wide-ranging speech to the "European youth" to define the stakes in Ukraine. He observed that the conflict was "a moment of testing for Europe and the United States and for the international order that we have worked for generations to build."[147] That order was built around a "particular set of [liberal] ideals" that originated in Western Europe and inspired the American Revolution.[148]

He, then, somewhat uncharacteristically, set forth what could be described as the credo of the liberal order: "Yes, we believe in democracy, with elections that are free and fair, and independent judiciaries and opposition parties, civil society and uncensored information so that individuals can make their own choices. Yes, we believe in open economies based on free markets and innovation and individual initiative and entrepreneurship and trade and investment that creates a broader prosperity."[149]

He concluded that the struggle in Ukraine is a "challenge to our ideals—to our very international order" and that "over the long haul, as nations that are free, as free people, the future is ours."[150] President Obama did not draw a red line over Crimea with Russia, and, indeed, he made clear that Ukrainians themselves should determine their future. Yet, in all his speeches, in all his rhetoric, he made clear that the crisis in Ukraine was a seminal moment for the transatlantic alliance, for the West, and for the liberal order. The problem, of course, was what to do about it.

In addition to transatlantic sanctions, the United States and EU engaged jointly in diplomatic efforts to try to resolve the conflict. These efforts, capped by nearly seven hours of negotiations led by Secretary of State John Kerry and High Representative Catherine Ashton, yielded an interim framework agreement in April, in the so-called Geneva format with Ukraine and Russia.[151] Although Ukraine had taken initial steps to comply with the agreement, Russia had not publicly endorsed any diplomatic track and the Geneva format did not advance much further.[152]

Alongside economic sanctions and diplomatic efforts, the United States reinforced NATO's eastern flank through pre-positioning of equipment in parts of Central and Eastern Europe and increasing U.S. military presence in Europe through the so-called European Reassurance Initiative (ERI). (The ERI would eventually grow fourfold, to $3.4 billion for fiscal year 2017.)[153] Meeting with regional leaders in Warsaw, Obama stressed that NATO allies "will never stand alone,"[154] echoing the same refrain later in Estonia where he affirmed that NATO's "Article 5 is crystal clear: An attack on one is an attack on all."[155]

Yet, viewing the conflict in Ukraine as a challenge shared by others, Obama also encouraged leadership from Europe. Symbolically, the G7 leaders moved the 2014 summit from its planned location in Sochi, Russia, to Brussels, where it was hosted for the first time by the European Union. On the margins of the seventieth anniversary commemorations of the D-Day landings in Normandy, German Chancellor Merkel and French President Hollande met with their Ukrainian and Russian counterparts, without Obama seeking a formal role. At the NATO summit in Wales, UK, in September 2014, the United States received political commitments from all twenty-eight allied leaders to increase defense spending toward 2 percent of GDP, addressing the issue of burden-sharing Obama had flagged at the beginning of his administration.[156] Citing the Ukraine conflict at the UN General Assembly, Obama emphasized his long-running theme that "all of us—big nations and small—must meet our responsibility to observe and enforce international norms."[157] At the end of his administration, he argued for "a strong Europe to bear its share of the burden, working with [the United States] on behalf of our collective security" because while the United States has "an extraordinary military, the best the world's ever known . . . the nature of today's threats means [it] can't deal with these challenges by [itself]."[158] The strategy of emphasizing the equality of partnership with Europe began to deliver, as European policymakers took greater initiative in addressing crises and bore larger shares of the burden.

This approach facilitated quick joint responses to new events. For instance, in mid-July, Russian-assisted separatists in eastern Ukrainian shot down Malaysia Airlines flight MH-17, which was flying close to the Russian-Ukrainian border (mistaking it for a military cargo plan), killing nearly 300 civilians. The United States imposed a range of new sanctions on Russian energy, arms, and financial sectors. Notably, the EU did, as well, having been previously reluctant to do so given the economic blowback it would involve. The transatlantic synergies meant "an even bigger bite" on the Russian economy.[159]

The collective responsibility approach also entailed downside risks. For instance, after the stalled Geneva format talks, a Trilateral Contact Group between Ukraine, Russia, and the OSCE agreed to the Minsk Protocols in September 2014. This accord consisted of a cease-fire and several obligations on both Ukraine and Russia regarding Ukrainian control over the border, exchange of prisoners, free and fair regional elections in eastern Ukraine, and decentralization. However, the cease-fire quickly broke down, and heavy fighting resumed over the next three months, with significant risk that the Russian-backed separatist groups would extend control into other major cities in eastern Ukraine.

To avert further escalation, the Normandy format leaders convened in Minsk in February 2015 to negotiate a new cease-fire. In effect, after nearly sixteen hours of negotiations among Merkel, Hollande, Petro Poroshenko, and Vladimir Putin, the parties agreed on the so-called Package of Measures to Implement the Minsk Agreements—the same basic bargain as before but with much stronger political backing. Ultimately, this accord also proved ephemeral.

Nonetheless, the Minsk Agreements from September 2014 and February 2015 became the organizing principle for economic pressure against Russia; as the G7 leaders noted, "duration of sanctions should be clearly linked to Russia's complete implementation of the Minsk agreements and respect for Ukraine's sovereignty."[160] EU sectoral sanctions became tied to Minsk implementation, and, thus, rollover of sanctions every six months—no easy feat given wobbly states susceptible to Russian pressure, such as Hungary, Cyprus, or Italy—proved nearly automatic. Moreover, the G7, in June 2015, endorsed a "Ukraine support group," convening the G7 ambassadors in Kyiv to facilitate economic and technical assistance to Ukraine.[161]

On the U.S. side, a number of high-level administration officials—most prominently Vice President Joe Biden, Secretary of State John Kerry, Deputy Secretary of State Antony Blinken, and Assistant Secretary of State Victoria Nuland—showed support for Ukraine through visits and speeches. However, President Obama viewed Ukraine as a matter for collective responsibility, and, notwithstanding numerous trips to Europe, he never visited Kyiv. Obama reportedly told aides that his presence in Ukraine would only antagonize Russia and escalate the conflict. The unavoidable implication was that others should bear the majority of the burden.[162]

In truth, President Obama believed the United States had limited concrete interests in Ukraine beyond supporting the principles of territorial integrity and state sovereignty. Though the promotion of democracy and human rights are central to the overall liberal order, the president's caution was supported by some commentators, who argued that Ukraine existed outside of the order due to its historical links with Russia. Ultimately, Obama's reticence to engage on Ukraine was difficult to justify given that he negotiated personally with other leaders on other collective issues, such as migration and climate change. He also convened high-level gatherings on shared challenges such as the Nuclear Security Summit in 2010 and the refugees summit in 2016.

One benefit of Obama's cautious approach was the emergence of French and German leadership on this issue. Given that Ukraine impacted security and economic interests of Europeans much more directly, it was only logical that they should lead the international response. On the other hand, the development of European leadership through the Normandy format was somewhat accidental; after all, other European countries, such as the UK or Poland, expressed greater interest in Ukraine than did France. Moreover, drawing clear conceptual distinctions between the interests of Europe and the United States on an issue such as Ukraine suggested there might be larger divisions between the two sides in the future.

Transatlantic policy toward Ukraine lacked active U.S. engagement at the highest level and, notwithstanding its overall effectiveness, sent the wrong message to Russia as well as European allies about the president's personal commitment to Europe's peace and security. To be sure, Obama sounded the right tones in speeches in Warsaw and Tallinn on the ironclad nature of NATO's collective defense clause under Article 5. Nevertheless, the overall misperception of U.S. disengagement from Europe—due to the reset with Russia, pivot to Asia, and inaction in Syria—continued to solidify.

NEW BEGINNINGS (T-TIP, JCPOA, EBOLA, AND CLIMATE)

Notwithstanding the continuing problems in Syria and other parts of the Middle East, there were a few significant achievements during the second Obama-Biden administration in collaboration with European partners. In 2013, on the margins of the G8 summit in Northern Ireland,[163] the two sides launched ambitious negotiations on a Transatlantic Trade and Investment Partnership Agreement (T-TIP), with important potential geostrategic and economic mutual benefits. Because the transatlantic economy was already deeply intertwined with nearly $1 trillion in trade supporting millions of jobs on both sides, the United States and the EU proposed to address complex regulatory and nontariff barriers.[164] Notably, it took more than eighteen months to even set an agenda—hardly an example of dynamism in the transatlantic relationship—yet President Obama argued that the U.S. "relationship with Europe remains the cornerstone of our freedom and our security . . . our partner in almost everything that we do."[165] He elaborated on this theme in a wide-ranging speech at the Brandenburg Gate in Berlin in which he declared that "our trade and our commerce is the engine of our global economy."[166]

However, T-TIP negotiations faced uphill political battles in Europe, with concerns over imports of chlorinated chicken from the United States into the EU and domination of critical economic sectors by American multinational firms. On the U.S. side, T-TIP always seemed secondary to TPP negotiations in the Asia-Pacific region, which were successfully concluded in February 2016. In the end, while negotiators made important progress, the T-TIP talks fizzled out because they ran out of time to work through the vast number of concerns and unsettled issues. A comprehensive trade agreement between the United States and Europe remains elusive, but looking to the future, both sides better understand the fault lines, and leaders, for the most part, recognize the enormous potential as well.

The main accomplishments of the transatlantic partnership during the remainder of Obama's tenure involved global security across a range of issues: countering the Ebola virus in West Africa, forging the Joint Comprehensive Plan of Action with Iran, and catalyzing the Paris Agreement on climate change.

The Ebola crisis first emerged in December 2013 in Guinea. A highly deadly though not easily transmitted disease, the virus gradually expanded to nearly forty-nine cases and twenty-nine deaths by March 2014, when the World Health Organization declared its official outbreak. In response to inquiries from President Obama, "a multiagency process was established that began to spin the wheels of [the United States] government response that would encompass agencies as diverse as the Centers for Disease Control and Prevention (CDC), the National Institutes of Health (NIH), the State Department, and the U.S. military."[167] By July 2014, Ebola expanded to neighboring countries Sierra Leone and Liberia. Over the following year, the three countries would experience over 15,000 cases of the virus, with more than 11,000 deaths. The disease also spread to seven other countries—Italy, Mali, Nigeria, Senegal, Spain, the United Kingdom, and the United States—but its impact was much more limited, with thirty-four cases and fifteen deaths. Part of the success in managing the Ebola outbreak was early action and coordinated transatlantic response.

Already, in June 2014, when the disease was still in its incipient stages, G7 leaders committed at their summit in Brussels to "working together, in close cooperation with WHO, to develop a Global Action Plan on antimicrobial resistance."[168] In August, President Obama held a previously scheduled U.S.-Africa Business Forum, at which he engaged with leaders from the affected countries to develop appropriate action. The U.S. government deployed medical first responders to West Africa and began working with the African Union to create "African Centers for Disease Control."[169] Obama noted that he was "surging not just U.S. resources, but [had] reached out to European partners and partners from other countries, working with the WHO."[170] In a visit to the CDC headquarters, Obama stressed that even though the U.S. risk exposure to Ebola was "extremely low," he treated it as a "national security priority" and, thus, mobilized the "largest international response in the history of the CDC."[171] At the request of Liberia's government, the United States established a military command center to coordinate civilian efforts across the region. With a staging area in Senegal, the United States created an airbridge to transport medical supplies and health workers into West Africa. The U.S. Public Health Service set up new field hospitals and trained thousands of health workers to support the public health systems in the region.

In September 2014, the UN Security Council, in its first emergency meeting on a public health crisis, established the UN Mission for Ebola Emergency Response and announced that the disease constituted a "threat to international peace and security."[172] At the meeting, President Obama warned that "if unchecked, this epidemic could kill hundreds of thousands of people in the coming months."[173] To further spur a sufficient international response, Obama organized a forty-four-country summit on Global Health Security, which led to over "100 commitments" to strengthen the security of public health systems.[174] By October, the United States had deployed 500 military personnel to West Africa, eventually expanding to 3,000 troops, which provided support to 10,000 civilian responders (including 100 CDC personnel) on the ground. Obama also appointed a special coordinator for Ebola response, and Ebola became a regular item for presidential briefings. Likewise, the EU appointed a high-level coordinator for the Ebola response and sent nearly 100 health personnel from the European Centre for Diseases Control and Prevention. During this period, the United States donated about $1 billion and the EU about $2 billion to finance nearly 75 percent of the overall international response.

By the end of 2014, the number of new cases decreased significantly, and the crisis had been effectively resolved by the time of the G7 summit in June 2015 in Germany. Through early and coordinated effort, the United States and Europe saved "hundreds of thousands, maybe a couple million, lives" in West Africa in "one of the most effective, if not the most effective, international public health responses in the history of the world"[175] and prevented the outbreak from spreading across the globe.[176] The following year, the White House also established within the National Security Council staff a Directorate for Global Health Security and Biodefense to analyze best practices from the Ebola outbreak and ensure adequate preparedness for the next epidemic. By May 2018, however, the Trump administration had closed the office and terminated the U.S. focus on pandemic risks, until the outbreak of COVID-19 in early 2020.

President Obama also prioritized limiting Iran's nuclear weapons program and, in April 2009, rejoined the P5+1 talks with Iran. However, the administration continued to apply economic sanctions on Iran that had first been initiated by President George W. Bush. In 2010, the EU imposed its own sanctions on Iran in the areas of trade, financial services, and energy. Two years later, after several attempts by Iran to stall the negotiations, the transatlantic economic squeeze tightened as the EU banned its member states from importing Iranian oil.[177]

Around this time, the Obama-Biden administration had opened a back-channel to Iran through Oman.[178] The two negotiating tracks, bilateral and P5+1, resulted in an interim agreement with Iran, the Joint Plan of Action, negotiated by Secretary of State John Kerry in early 2014 and, eventually, in the JCPOA in July 2015. The Iran nuclear negotiations succeeded for several reasons, but transatlantic economic sanctions, particularly on behalf of Europe, provided critical leverage. Indeed, the EU took so much ownership over the JCPOA that it has premised its credibility on saving the deal during the Trump administration.

Similar transatlantic dynamics occurred in reaching the Paris Agreement, also negotiated by Secretary Kerry. Alongside transatlantic support, there was a separate U.S. bilateral negotiating track, this time with China. Yet, the deal would not have been possible without strong coordination behind the scenes among the transatlantic partners.[179]

INTERNATIONAL ORDER

In his penultimate UNGA speech, Obama argued that the global order had "underwritten unparalleled advances in human liberty and prosperity," pointing to the "diplomatic cooperation between the world's major powers," a "global economy that has lifted more than a billion people from poverty," and international rules and norms that "have helped constrain bigger countries from imposing our will on smaller ones and advanced the emergence of democracy and development and individual liberty on every continent."[180] Notwithstanding President Obama's inspiring words, as his administration was winding down, the accumulation of international crises threatened to upend the global order built by the West over the previous seven decades.

Russia's aggression in Ukraine, alongside ISIL-inspired terrorist attacks in the United States and Europe, shook the foundations of transatlantic security. The escalation of violence in Syria between 2014 and 2016 resulted in the worst humanitarian crisis since the end of World War II. In 2014, the number of Syrian refugees doubled, to 3.8 million; two years later, that number had swelled to more than 5 million. Within Syria, in 2014, there were 6.5 million IDPs; by 2016, half of the Syrian population had been forcibly displaced.

For the initial three years of the Syrian conflict, the refugees stayed in the neighboring countries of Turkey, Jordan, Lebanon, and Iraq. In 2015, with no end to the war in sight, escalating violence from Assad and ISIL, and insufficient humanitarian funding, displaced Syrians searched for refuge elsewhere, and migrated to Europe, particularly to Germany. Other refugees, from Iraq and Afghanistan, as well as economic migrants, followed. In total, approximately 2 million refugees and economic migrants traveled into Europe in 2015 and 2016, often through dangerous and sometimes deadly irregular channels. The mass scale of the migration overwhelmed European political systems, quickly becoming the main concern of local populations and fuel for xenophobia and populism. The migration crisis in Europe also became a "major national security issue" for the United States because of its potential effects on stability, the transatlantic economy, and collective security.[181]

As the fabric of international order seemed to pull apart, EU leaders argued that their primary task should be to protect and preserve the core of the transatlantic alliance. On the margins of the NATO summit in Warsaw in July 2016, the new president of the European Council, Donald Tusk, declared: "There is no freedom in Europe without Atlantic solidarity. Caring for the unity of the whole political community of the West is key."[182] Likewise, European Commission President Jean-Claude Juncker argued: "Our first duty is to show unity and reaffirm the values we share: human rights, freedom, democracy, and the keystone on which the other rests, the rule of law . . . The United States, NATO, and European Union are central pillars of the global order. We complement each other and together provide peace and stability in Europe, our neighborhood, and beyond."[183]

Only months earlier, President Obama, in a speech in Hanover, Germany, had tried to place the transatlantic alliance in a historical context, declaring that Europe's "accomplishment—more than 500 million people speaking 24 languages in 28 countries, 19 with a common currency, in one European Union—remains one of the greatest political and economic achievements of modern times."[184]

Anxious to place his presidency in the context of this extraordinary achievement, the president highlighted accomplishments of the alliance during the previous eight years:

> Pulling the global economy back from the brink of depression and putting the world on the path of recovery; a comprehensive deal that's cut off every single one of Iran's paths to a nu-

clear bomb, part of a shared vision of a world without nuclear weapons; in Paris, the most ambitious agreement in history to fight climate change; stopping Ebola in West Africa and saving countless lives; rallying the world around new sustainable development, including our goal to end extreme poverty. None of those things could have happened if I—if the United States—did not have a partnership with a strong and united Europe.[185]

Notwithstanding the mutual statements praising the liberal order and the transatlantic community's role in establishing and enlarging it, the tide of history seemed to veer in a different direction. At his last speech to the UN General Assembly, in September 2016, President Obama remarked on the "growing contest between authoritarianism and liberalism."[186] However, only months later, with the election of Donald Trump in November, a new era of "American carnage" would emerge.[187]

———

President Obama made the transatlantic alliance stronger than it had been since the 1990s. He helped foster an equitable partnership with greater sharing of the burdens as well as credit for global leadership. Along with European allies, the United States elevated the G20 to the leaders' level as the premier forum for international economic cooperation to prevent an economic depression. Obama joined Hollande and Cameron in launching NATO's intervention in Libya to prevent mass atrocities. In response to Russia's aggression in Ukraine, NATO leaders committed to increase defense spending and establish deterrence measures in the eastern flank through enhanced forward presence of troops and equipment. The United States and the EU also brokered the Iran nuclear deal, through joint economic and diplomatic leverage, and served as the core for the Paris climate agreement. Perhaps no American leader since George H. W. Bush had been as admired and respected by Europeans as Obama.

Notwithstanding President Obama's popularity among Europeans, transatlantic achievements were increasingly difficult to distinguish from global achievements, ranging from nuclear nonproliferation to climate change. The only distinctly transatlantic project, T-TIP, was not successful. NATO's enlargement to Montenegro did not compare in significance to the expansions of the 1990s or 2000s. And as the transatlantic partnership became more equitable, it also made it more possible that the two sides could drift apart.

For all their personal affinity for Obama, Europeans are more likely to recall the reset with Russia, the red line in Syria, or the pivot to Asia as the main U.S. policies that affected them, rather than any of the joint global successes. Obama's Nobel Peace Prize was not followed with the Charlemagne Prize, awarded for work done in the service of European unification; the last American to receive that award was Bill Clinton in 2000. Yet, Obama helped fortify the transatlantic alliance, the resilience of which would be severely tested by the assaults of his successor.

3

The Unraveling of the West (2017–2020)

The election of Donald Trump as president stunned the world. An unlikely candidate with no prior public service and no concept of international relations beyond investing in golf courses, Trump defeated eleven opponents in the Republican primaries, and later eked out a victory over Democratic opponent Hillary Clinton, whom President Obama described as the most qualified person to ever run for the American presidency.[1] Trump's inaugural address was equally surprising, centered on an assessment that the United States—at its peak of material wealth and with geopolitical preeminence unparalleled since the ancient days of the Roman Empire—was undergoing a period of "carnage" that required placing "America First."[2] This was widely perceived as signaling a transformation in U.S. foreign policy and alliances.[3]

Fortunately, the Trump administration was not sufficiently disciplined to implement any significant shifts in long-standing U.S. policy toward Europe. Astute observers noticed at the outset of the Trump administration that it had no grand strategy whatsoever, much less fully formed policies on various issues; instead, President Trump made random statements and decisions that lacked coherence and often defied logic.[4] President Obama, after meeting with Trump during the transition, reportedly concluded in private: "He knows absolutely nothing."[5]

This basic incompetence, which could have been written off at the beginning of the administration as a redressable issue due to lack of experience, persisted throughout Trump's term. Even beyond the inconsistent, often inherently contradictory, decisionmaking on complex policy issues such as Syria, Iran, or North Korea, Trump seemed to have difficulty with simple facts. For instance, on his focal issue of burden-sharing within NATO, he confused increased *cumulative* defense spending of $130 billion between 2016 and 2019 with *annual* amounts, repeating the mistake even after the NATO secretary-general corrected him.[6] When asked whether the United States supported protesters in Iran, he responded "no" in one press briefing, only to reverse himself in the very next briefing.[7] His incapacity to absorb and repeat basic facts was exacerbated by his willingness to make stunningly false or misleading claims: estimated at over twenty *per day* in 2019 by the *Washington Post*.[8] It suggested a peculiar inability to process reality accurately and make rational decisions over time.

In one bizarre press conference, Trump insisted that he was a "very stable genius,"[9] but the consensus view in Europe early on was that the new American president was "unpredictable," with, at best, an "amorphous" foreign policy and, at worst, no real policy at all.[10] As Fareed Zakaria noted recently, the problem with Trump was not any specific decision but, rather, that he did "not have a foreign policy," just a "series of impulses—isolationism, unilateralism, bellicosity—some of them completely contradictory."[11]

Despite the glaring foreign policy gap at the top, various officials within the Trump administration sought to maintain elements of continuity from the Obama-Biden administration in terms of strategy toward Europe. For instance, former Secretary of Defense Jim Mattis and former National Security Advisor H. R. McMaster were instrumental in strengthening U.S. troop presence in Europe as part of the European Deterrence Initiative. Likewise, former Assistant Secretary of State for European and Eurasian Affairs Wess Mitchell, during his brief tenure, gave several speeches on the importance of Europe and the Western alliance.[12] But their efforts never had genuine presidential commitment, reflecting stable U.S. policy. Cognizant that any strategy could always be undermined or reversed by a Trump tweet or impulsive decision, these officials ultimately left the administration.

From the beginning, U.S. allies in Europe were particularly concerned about Trump's claim during the campaign that NATO was "obsolete"[13] and about his overall commitment to NATO, as well as about his apparent affinity for Russia and Vladimir Putin.[14] Russia's shadow loomed large over the

Trump administration, raising doubts and anxieties over long-standing pillars of U.S. foreign policy and its commitment to the transatlantic alliance.

THE KREMLIN CANDIDATE

Shortly before Donald Trump assumed office, the U.S. intelligence community released a declassified report on Russian interference in the 2016 U.S. presidential elections. It concluded with "high confidence" that Putin sought to "undermine public faith" in U.S. democracy, harm Clinton's electability, and help Trump's chances when possible by discrediting Clinton.[15] One former acting CIA director described Trump as "an unwitting agent of the Russian Federation."[16] The day after the U.S. presidential elections, Russians celebrated in Moscow by singing "we are the champions of the world."[17] Yet, the fact that Trump was the Kremlin's preferred candidate still left open the question to what extent Trump reciprocated the loyalty to Putin, whom he singularly praised several times as a strong leader.[18]

Once in office, Trump was unusually sensitive about his relationship with Putin and Russia. He admonished his staff for not informing him about a call from Putin,[19] which he then immediately had scheduled for the following day.[20] In the one-hour-long "congratulatory" phone call, Trump and Putin discussed counterterrorism and nonproliferation, but avoided issues such as Russian electoral interference or U.S. sanctions against Russia for its aggression in Ukraine.

In July 2017, Trump met with Putin for the first time on the margins of the G20, also under mysterious circumstances.[21] They initially met for two hours, but without any remarks or readout afterward; indeed, Trump took away his interpreter's notes and forbade her from speaking to anyone about the meeting. Later in the day, Trump and Putin spoke again, for another hour after the G20 dinner, this time including only the Russian leader's interpreter. Shortly after the meeting, given the ongoing concerns stemming from Russian interference in the 2016 elections and the affinity between Trump and Putin, the U.S. Congress codified into law sanctions against Russia, through the Countering America's Adversaries Through Sanctions Act (CAATSA).

Subsequently, Putin met with Trump twice, further adding to existing suspicions. On the margins of the Asia-Pacific Economic Cooperation (APEC) forum in November 2017, Trump questioned the credibility of U.S.

intelligence agencies regarding their assessment on Russian interference and seemed to "really believe" Putin's denials.[22] He later reversed himself, but the damage was already done.[23]

In July 2018, Trump met with Putin in Helsinki for two hours, which was followed with equally bizarre statements. First, Putin led the press conference with opening remarks and revealed that he had wanted Trump to win the 2016 elections.[24] Then, Trump again equivocated between the U.S. intelligence agencies and Russia, saying he had "confidence in both parties."[25] The following year, at the G7 summit in Biarritz, France, Trump suggested he might invite Putin to the next G7 summit, which the United States would be hosting.[26] He also floated the possibility of attending the May Day parade in Moscow in 2020, calling it a "very big deal."[27]

To paraphrase Churchill's famous line about the Soviet Union, the Trump-Putin relationship remained "a riddle, wrapped in a mystery, inside an enigma" but without a key, thus far, to unlock it.[28] Two years of investigation by Robert Mueller, the former FBI director appointed by the Justice Department as special counsel for the inquiry into Russian electoral interference, found nearly 300 contacts between the Trump campaign and Russia-linked operatives, including at least thirty-eight meetings.[29] Former National Security Advisor John Bolton asserted that Putin "plays Trump like a fiddle."[30]

While the Trump administration boasted about great power competition with Russia, America isolated itself and, in the process, allowed Moscow to expand its influence across the Middle East, Africa, Asia, and even in Latin America. The takeover by Russian troops of U.S. bases in northern Syria provided the paradigmatic image of the evisceration of the U.S. position in the world, as American troops withdrew and the Russians advanced on the same highway. Ongoing ambiguity as to whether Trump was the Kremlin's unwitting agent, or Putin's puppet, created anxiety among the foreign policy establishment in the United States and around the world, particularly in Europe. Trump's overtures to Putin reopened debate among European leaders on Russia policy, but this was largely overshadowed by the unprecedented barrage of criticism and threats from its traditional transatlantic ally.

EUROPE AS FOE

As noted, the challenge in analyzing the Trump administration is that there was no real foreign policy; instead, there were disparate declarations on trade, unilateralism, and "endless war." However, even in these areas, Trump's actions had little consistency, coherence, or coordination.

On occasion, officials in the Trump administration expressed interest in maintaining a strong transatlantic relationship. For instance, Senator Kay Bailey Hutchinson, at her confirmation hearing for U.S. ambassador to NATO, affirmed (as would most similar candidates in other U.S. administrations) that "NATO allies are our core partners in diplomacy and on the battlefield, our partners of first resort in dealing with old and new threats to the security of our people."[31] Trump's first foreign visitor was British Prime Minister Theresa May, and the first official state visit was with French President Emmanuel Macron.[32] The first trip by Vice President Pence was to the annual transatlantic gathering at the Munich Security Conference, where he confirmed that the United States "strongly supports NATO and will be unwavering in our commitment to this transatlantic alliance."[33] Notwithstanding Trump's overblown, hostile rhetoric during the campaign, the initial statements from members of the administration seemed to indicate that it would place a high value on sound transatlantic relations.

In his first foreign policy speech, while visiting Saudi Arabia, President Trump embraced a philosophy of "principled realism rooted in common values, shared interests, and common sense."[34] While Trump never mentioned Europe, his words, on their face, bore a striking resemblance to the 2016 EU Global Strategy's philosophy of "principled pragmatism." Nevertheless, Europeans remained skeptical given candidate Trump's hostile remarks about NATO and the EU. In February 2017, European Council President Donald Tusk met with Vice President Pence and declared, "too many new and sometimes surprising opinions have been voiced . . . about our relations and our common security for us to pretend that everything is as it used to be."[35] Tusk asked the vice president for reassurances on three issues: whether he believed in preservation of the rules-based international order as in the interest of the West; the importance of NATO and transatlantic cooperation to mutual security; and U.S. support for the European Union. The vice president affirmed the importance of all three, but also referenced the debate over transatlantic burden-sharing, noting that "the patience of the American people will not endure forever."[36]

Other leaders sought to exploit the emerging vacuum within the transatlantic community. At the World Economic Forum in Davos, Chinese President Xi Jinping outlined his country's commitment to defend globalization, free trade, and the rules-based international order.[37] Russia's foreign minister Sergey Lavrov called for a "post-West order" during his remarks at the Munich Security Conference.[38] Sensing weakness within the West, both China and Russia began to expand their global influence across Africa, the Middle East, and even in Latin America (in the case of Venezuela). They have also further developed their bilateral partnership; in late 2019, more than 100,000 Russia and Chinese troops participated in joint military exercises.

The change in the U.S. approach to Europe became evident the following month when President Trump met with German Chancellor Angela Merkel and reportedly informed her that Germany had accumulated a $300 billion debt to the United States for defense spending.[39] In a later meeting with EU leaders, he described Germany as "bad, very bad."[40] Trump linked the so-called defense deficit with the trade deficit the United States had with Germany and Europe. However, his fixation with trade deficits ignored the U.S. trade *surplus* in services with the EU, which largely canceled out the trade deficit in goods.

At the NATO summit in May, Trump refused to endorse the collective security guarantee under Article 5, even though his staff had included language supporting collective security in his speech.[41] Instead, the president scolded NATO allies for "not paying what they should be paying" and owing "massive amounts of money from past years."[42] He withdrew from the Paris Agreement, a seminal achievement of transatlantic diplomacy during the Obama-Biden administration.[43] And he appeared to snub EU leaders by not holding a press conference with them and releasing only a bland readout from their meeting.[44] After feverish damage control by his staff, Trump finally endorsed his commitment to Article 5 the following month.[45] He also had previously reversed his position on NATO, describing it as "no longer obsolete."[46] However, he privately threatened to leave NATO and publicly confirmed his authority to do so.[47] At a private dinner with NATO leaders, his comments were later described as "awful" and a "train wreck."[48] According to Rose Gottemoeller, the former NATO deputy secretary-general, European leaders took these threats "extremely seriously" because they marked a potential "existential" crisis.[49]

In Europe, Chancellor Merkel sounded the alarm bell, noting that the "times in which [Europeans] could completely depend on others are, to a certain extent, over" and that "Europeans truly have to take our fate into our own hands."[50] As the longest-serving leader in Europe, Merkel, an astute politician, sized up Trump quickly; she noted that, "it is not the case that the United States of America will simply protect us. Instead, Europe must take its destiny in its own hands. That is our job for the future."[51] However, French President Macron, who had just been elected in an over-whelming victory, adopted a different approach to dealing with the unpredictable president.

Seeking to appeal to Trump's affinity for showmanship, President Macron invited the U.S. president to the Bastille Day military parade and to dinner atop the Eiffel Tower. The two leaders appeared to get along personally, and Trump would rave subsequently about the parade, copying it, in part, for the Fourth of July celebrations in 2019, which featured for the first time an extensive display of military equipment.

Trump reciprocated by hosting Macron in April 2018 for the first official state visit during his administration. The United States, France, and the United Kingdom had just jointly launched airstrikes against chemical weapons sites in Syria to preserve the norm against the use of chemical weapons—a brief intervention that had bipartisan support in the United States and could have served for wider transatlantic cooperation on Syria (but, ultimately, was mere political theatrics).[52] To commemorate the visit, Macron brought a tree from the Belleau Forest, where U.S. soldiers fought during World War I, to plant at the White House as "a symbol of the sacrifice and the common battles that France and the United States have led together" and "the foundation on which we shall continue to build and write together, side by side, the chapters of our modern history, forge the Western world, and aspire to universality."[53] Yet, in a sign of things to come, the "friendship" tree would die a year later.[54]

Notwithstanding a moment of good feelings between the United States and France, Trump could not resist verbally assaulting the European Union, stating that the EU "has not treated us well" in a "very, very unfair trade situation."[55] He criticized the EU for its trade surplus of $151 billion with the United States and threatened steel and aluminum tariffs against the EU if the balance did not shift.[56] And in a fundamental breach with long-standing U.S. policy, Trump asked Macron when France would leave the EU[57] because he would "rather deal just with France" instead of the EU.[58] In a subsequent meeting with NATO Secretary-General Jens Stoltenberg, Trump continued his harangue: "The European Union has been terrible to the United States on trade. They've been terrible to our workers. The European Union—last year, we had a trade deficit of $151 billion. . . . The European Union—outside of China and a couple of others—treats us, on trade, as badly as you can be treated."[59] By mid-summer, Trump had concluded: "the European Union is a foe."[60]

Trump's rhetoric toward NATO and the EU, his tariff threats, his decision to leave the Paris Agreement, and, finally, the U.S. withdrawal from the Iran nuclear deal[61] prompted Tusk to ask: "With friends like that, who needs enemies?"[62] Tusk criticized Trump for his "capricious assertiveness" and sarcastically thanked him for helping Europe get "rid of all illusions," noting, "if you need a helping hand, you will find one at the end of your arm."[63] He still called for Europe to "do everything in its power to protect, in spite of today's mood, the transatlantic bond," but also to prepare for "those scenarios, where [it] will have to act on [its] own."[64]

Transatlantic tensions escalated further throughout the summer of 2018. In June, at the G7 summit in Charlevoix, Canada, Trump refused to sign the communiqué because it mentioned the rules-based international order that the European and other G7 leaders insisted on.[65] The following month, at the NATO summit in Brussels, he linked criticism of Germany's defense spending to its Nord Stream II oil and gas pipeline project with Russia, arguing that it was "very inappropriate" for the United States to pay billions for NATO to protect against Russia when Germany then pays billions to Russia for oil and gas.[66] He also criticized Theresa May's approach to Brexit negotiations, declaring that the UK seemed to be "getting at least partially involved back with the European Union."[67]

In July 2018, European Commission President Jean-Claude Juncker met with Trump at the White House and managed to calm the latter's caustic rhetoric. In a nutshell, Trump withdrew his tariff threats and Juncker committed that Europe would buy additional U.S. goods, including (prominently, if strangely) soybeans.[68] Uncharacteristically, Trump quoted from the EU-U.S. joint statement in paying homage to "a new phase in the relationship between the United States and the European Union—a phase of close friendship; of strong trade relations in which both of us will win; of working better together for global security and prosperity; and of fighting jointly against terrorism."[69]

In practice, the deal merely preserved the status quo and opened dialogue for future negotiations. And only five days later, Trump returned to his prior rhetoric, accusing the EU of "totally tak[ing] advantage of the United States" that was "not fair."[70] The president continued to condemn European trade practices throughout the following year.[71] His newly appointed Secretary of State, Mike Pompeo, backed up the president, delivering a speech in Brussels that was widely viewed as a wholesale attack against the European Union itself. Pompeo questioned whether the EU was "ensuring that the interests of countries and their citizens are placed before those of bureaucrats here in Brussels" and argued that "multilateralism has too often become viewed as an end unto itself."[72] And Trump's ambassador to the EU, Gordon Sondland, claimed that his job was "to destroy the European Union."[73]

In 2017, Europe's leaders explored whether they could do business with President Trump, and by 2018, they had their answer: the president viewed international relations—even with long-established allies—as a zero-sum game. If President Trump did not have the upper hand in trade, in negotiations over burden-sharing, even in media coverage, then Europe was of little use to him. It proved to be a wake-up call, if not a shock, to the transatlantic community. By 2019, the Europeans focused on maintaining the status quo wherever possible, limiting potential disagreements and preserving the rules-based international order until the 2020 presidential elections in the United States. That meant denying President Trump, when possible, any transatlantic platform where he might further denigrate either the EU or NATO. For instance, the seventieth anniversary of NATO was celebrated substantively at the foreign ministerial level, whereas the leaders event was downgraded from a summit to a meeting. Likewise, in hosting the G7 summit in France, Macron opted for a terse communiqué—a mere 6 percent of the length of the 2018 communiqué—that masked any substantive disagreements.

But no amount of diplomatic avoidance or masking of differences could completely mitigate the risk of miscalculation and mismanagement. One particular episode stands out as striking at the heart of the transatlantic relationship.

KURDS

In October 2019, Turkish President Recep Tayyip Erdogan sent troops into northern Syria to deal with what he perceived as an existential problem for his country: Kurdish armed groups (People's Protection Units, YPG) with political ties to the Kurdistan Workers' Party (PKK) inside Turkey. Turkey had long viewed the PKK as terrorists and opposed Kurdish groups in Syria. Erdogan did not base his decision on any development within Turkey or within Syria but, rather, on Trump's implicit "green light" after withdrawing U.S. troops from the region and reversing U.S. support for the Kurdish forces.[74]

The decision to withhold further assistance to the Kurds—who sacrificed more than 10,000 soldiers in the coalition fight against ISIS—not only "shocked" U.S. allies in the region but in Europe, as well. As Rose Gottemoeller put it, "it crystallized for the Allies a general anxiety, that feeling that the United States is now unpredictable and cannot be counted on to take the key strategic decisions that will point the Alliance in the direction it needs to go."[75] Moreover, Trump did not consult any of the allies and, in announcing U.S. withdrawal of troops, seemed oblivious to both the immediate and long-term consequences. For countries that depend in some measure on U.S. protection, Trump's decision to turn his back on the Kurdish allies severely undercut the credibility of U.S. security guarantees elsewhere.

By the time President Trump appeared at the World Economic Forum in Davos, Switzerland, in January 2020, he had become something of "a marginal figure" among other world leaders. According to one former British foreign minister, "much of the rest of the world has simply moved beyond the Trump drama."[76] Indeed, he was jeered by world leaders during his 2018 speech at the UN General Assembly when he stated: "In less than two years, my administration has accomplished more than almost any administration in the history of our country."[77] Similarly, at a reception during the 2019 NATO summit, the leaders of the UK, Holland, France, and Canada were caught on camera laughing about Trump's histrionics. One German foreign policy expert argued that Europeans "have a special place of disdain for Trump for all kinds of reasons that go way beyond what he did."[78] When "Trump looks like he is destroying American democracy, at least for many Germans, that means for us that the master that we learned from all of a sudden is going over to the dark side and that makes us nervous about ourselves."[79]

There is little doubt that the "Trump drama" has left the transatlantic relationship in disarray, but it is not without historical precedent. For instance, according to Gottemoeller, the crisis over U.S. troop withdrawal from northern Syria did not reach the "low points" of Charles de Gaulle's withdrawal from NATO's military structures in 1966, when the French president ejected NATO staff from France, or of the rifts from the 2003 Iraq War, when allies shouted at each other during sessions of the North Atlantic Council.[80] Others argue that prior disagreements were over policy rather than the importance of the alliance itself.

However, the concern in Europe was that, as fractured as the relationship appeared to be currently, if President Trump won a second term, it could have gotten even worse. Wolfgang Ischinger argued that the malaise reflected "a particularly severe case of a lack of coordination and consultation on a number of issues."[81] One senior German official described the challenge as "different in kind" and "existential," arguing that a second Trump administration would have required Europe to significantly reconsider the transatlantic relationship.[82] Still others argued that if Europeans "do soul-searching, thinking that they have to rethink their relationship with the United States, they will not get very far as the issue would become very divisive within the EU."[83] Atlanticists feared what would happen if Trump was reelected and able to pursue an alternative reality for the West. Underneath the continual chaos of Trump's rhetoric and decisions, there were the constant themes of jingoism, nationalism, populism, and protectionism. In fact, Trump's worldview stood in stark contrast to the traditional visions of the West based on democracy, human rights, capitalism, and rule of law.

ALTERNATIVE REALITY FOR THE WEST

President Trump outlined an alternative vision for the West early in his administration during a speech in Warsaw. In prepared remarks styled in populist terms to the "People of Poland," Trump spoke with near-spiritual emotion about the need "to summon the courage and the will to defend our civilization."[84] He called for "a strong alliance of free, sovereign and independent nations" as "the best defense for our freedoms and for our interests." He continued in dramatic overtones: "The fundamental question of our time is whether the West has the will to survive. Do we have the confidence in our values to defend them at any cost? Do we have enough respect for our citizens to protect our borders? Do we have the desire and the courage to preserve our civilization in the face of those who would subvert and destroy it?" He closed with a jingoist vision for the West: "let us all fight like the Poles—for family, for freedom, for country, and for God."

As noted, the president's statements did not add up to a policy, let alone a strategy for the West. However, in emphasizing national sovereignty and national interest as primary organizing principles, Trump provided some insight into his thinking about international relations.

In his first speech to the UNGA, he stressed that he "will always put America first, just like you, as the leaders of your countries will always, and should always, put your countries first."[85] Although Trump attempted to make a somewhat more nuanced argument, "America first does not mean America alone,"[86] he found few supporters of this incipient vision beyond a few autocrats, such as Russia's Vladimir Putin or Hungary's Viktor Orban.

European leaders tried to outline a different vision for the West that reflected its traditional values and universalist aspirations. Speaking before a joint session of Congress in April 2018, President Macron argued that the United States and France "have worked together for the universal ideals of liberty, tolerance, and equal rights."[87] But, he argued, "our Western values themselves are at risk," and he offered two potential options for the West. The first entailed choosing, like Trump, "isolationism, withdrawal, and nationalism." However, according to Macron, this path would imply that "international institutions, including the United Nations and NATO, will no longer be able to exercise their mandate and stabilizing influence" and the West "would then inevitably and severely undermine the liberal order [it] built after World War II." He called, instead, for another path, "a more effective, accountable, and results-oriented multilateralism" to build the "21st century world order." He argued that this "strong multilateralism will not outshine our national cultures and national identities" but, rather, "allow our cultures and identities to be respected, to be protected and to flourish freely together." In a subsequent speech at the Paris Peace Forum on the 100th anniversary of the armistice ending World War I, he placed nationalism in the same category as racism, anti-Semitism, and extremism, as "grim passions" to be rejected.[88]

Likewise, Merkel presented her vision for the West speaking before the European Parliament. Noting that "old allies are calling tried and proven alliances into question" and emphasizing that "tolerance is the soul of Europe," she called for solidarity as the core value of "European DNA": "solidarity as a universal, fundamental value; solidarity as a responsibility for the community; and solidarity in terms of one's own rational interest."[89] Again rejecting Trump's vision, she stressed that "nationalism and egoism must never again be allowed to gain a foothold in Europe" and, instead, "tolerance and solidarity are our common future."

Unrepentant, Trump continued to focus on the attractiveness of nationalism in international relations. In his third appearance before the UN General Assembly, he expounded on his earlier themes with even greater bombast and thrust: "Wise leaders always put the good of their own people and their own country first. The future does not belong to globalists. The future belongs to patriots. The future belongs to sovereign and independent nations who protect their citizens, respect their neighbors, and honor the differences that make each country special and unique."[90]

Trump's former speechwriter, Michael Anton, tried to spin the president's desultory ruminations into a coherent "Trump Doctrine,"[91] but without much success. Equating globalization with imperialism, Anton argued that both equally threaten democracy and liberty. Even more striking, he claimed that the EU was "the most illustrative example" of this phenomenon and "a fraud from the beginning." Thus, the EU's purported threat to "nationalism and national sovereignty . . . provoked a populist revolt, embodied by the rise of the yellow vest movement in France, Italian Interior Minister Matteo Salvini, Poland's Law and Justice party, the Brexit process, and Hungarian Prime Minister Viktor Orban."[92]

Undoubtedly, Trump's nationalism and populism resonate in some parts of the world. But it remains to be seen whether these movements are long-term trends or merely transient moments in history. As Henry Kissinger noted pointedly, "Trump may be one of those figures in history who appears from time to time to mark the end of an era and to force it to give up its old pretenses. It doesn't necessarily mean that he knows this, or that he is considering any great alternative. It could just be an accident."[93] Indeed, after four years in office, his most remarkable imprint on international relations was an obsession with former President Obama's multilateral diplomatic achievements, seeking to undo the Iran nuclear deal, the

Trans-Pacific Partnership, and the Paris Agreement. In the realm of foreign policy, Trump did not accomplish anything of enduring significance during his term in office. He often peppered his speeches with recycled notions of nationalism and sovereignty but without any broader coherence or practical policy implementation.

LOST AT THE UN

In addition to weakening the EU and eviscerating NATO, the Trump administration seemed intent on starving the United Nations (one of the EU's "core partners" according to its 2016 Global Strategy, along with the United States and NATO), though, again, this was largely unsuccessful. The U.S. Senate confirmed former South Carolina governor Nikki Haley as U.S. ambassador to the UN only a week into the new administration, the third cabinet member to be confirmed (after Defense Secretary Mattis and CIA Director Pompeo). In contrast to both Presidents George H. W. Bush and George W. Bush, who viewed the U.N. ambassadorship as a sub-cabinet post, Trump included Haley in the cabinet and on the principals committee of the National Security Council. With this backing from the president, Ambassador Haley announced immediately that the administration would "look at the UN, and everything that's working, we're going to make it better; everything that's not working, we're going to try and fix; and anything that seems to be obsolete and not necessary, we're going to do away with."[94]

At a minimum, for any policy to be successful, the rhetoric must be matched by concrete action. However, no coherent U.S. policy toward the UN emerged from the administration. Indeed, for a period of time, it seemed as though Ambassador Haley's public statements did not correspond to President Trump's views on particular issues, such as Russia or Syria, because she failed to clear her statements with either the White House or the U.S. State Department.

Moreover, heightened diplomatic activity around crises, such as Syria's use of chemical weapons in April 2017, failed to yield any significant results at the UN. Instead, the president engaged in symbolic one-off actions (such as missile strikes) that did not translate into any diplomatic process at the UN or elsewhere. With the notable exception of increased UN Security Council sanctions against North Korea, which apparently have had little effect on Pyongyang's nuclear development program, there was no significant multilateral engagement within the UN.[95] Instead, the overall theme of Trump's approach to the UN appeared to be that less is more.

In April 2017, in the run-up to holding the rotating presidency of the Security Council, Ambassador Haley outlined her two main objectives: prioritizing human rights and reducing and reforming peacekeeping operations. In a speech to the Council on Foreign Relations, she noted that the Security Council had never held a session dedicated to human rights and security. She called the Human Rights Council (where these issues are addressed) "corrupt" and said that the United States would reconsider its membership in that body. She argued that the council paradoxically included human rights violators, such as Venezuela and Cuba, while unfairly targeting Israel. Her remarks might have had greater impact had President Trump ever called out the many authoritarians around the world—whom he seemed to admire—for their human rights abuses. Human rights, a pillar of American foreign policy since President Jimmy Carter, were cast aside by the Trump administration.

Regarding peacekeeping, one of the UN's most important multilateral activities, Haley argued that many missions lacked an exit strategy, and that operations in war-torn countries such as South Sudan, the Democratic Republic of the Congo (DRC), and the Central African Republic had "no political solution in sight."[96] She insisted on five guiding principles for future peacekeeping missions: supporting political solutions; host country cooperation; realistic and achievable mandates; exit strategy; and adjustments when situations improve or fail to improve.[97]

While these guidelines may have appeared reasonable on the surface, Haley failed to note other critical factors. For instance, peacekeeping missions often seek to promote options for a political solution rather than simply support an ongoing process. Moreover, to protect civilians from atrocities perpetrated by host governments, some missions operate without the cooperation of those governments. Mandates can combine realistic short-term deliverables with aspirational long-term goals that are achievable beyond a mission's duration (promoting rule of law, for example). Exit timetables must be balanced against other objectives, such as preserving the peace or protecting civilians. Finally, missions need not be micromanaged through constant mandate reviews but, instead, require clear political guidelines from the Security Council along with operational flexibility for local UN officials staffed with sufficient resources.

Haley also focused on cutting, and in some cases closing, peacekeeping operations, primarily to reduce the share of U.S. contributions from 28.6 percent to 25 percent (a cut of $283 million out of the $7.87 billion for the 2016–2017 fiscal year) as legislated by Congress. However, in his initial budget proposed to Congress, President Trump demanded even steeper cuts, amounting to 18 percent (a cut of $834 million), a 40 percent reduction in overall U.S. contributions. In theory, spending less money could yield more desired outcomes by forcing greater clarity of priorities and efficiency of operations. In practice, however, fewer resources and listless diplomacy only contributed to more festering crises and global disorder. Haley's focus on spending cuts at the UN, specifically the peacekeeping function, was undermined by the president's acknowledgement that the UN's budget is "peanuts."[98]

In the end, Ambassador Haley failed to make a lasting impact on either human rights policy or bureaucratic reform at the UN. The reduction in U.S. contributions to the UN, while producing modest savings to the U.S. government, needed to be weighed against the opportunity costs from failure to address the growing number of festering crises around the world.

Missed diplomatic opportunities are difficult to assess, but it is clear that the United States abdicated leadership during the worst global humanitarian crisis since the Second World War, with over 25 million refugees and over 70 million forcibly displaced people around the world. Just as Haley did not highlight these issues in public, there is no evidence she urged a more forceful response within U.S. interagency government discussions or in her interactions with foreign counterparts and leaders. Yet, diplomacy is essential to avoid even larger problems in the near-term future.

UN Secretary-General António Guterres, a former Portuguese prime minister, argued in his first remarks to the Security Council that the rules-based international order is under "grave threat."[99] He viewed the order as challenged not only by external threats, such as international terrorism or climate change, but also by internal doubts raised by traditional supporters of the UN system, such as the United States and parts of Europe. As the international system has evolved from the unipolar moment of the 1990s and early 2000s to the multipolar world of 2020, Guterres argued that the greatest danger is not conflict due to power struggles but, rather, the prospect of perpetual instability in a world with no global leadership, no rules, and no norms.

The absence of U.S. leadership at the UN, especially from a founding member and traditional anchor such as the United States, meant more instability in a deteriorating strategic context. European leaders, also founding members, sought to continually affirm the core values and principles of the UN Charter that provided the foundations for the international system. Given the onslaught of negative press about a chaotic and dangerous world, they wisely chose to project a strategic narrative of order and control, as well as offer a vision of hope and opportunity. With the United States on the sidelines, Europe needed to identify ways in which the UN system could be renewed and adapted to new challenges. Ambition and creativity—rather than "wistfulness" about "westlessness"[100]—are required to develop new norms and institutions to preserve and strengthen the core values of the UN Charter and, with it, the liberal order. Beyond financial contributions, the main challenge will be the international community's intellectual efforts and the scope of its imagination.

———

In short, the past four years marked numerous missed opportunities. Trump's foreign policy made it much more difficult to mobilize European support on clear areas of common interest, such as confronting the rise of China, and more difficult to have a constructive dialogue on issues where there is obvious disagreement, such as the most effective way to prevent Iran from developing a nuclear weapon. Notwithstanding Trump's "maximal pressure" on Iran and withdrawal from the JCPOA, the nuclear deal has persisted on a lifeline thanks to European support, illustrating the mutual dependence of the United States and EU in achieving their foreign policy goals. Yet, the Europeans have grown much more distrustful not only of Trump but the U.S. government, and increasingly question U.S. representations on technical issues, such as risk factors surrounding 5G.

Moreover, the Trump-induced transatlantic rift has opened the global space for greater influence by Russia and China, whether in Syria, Libya, Africa, or even Latin America. Even in Europe, some leaders, such as Macron, view the United States in the same category as Russia or China, as another great power that Europe should balance against to maximize its own interests.

Perhaps most importantly, some Europeans increasingly misperceive Trump's erratic leadership as the "new normal." More disturbingly, others view it as all too consistent with long-term U.S. trends. Former EU Ambassador to the United States David O'Sullivan argued that the United States and the EU have "had a very troubled relationship in the last 20–30 years," as a result of "support for Pax Americana" combined with "a lot of disagreements" over issues such as Iraq and trade. Likewise, the Cold War was no "golden age" of transatlantic relations: after all, in the Vietnam War, "the Europeans offered no support to the Americans." Thus, U.S. policy, O'Sullivan argues, may be actually "reverting to type," whereby the period 1945 through 2008 is the exception and isolationism the rule.[101]

Similarly, one senior EU official argued that the "United States has always had a certain level of ambivalence in its relationship towards the European Union."[102] When asked about Trump's view of the EU as a foe, he interpreted this view as "deeply ideologically rooted" in the "American soul and Constitution," whereby a political project such as the EU is a "nightmare."[103] He stressed that the "transatlantic relationship remains a vital relationship for the European Union and for its member states," but noted that the United States has a doctrine of "predominance: it wants to be the top power in the world."[104] On the one hand, the "United States has a strategic outlook that differs from the one of the European Union: it can take decisions, be it in Afghanistan, the Middle East or even Africa—surrounding Europe—that will not affect its security directly, but can impact Europe's physical security and control of borders."[105] On the other hand, other EU officials emphasize the need to "distinguish between Trump and the United States," noting that it is "quite surprising how destructive his personal behavior has been on certain foreign policy areas, but it has been virtually unseen in other areas where basically there has been a lot of continuity."[106] Nonetheless, even they did not expect "things to revert to normal" if Trump lost the 2020 election, as "America is going to pivot away from the European Union and will have other more pressing immediate interests."[107] Instead, they argued, "America will go back to its old normal: offshore balancing, defending its core interests, rather than being the global police officer"—again viewing the years 1941–2008 as "the exception to the rule rather than the rule."[108]

The main challenges to the United States and Europe will not be resolved by resurrecting the spirit of nationalism. The Trump administration correctly identified the rise of China as an ongoing foreign policy concern, but only a few of its officials argued that Western cooperation is a necessary condition for future success in meeting that challenge.[109] And as President Eisenhower once said, "we are concerned not only with the protection of territory . . . but with the defense of a way of life."[110] That is where the real contest of the future will lie—the struggle between liberalism and authoritarianism, in which the Trump administration squandered four years of potential transatlantic cooperation.

4

Internal and External Challenges to the West

Underlying the crisis of the West are both internal and external challenges. Within the transatlantic community, various fissures have emerged due to growing income inequalities that have built up in parts of Europe and, especially, in the United States, such that the basic bargain is deemed by some domestic constituencies to be fundamentally unfair. Trump, as well as European populists, rose to power on a wave of legitimate grievances but without any viable domestic or international solutions. Outside of the West, illiberal states such as China and Russia have proffered a different model for global success, one based on authoritarianism and state capitalism, and have sought to gradually extend this model into parts of the West and the rest of the world. Both internal and external challenges need a coherent response as part of the overall defense of the liberal order.

INEQUALITY AND IDENTITY

There is consensus among policymakers, political scientists, and the general public that for the last seventy years the liberal order has successfully delivered broad benefits to its members in terms of peace, prosperity, and political inclusion.[1] In fact, Western populations have steadily grown wealthier; average annual growth in GDP per capita in the European Union and the United States has exceeded global growth since 1960. China and India grew at an even faster pace; they, too, have benefited from the liberal order, though, in many respects, they are outliers, and the durability of their models remains unproven.

While the achievements of the liberal order have been impressive, they have also obscured a diversity of outcomes, some of which have negatively impacted certain groups.[2] Globalization, one of the economic pillars of the liberal order, has lifted millions of people out of poverty, most notably an estimated 500 million in China alone. However, the process also has enriched a global elite while simultaneously squeezing the world's middle class.

In particular, real wages in the United States stagnated for most workers in recent decades, with significant gains only for the top earners.[3] As a consequence, since 1980, income inequality in the US has risen significantly, as shown in figure 4-1. The growing economic gaps between rich and poor became one of the central critiques of populists, who argued that the system was rigged in favor of the elites, which captured most of the economic growth at the expense of a hollowed-out middle class.[4] For instance, in 2000, when adjusted for inflation, the range of household incomes in that middle 20 percent started at $38,000 a year. Nineteen years later, that figure had slipped from $38,000 a year to $33,000 a year. Now at the high end of the range, household income for that middle 20 percent fell from about $68,000 a year in 2000 to $66,000 a year in 2019. Moreover, America's industrial base has largely evaporated, as hundreds of thousands of manufacturing jobs have been lost to Asia and Latin America, where workers are paid far less. American workers in the manufacturing sector generally blame Washington politicians for having sold them out in bilateral and multilateral trade deals.[5]

However, Europe's experience over the past four decades demonstrates that economic discontent stemmed more from domestic tax and spending policies than foreign policy, or even trade policy. In fact, income inequality in the EU has increased only slightly compared to the 1980s. And it has gradually decreased since the 1990s, as Central and Eastern European states have grown quickly in terms of GDP per capita compared to Western European states. Currently, there is a range of income inequality within Europe, but all EU member states currently have more income equality than the United States. Since the EU's enlargement across Central and

FIGURE 4-1. Income Inequality in Europe and the United States

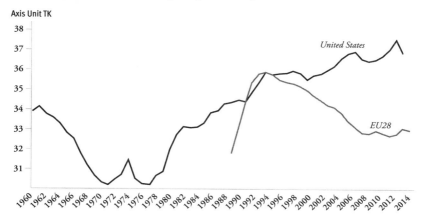

Source: Gini coefficients adapted from Bruegel (2016). Data from US Standardized World Income Inequality Database (SWIID), while EU28 data is from Darvas (2016), based on individual country data from Solt (2016).

Eastern Europe in 2004, inequalities within the EU have fluctuated only marginally, with marked deterioration only in the United Kingdom and Portugal and significant improvements in some countries, such as Poland, as shown in figure 4-2.

Growing income inequality has contributed to the rise of populism and nationalism in both the United States and Europe, but it is only one source of global malaise about the liberal order. There are other factors that are somewhat more difficult to quantify. As the forces of globalization overpower individual initiative, many sense the loss of national identity and control over their future.[6] More important, an increasingly accepted narrative has emerged that the current institutional structures, both in the United States and in Europe, are not delivering solutions. The result is that a wholesale set of complaints, claims, and challenges to long-established rules and institutions now threatens the very foundation of the liberal order. The psychological need for simplicity and clarity, rather than complexity and ambiguity, is an ineluctable feature of modern politics and needs to be acknowledged with empathy and addressed through exchange and dialogue. Criticisms are not often framed as debates about the West and the liberal order, but are driven, instead, by local, regional, or national concerns or issues. However, a general narrative has emerged that the current institutional structures—by whatever name they are called—are not delivering

FIGURE 4-2. Income Distribution in Europe.

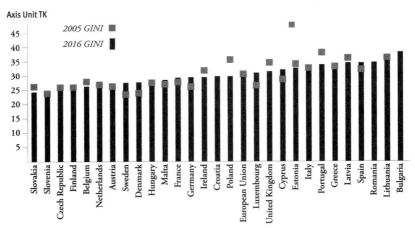

Note: 2005 data not available for Bulgaria, Croatia, and Romania.

Source: Eurostat (2020).

for the general populations in either the United States or Europe. A single change in one or another policy would not be viewed as an attempt to overturn the liberal order, but a wholesale set of claims to unravel many of the long-established norms, rules, and institutions can be viewed from this wider perspective as a systemic challenge.

Spurred by the likes of Stephen Bannon, Nigel Farage, and Marine Le Pen, critics have conflated a wide range of concerns (with income inequalities in the United States as the most measurable and palpable one) as grounds for revisiting fundamental commitments to the liberal order and its underlying norms. The basic political fault lines, instead of traditional distinctions between right and left, have become reoriented around divisions between those favoring open and liberal societies versus closed and illiberal societies. For the critics, the argument seemed simple: if the order has not delivered in terms of their prosperity and political inclusion, why should they support it? And more important, why should taxpayer funding be allocated for global efforts when there are so many problems at home? These internal tensions will need to be resolved if America and Europe hope to deal with both near-term and long-term threats from Russia and China.

GREAT POWER COMPETITION

After roughly a quarter of a century of great power consensus, the rivalry between autocracy and democracy has returned and is reshaping the twenty-first century's geostrategic landscape. Indeed, since 1989, relations among Europe, the United States, China, and Russia have been not only (mostly) peaceful but also premised—at least by Western leaders—on a degree of political and economic convergence over time. At the turn of the twenty-first century, Russia was viewed as an emerging democracy and, briefly, even as a potential candidate for NATO membership, while China's emergence on the global stage was viewed as a possible harbinger of greater liberalization. However, both Russia and China pose structural challenges to the liberal order, though in distinctly different ways, given their vastly different scale, scope, and strategic goals.[7]

After the break-up of the Soviet Union and dissolution of the Warsaw Pact, Russia and the United States enjoyed a period of harmonious relations. Of course, as has been noted, there were exceptions to these halcyon years, most conspicuously the divisions over NATO's intervention in Kosovo in 1999 and the U.S.-led war in Iraq in 2003. But the general sense of convergence enabled significant great power collaboration on a number of issues. For example, Russia joined the Council of Europe in 1996 and the following year, the G7 included Russia, to become the G8. Most significant, Russia acquiesced to the enlargement of both NATO and the EU to include former members of Comecon and the Warsaw Pact.

This remarkable post–Cold War convergence was interrupted in 2008 by Russia's war with former fellow Soviet republic Georgia. However, the West was anxious to move past the conflict as quickly as possible, and after condemning Russian aggression, a number of positive steps followed. The United States and the EU encouraged the accession of Russia to the World Trade Organization. In 2010, the United States and Russia successfully negotiated the New Strategic Arms Reduction Treaty. Russia permitted the United States to use its supply routes into Afghanistan. And finally, in 2011, Russia acquiesced to the UN Security Council's authorization of NATO's intervention in Libya.

Relations between the United States and Russia became severely strained when Vladimir Putin returned as president of Russia in 2012. The standoff over Russia's illegal annexation of Crimea and destabilization of eastern

Ukraine in 2014 marked a severe breach of the international order. This was subsequently compounded in Syria, where Russia's intervention with troops and military equipment in 2015 in support of the Assad regime was in direct opposition to European and U.S. objectives to restore stability and facilitate a Syrian-led political process in the war-torn country. Russian interference in the U.S. presidential elections in 2016, and subsequently in European elections, showed that it felt few constraints in pushing back against what it perceived as an existential threat: the global convergence around democracy, human rights, rule of law, and market economy. Russia's very likely use of a nerve agent to poison one of its former spies living in the UK—the kind of covert murderous act not seen since the end of the Cold War—is only the latest example of its willingness to create tension with the West.

Rather than democratizing, Russia embraced some capitalist principles to expand its material base and enrich its oligarchy but, ultimately, grew more authoritarian. Economic growth in the Soviet Union was difficult to assess, but available figures for Russia in 1989–2016 show a meager 0.50 percent growth in GDP per capita—effectively nearly two decades of stagnation. However, it is estimated that there are nearly twice as many billionaires in Russia as there are in the United Kingdom.

Given its recent history, Russia will likely continue to pose the most overt challenge to the liberal order's objectives and policies. First in Georgia in 2008 and then in Ukraine in 2014, Russia sought to forestall EU and NATO engagement in the region by invading parts of both countries and supporting separatist movements. Indeed, Russian decisionmakers now view the EU and NATO as two sides of the same Western coin and, over the long term, seek the evisceration and hollowing out of both institutions. The Kremlin's latest national security strategy, published in December 2015, explicitly blamed NATO's expansion as "creating a threat to [Russia's] national security." It also sought to defend "traditional Russian religious and moral values" against "external expansion of ideologies and values." Russia's sizable military force still enables it to play the role of a spoiler in destabilizing the liberal order. Yet, given its dearth of material resources, Russia cannot even pretend to overturn the order.

Over the long term, China presents a transformational challenge to the liberal order, as shown in table 4-1, given its economic heft, extraordinary prosperity gains, and rapidly expanding military. President Xi Jinping's outline of the "Chinese Dream" in speeches during 2017 emphasized the role of Communist "Party leadership," "consultative democracy," and "democratic dictatorship" in driving China's economic success. President Xi's elimination of term limits enabling him potentially to remain in power for life further cements China's authoritarian model. China has begun to flex its muscle in the South China Sea, building a world-class navy, and is seeking to build or buy forward operating bases around the world. Through the Belt and Road Initiative, China is also seeking to string together a global trading network.[8]

With an increasingly powerful military and economy, China has the potential to create a new global order—rules-based and predictable, but not liberal—without protection of human rights, provision of rule of law, promotion of democracy, or preservation of market capitalism. However, in the near term, notwithstanding the brazen attempt to subsume Hong Kong in violation of its treaty with Britain, it will be difficult for China to reshape

TABLE 4-1. Russia's and China's Challenges to the West

Challenge	Russia	China
Type	Spoiler	Transformational
Scale	Limited	Systemic
Duration	Near- and medium-term	Medium- to long-term
Scope	Regional and beyond	Global
Instrument	Military and hybrid threats	Economic and military
Institutional initiatives	Stagnating (for example, Eurasian Economic Union)	Flourishing (for example, Asian Infrastructure Investment Bank, Belt and Road Initiative, 17+1 Format)
UN Security Council activity	Frequent use of veto to block action	Largest P5 contributor of peacekeeping troops and second largest donor for peacekeeping

the liberal order, given institutional resilience. Over time, however, given its commensurate economic scale and growing military might, China could find success in promoting authoritarianism and illiberal values around the world (for example, in Venezuela or Brazil) just as the West promoted democracy and liberal values during the second half of the twentieth century.

MANAGING RUSSIA'S DECLINE

Although rising powers historically create security challenges, it is Russia's decline, like a supernova, that has destabilized the foundations of Western security and that will need to be managed over time.[9] To the extent that the "near-absolute priority of domestic stability and external security considerations" historically explain Russian foreign policy,[10] the Kremlin's insecurity about being able to remain in power as an authoritarian regime largely explains its policies abroad, particularly in Ukraine.

As previously noted, Russia's role in the world is often as a spoiler. While Russian dreams of *Novorossiya* propagated throughout 2014 and 2015 with threats to carve up Ukraine, Moscow failed in its objectives. Notwithstanding more than 13,000 casualties in eastern Ukraine, the democratically elected government in Kyiv is still in power, and its civil society has shown extraordinary resilience and resolve over the past five years. And the Kremlin's fundamental concern—its continued viability—has been invalidated: democrats in neighboring Kyiv are no more a threat to Moscow than those in Vilnius, Tallinn, or Riga. In contrast to setbacks in Ukraine, Russia's 2015 intervention in Syria on behalf of the Assad regime was a "success" by its own standards: the tactical demonstrations of force served to bolster Russia's international image as a great power, stabilized the Assad regime, and destabilized Europe with a massive exodus of Syrian refugees.

Russia, notwithstanding its outsized geography and self-image, has been, by and large, at a standstill in terms of material power over the past twenty-five years, and it is likely to continue to remain so. Its population, uniquely for a developed country, actually shrunk for nearly two decades during the 1990s and 2000s, and its GDP per capita is only marginally higher than at the end of the Cold War. Its limited economic base of only 2 percent of global GDP (less than South Korea and comparable to Australia) and meager economic performance over the past quarter-century severely constrain its ability to attract new adherents to its model. It has few close allies, and its key institutional initiative in the form of the Eurasian Economic Union has plateaued.

By all objective measures of material resources, Russia is arguably no longer a great power but, rather, a regional power with localized influence. Nonetheless, it continues to strive for great power status and, in some parts of Europe, is perceived to be one.[11] Russia has been investing in its military, with expenditures growing at 10 percent annually between 2011 and 2016 and accounting for 4.3 percent of Russian GDP in 2017—against 3.1 percent in the United States, 1.9 percent in China, and 1.5 percent on average in the EU. Yet, this spike in military spending is likely to be unsustainable, and Russia may need to revert to its 3 to 4 percent historical average, as shown in figure 4-3.

Notwithstanding the West's ultimate objective of compelling Russia to end the conflict in Ukraine according to the Minsk agreements, peace has yet to be achieved. However, Russia's capacity to inflict damage is today more limited than when it first invaded Ukraine. The West has imposed a python-like strategy of squeezing Russia, which depends on close transat-

FIGURE 4-3. Russia's Military Spending Under Pressure

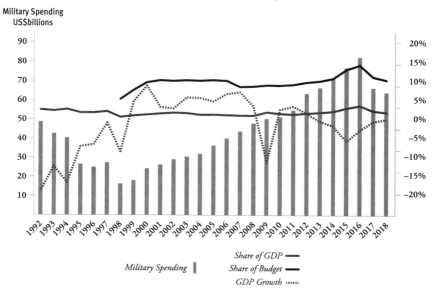

Notes: Left axis is military spending in USD billions.

Sources: SIPRI (2020) for military spending; World Bank (2020) for GDP.

lantic coordination. Indeed, as shown in figure 4-3, transatlantic sanctions against Russia have deprived the Russian economy of 1 to 1.5 percent of its GDP annually, or more than $100 billion, since 2014. Economic pressure against Russia has constrained its military, forcing Moscow to cut defense spending drastically, by 20 percent in 2017.

Mirroring the Obama-Biden administration's strategy toward Russia,[12] the EU's 2016 Russia strategy is based on firmness and engagement, as reflected in five principles:

- full implementation of the Minsk agreements as a key element for any substantial change in the EU's relations with Russia;

- strengthening relations with the EU's Eastern Partners and other neighbors;

- strengthening internal resilience of the EU;

- selective engagement with Russia on foreign policy and global issues and other areas where there is a clear EU interest; and

- willingness to support Russian civil society and invest in people-to-people contacts.

The current strategy, which could be summarized as "confront where we must and cooperate when we can," remains sound.

An additional guiding principle might include close policy coordination with other G7 partners, such as Canada and Japan. Though this norm has operated in the background, it is critical to the success of any strategy toward Russia. Russia's attempts to divide the transatlantic community have largely failed and, instead, have had the opposite effect of nations closing ranks within the West. But neither transatlantic nor European unity with respect to Russia happened automatically and should not be presumed in the future. Alliances need to be continually maintained and coordinated. As former Secretary of State George Shultz often said, "if you have a garden, and want to see it flourish, you have to tend it."

In particular, President Trump's overtures toward Putin encouraged other European leaders, notably Emmanuel Macron and Angela Merkel, to explore some sort of rapprochement with Moscow. Indeed, many leaders at the 2019 G7 summit seemed inclined toward inviting Russia back into the fold, perceiving Moscow as relevant to key common challenges, whether in Syria, Libya, or Iran. Most recently, Trump invited Putin as a guest to the G7 summit in Camp David in September 2020, which European leaders, fortunately, opposed; in any event, the meeting was postponed due to COVID-19 as well as the presidential election. Western relations with Russia cannot be normalized while the Kremlin wages war in Ukraine, props up a ruthless dictator in Syria, sows chaos in Libya, and spreads disinformation campaigns in Europe and America. Returning to the status quo before Trump would also be insufficient, as the economic sanctions against Russia have not succeeded in changing its behavior and, in fact, Moscow's transgressions and threats now go beyond its aggression in Ukraine.

In developing a robust strategy to push back against Russia, the United States and its allies will be constrained in identifying creative new methods of influencing Moscow. Given that transatlantic sanctions against Russia have succeeded in limiting Russia's military spending, they remain the primary lever of pressure against the Kremlin and should be expanded to limit Moscow's ability to cause damage abroad. The EU's current focus on developing a human rights sanctions regime could be leveraged in particular against the Kremlin. Moreover, continued Western financial and political support for transformative change in Ukraine, Georgia, and elsewhere in the region—as well as renewed engagement with Belarus, Kazakhstan, and others—will likely redound over time to the West's advantage, as it would expand the scope of free institutions.

U.S. efforts to wean Europe off its dependency on Russia's fossil fuels are challenged in the short term by the relative cost structure of liquefied natural gas (LNG). Over the long term, using appropriate financial incentives, it could be profitable for both Europe and the United States to challenge Russia's energy dominance on the continent, especially as limiting Russian gas exports will further weaken Moscow's ability to inflict damage abroad. However, both the EU and the United States are constrained by relative fatigue with international commitments, so it is doubtful that either will exert greater pressure on Russia. Given the drop in oil prices, Russia's failure to set prices with Saudi Arabia, and many EU members' commitment to alternative fuels, Russian leverage may atrophy even without prodding from the United States.

As a matter of necessity, these potential areas of confrontation will need to be balanced with potential, though limited, areas of cooperation. Hopes for U.S.-Russian coordination in Syria, already tenuous in 2015 and 2016, are now belied by the years of conflicting interests and objectives in the Middle East. While Bashar al-Assad and Putin may have prevailed for the time being in Syria's civil war, their cooperation does not make them partners for the West. The same applies to the current conflict in Libya, where Russia and the United States nominally supported Haftar but have separate interests and objectives.

For the foreseeable future, the West's relations with Russia are likely to remain limited to a small set of core common interests, such as counterterrorism, climate change, and nuclear nonproliferation (notwithstanding the recent fallout over the status of the Intermediate Nuclear Forces treaty, which the United States says Russia violated with deployment of certain missiles and Russia says the United States violated first with its missile defense shield). President Putin's decision to rewrite the Russian constitution and continue in office post-2024 suggests that the Kremlin's policies will persist as he seeks to protect the regime from internal opposition. Reconciliation with the West requires fundamental change in Russian policy, and is highly unlikely because any moderation of behavior, ultimately, cuts against the Kremlin's principal objective to remain an authoritarian regime. Ideally, future relations with Russia might resemble those during the 1990s, when there was genuine cooperation. Even the first decade of the twenty-first century offered a precedent for greater stability and predictability.

Overall, the West needs to maintain its resolve and strategic persistence. In this endeavor, its decisionmaking process—slow, deliberate, consensus-driven, and rules-based—is key to its competitive advantage. Like a grand flotilla, the West and its component parts take time to chart a course, but once established, they are most successful when they stay the course. The main challenge from Russia lies in its sizable military instrument, which still enables Russia to play the role of a spoiler in destabilizing the liberal order. Moscow will, undoubtedly, continue to opportunistically exploit strategic openings, whether in Libya, Yemen, Afghanistan, or elsewhere, to destabilize Europe, the West, and the liberal order.

SUPPORTING UKRAINE'S TRANSFORMATION

Western strategy toward Russia, in turn, is inextricably intertwined with its strategy toward Ukraine, the largest country in Europe; sixth in population, with 42.5 million. As the late Zbigniew Brzezinski argued, without

Ukraine Russia ceases to be an empire. And as former European Council President Donald Tusk noted in his remarks to the Ukrainian Rada, the future of Ukraine will shape profoundly the future of Europe.[13] In many ways, Ukraine is also the fulcrum on which the fate of the liberal order rests.

The Ukrainian government's decision to suspend the signing of an association agreement with Europe inspired the initial protests in Ukraine in late 2013 and early 2014. Many of the demonstrators carried EU flags during the three-month daily occupation of Kyiv's Euromaidan. Dozens of protestors were killed and hundreds more were injured. In the six years since the Euromaidan Revolution, Ukraine has become a central arena for the West's vision of a world order organized around the principles of democracy, human rights, rule of law, and market capitalism. As the 2019 EU strategy report describes it, the West has an "existential interest" in Ukraine.[14] But the struggle has also been a test case for the credibility of Western foreign policy: whether the United States and the EU, given the scale of material resources and political attention collectively committed to Ukraine, can accomplish the objectives they set out. Although Trump sought to use Ukraine for domestic political purposes, to solicit damaging information on his Democratic political rival Joe Biden,[15] he was largely unable to displace the long-term transatlantic commitment to Ukraine.

Ukraine has surprised most observers with its reforms and the willingness of its citizens to make significant sacrifices. President Volodymyr Zelenskyy has tried to fulfill his campaign pledges, though some of his recent decisions raise questions about the future. His early appointment of Andriy Bohdan as his chief of staff, given the latter's connections to oligarch Ihor Kolomoyskyi, tainted his image. In March 2020, his political standing suffered another blow when Ukraine's prosecutor general was replaced, apparently because he refused to prosecute former president Petro Poroshenko. The Ukrainian government was completely reshuffled, with a new prime minister and new ministers in charge of foreign affairs, defense, and finance. The jury is still out on the new team, but the expectations are bleak in the near term. For instance, the new finance minister Ihor Umansky questioned the value of working with the IMF at a time when Ukraine was seeking to secure a new $5.5 billion loan agreement with the fund.

For well-documented historical reasons, Russia also has interests in Ukraine, where nearly 30 percent of the population speaks Russian as their native language. Russia's seizure and subsequent annexation of Crimea was, according to President Putin, prompted by a "shared history and pride." Indeed, he has questioned whether Ukraine is a sovereign state. Putin also wanted to preserve access to Sevastopol, the sole warm water port for Russia's Black Sea Fleet. He maintained that, had he not acted, "NATO's navy would be right there in this city of Russia's military glory." Russia's ongoing military presence and support for separatists in Donetsk and Luhansk are driven by the same historical rationales and concerns about Ukraine's integration with the West.

Democratic and free-market reforms have made significant progress in Ukraine. According to the World Bank, for two years after the Euromaidan Revolution, GDP in Ukraine decreased by a total of 12 to 16 percent, but during the subsequent years, notwithstanding the costly war in the east, the country has made steady political and economic gains. As then European Commission President Juncker noted at the EU-Ukraine summit in 2018, Ukraine has made more reforms since 2014 than in the previous two decades of independence. And, indeed, the list of reforms is long, and it includes many sectors: banking, energy, military, procurement, courts, and law enforcement. Nearly every single aspect of political, economic, and social life in Ukraine has changed, though substantial work remains (primarily on anti-corruption and privatization).

Economically, Ukraine is poised for long-term growth, although it has yet to achieve high rates. Just as Poland managed to quadruple its average income relative to the EU since the fall of communism, so could Ukraine, if similar favorable conditions and external financing exist. Ukraine's GDP per capita approximated Poland's in 1990 but now is only one-fifth. Ukraine has the potential to experience decades of high economic growth as it recovers from its historic losses. It is often rightly said that even with conflict continuing in Donetsk and Luhansk (3 percent of Ukraine's territory) and the ongoing unlawful seizure of Crimea (4 percent of its territory), Ukraine can be considerably successful. The international community's economic and technical assistance to Ukraine has been conducted quite effectively through the G7+ format, which has also coordinated sanctions policy against Russia.

Politically, the Minsk Agreements from 2014 and 2015 remain the organizing principles for any potential resolution to the crisis and the lifting of Western sanctions. Negotiations among Ukraine, Russia, Germany, and France—known as the Normandy format—have occurred only twice at the leaders level over the past four years: in 2016 and, more recently, in December 2019. While there is not much confidence in the Normandy format leading to a resolution of the conflict, neither are there any apparent better alternatives. Several ideas, such as adding the EU or the United States formally to the negotiations, have been explored in the past (through the so-called Geneva format) but are unlikely to change the underlying dynamic. Both the EU and the United States are regularly consulted on the negotiating terms and strategies. Moreover, the U.S.-Russia negotiating channel, initiated during the Obama-Biden administration by Assistant Secretary of State Victoria Nuland, and continued with Special Representative for Ukraine Negotiations Kurt Volker (until his resignation in September 2019), was conducted in sync with the Normandy format discussions, without much effect on the overall peace process.

While Russia's threat to the liberal order will be tested primarily in Ukraine, China's challenge will be more global in scope and likely more durable.

COUNTERING CHINA'S ASSERTIVENESS

Since joining the World Trade Organization in 2001, China has become a global economic player, as shown in figure 4-4; no longer viewed simply as a hub for low-cost manufacturing, it is now one of the world's most significant international investors and trading partners. Moreover, with the appointment of Xi Jinping as president in 2013, China ushered in a new era in international economic and political relations.[16]

In response to the rise of China, the Obama-Biden administration's strategy focused on building up America's diplomatic and economic presence in the Pacific region through "forward-deployment."[17] The Trans-Pacific Partnership represented the cornerstone of President Obama's rebalance to Asia. The multilateral trade agreement did not target China directly; instead, it would have preempted Beijing by introducing U.S. economic standards to a number of Asian and Latin American countries before China brought its own standards. Nor did the agreement presume a change to China's domestic order according to liberal principles of democracy and human rights but, rather, only the assurance that China could not reshape countries in its neighborhood.

As noted earlier, the Trump administration withdrew from the TPP in

FIGURE 4-4. Russia's Stagnation and China's Surge

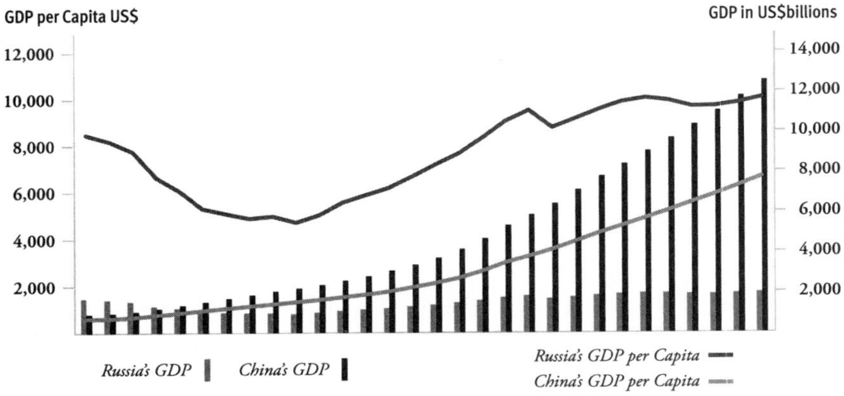

GDP per Capita US$ GDP in US$billions

Russia's GDP ❙ China's GDP ❙	Russia's GDP per Capita ▬ China's GDP per Capita ▬

Notes: GDP per capita in USD (left axis) and GDP in USD billions (right axis)
Source: World Bank (2018).

April 1018, and adopted a much more aggressive approach toward China, imposing tariffs on $550 billion of Chinese imports. But it was unclear what interests or objectives the administration was pursuing through its Indo-Pacific strategy, as it oscillated between trade wars and olive branches to Beijing. Former EU Ambassador to the United States David O'Sullivan argued that the Trump administration wanted to preserve U.S. "dominance" on the world stage, which it enjoyed since the collapse of the Soviet Union and which China uniquely threatens.[18] This, of course, is completely consistent with Trump's "America First" bromide but hardly represents a coherent strategy.

Europe's strategy to Asia is, likewise, somewhat ambiguous, but is developing in response to three geopolitical factors—the return of great-power rivalry, China's growing assertiveness, and emerging U.S.-Chinese tensions. Europeans are struggling to define their core interests and objectives in the region: How much commonality or diversity of interest is there between Europe and Asia? What are the main instruments that the EU or individual member states have at their disposal to serve their interests in Asia? And, who are Europe's potential partners and competitors in the region?

It is unlikely that European policymakers—representing 500 million people and nearly thirty countries—will be able to coalesce around a single strategy toward Asia, a region of 4.5 billion people and more than fifty countries. However, the EU's 2016 Global Strategy provided a general framework for Europe's policies toward the wider Asia-Pacific region.[19] It argued that there is a "direct connection" between European prosperity and Asian security, and sought "to make greater practical contributions to Asian security" through partnerships with Japan, South Korea, and others.

Implementing these political guidelines, the European Commission and the European External Action Service issued a joint communication to the European Parliament and Council in September 2018 proposing concrete policies to improve connections between Europe and Asia. The communication focused on interoperable transport, energy, and digital networks[20] and was generally perceived as a response to China's Belt and Road Initiative. While European strategies toward Asia appeared compatible with the Trump administration's free and open Indo-Pacific strategy, some tension between the two approaches were likely, given Trump's trade war with China.

For Europe, the central dynamic in Asia has been the region's rapid economic growth, particularly in China, and the opportunities for trade and investment. Asia, with roughly 60 percent of the world's population, accounts for 35 percent of the EU's exports (€618 billion) and 45 percent of the EU's imports (€774 billion).[21] Between 1989 and 2016, GDP per capita growth rates in Asia were more than double those in the EU and the United States (3.25 percent compared to 1.47 and 1.39 percent, respectively); and people in China and India grew wealthier on average by 8.76 and 4.85 percent, respectively.[22] Recently, the EU concluded trade and investment protection agreements with Vietnam and Singapore, as well as a strategic and economic partnership agreement with Japan. It has also opened trade talks with Australia and New Zealand.

Notwithstanding increased opportunities for trade and investment, the security situation in Asia is tense due to the ongoing crisis with North Korea over its nuclear weapons program. There is also tension over China's territorial claims in the South China Sea, where it has militarized newly constructed artificial islands, and between China and Japan over the Senkaku/Diaoyu islands. Europe has relied on U.S. military primacy in Asia to provide regional security and stability,[23] but any escalation of these conflicts has the potential to disrupt European trade in Asia.

Due to its economic power, Europe's statements carry weight with actors in the region, and the EU has been increasingly vocal in support of international law and a rules-based order. For example, the EU protested the introduction of an air defense identification zone by China in the East China Sea, and supported the judgment against China by the Permanent Court of Arbitration with regard to the South China Sea dispute. France has periodically run freedom-of-navigation operations in the region, which could be deemed by outside observers as a type of EU rule-of-law mission, to contest China's claims and to support the international law of the sea.

Europe generally has good relations with many countries in Asia, particularly India, Japan, Australia, and New Zealand. Interactions with China, however, have gone through a significant evolution in recent years, given the country's rapid rise in economic, military, and political power, and its growing assertiveness. With respect to China, the EU's 2016 strategy recommended engagement based on "respect for rule of law, both domestically and internationally."[24]

China respects the EU as an institution, but views Europe as a region divided into four parts:

- Big states: Germany, France, and the United Kingdom;

- Northern Europe: the Scandinavian states, Ireland, Iceland, etc.;

- Central and Eastern Europe: Poland, Lithuania, Latvia, Estonia, etc.; and

- Southern Europe: Greece, Italy, Spain, Portugal, Malta.[25]

China's 17+1 format for engaging with seventeen countries of Central and Eastern Europe has been a success of its diplomacy, yet enthusiasm has been curbed by China's failure to deliver on the high (and sometimes outsize) expectations of the participating nations. The countries involved form a diverse group, including EU member states and accession candidates in the Balkans. China's Belt and Road Initiative is a central mechanism for the expansion of its economic and political influence, with around eighty countries now participating, but here, too, many large-scale projects have stalled, notwithstanding signed memoranda of understanding.[26]

China's December 2018 policy paper on the EU is a laundry list of demands and instructions (such as treating Taiwan and Tibet as taboo subjects, and being granted market-economy status), and largely tone deaf in terms of building a relationship with the European Union. China reportedly also has funded various think tanks and academic initiatives in Europe to ensure that a pro-China line emerges within public debates. Globally, its growing economic and political presence also manifests itself in international organizations, such as the UN, where any criticism of the country is actively countered. Yet, notwithstanding its material prowess, China has few real friends and allies in Europe.

An overarching strategic concern for Europe is the evolving U.S. policy in the Pacific region, particularly toward China. Generally, the U.S. strategy is more confrontational toward China than is Europe's. While the United States views China as a direct strategic competitor and potential military adversary, Europe has focused on promoting economic prosperity through direct and portfolio investment in China. This interest is both immediate and long-term, and likely to overshadow other interests related to democracy promotion, human rights, or security in Asia. It may even become accentuated over time as China expands its economic presence in Europe and turns its trade and investment relationships into political leverage. For some European countries—particularly France, Germany, and the United Kingdom—economic interest also includes arms exports to the region.

Second, Europe has a vital interest in protecting its way of life and the wider liberal order—based on democracy, human rights, rule of law, fair trade, and a social market economy—from illiberal forces. But it is an open question whether China poses the same political threat to Europe as does Russia, or whether China simply wants mutual noninterference in internal affairs. After all, democracy and human rights in Europe do not, *ipso facto*, pose a threat to China's political and social structure. Apart from heightened sensitivities over Tibetan sovereignty, and over Taiwan and the one-China policy, China's regime faces few domestic political challenges. One-party rule can be expected to continue for decades.

Third, with respect to regional security, Europe prefers the status quo of U.S. military primacy in Asia as the best-case scenario. It also has a particular interest in the credibility of U.S. security guarantees to its Asian allies, such as Japan or South Korea, as an indicator of the credibility of U.S. guarantees to NATO. For this reason, it has a unique stake in the outcome of the North Korea crisis, and would view a deal that addresses only Pyongyang's long-range missile threat as unsatisfactory (as it would be perceived to serve U.S. interest over allied interest). After all, if the United

States overlooks South Korea's concerns in this crisis, what guarantee would Europeans have that the United States would consider their concerns in a subsequent crisis? In the event that military tensions increase between the United States and China, Europe, beyond offering diplomatic support, is likely to remain neutral and avoid becoming involved in any conflict in the region. Many Europeans recall the Vietnam War experience, and it remains a relevant analogy for them.

Fourth, Europe wants to promote the so-called rules-based global order, which provides for a degree of predictability and stability in interactions with Asian countries and can help guide the rise of China toward positive global contributions. But any positive changes are likely to be gradual and to involve numerous setbacks along the way, rather than transformational change akin to the 1989 democratization wave in Central and Eastern Europe.

Over the next five years, Europe's primary policy instrument in Asia is likely to be economic, through trade and investment agreements. Traditionally, European economic policy has been used to maximize prosperity and commercial opportunity. However, Europe wants to promote universal values in Asia and may be able to leverage its trade and investment agreements there to promote better labor regulations, anti-corruption mechanisms, legal reforms, and political transparency. Its partnership agreements with Japan, Australia, and New Zealand provide a useful model. In addition to bilateral treaties with countries in the region, the EU could join the Comprehensive and Progressive Agreement for Trans-Pacific Partnership with eleven Pacific states as a way of reviving the high standards that characterized the prior TPP from which the Trump administration withdrew. In navigating new trade deals, the EU will need to contend with the new U.S. policy to isolate "nonmarket" countries, such as China, through a so-called poison pill in the new United States–Mexico–Canada Agreement (which gives the other signatories the right to withdraw if one signs a free trade agreement with a nonmarket country).

Beyond trade and investment policies, the EU-Asia Connectivity Strategy provides a wider framework for economic engagement with Asia and for responding to China's Belt and Road Initiative. Recognizing that the Belt and Road Initiative has been successful in messaging, but less so in terms of providing concrete deliverables, Europe will, undoubtedly, be closely watching the extent to which China funds energy, infrastructure, communications, and digital projects.

Europe is also considering a new set of policies to protect its way of life from illiberal forces. For instance, efforts to screen foreign direct investment into Europe for security concerns has quickly gained steam. As a consequence, Huawei's 5G technology, though cost-competitive and advantageous in terms of communications speed, may be rejected in European countries because it potentially facilitates surveillance by China's security services. The same dynamic will characterize other decisions related to scientific cooperation, particularly in areas such as artificial intelligence. Another policy option would be to obtain credible mutual guarantees of political noninterference, which may be possible between Europe and China. However, this would require Europe sacrificing its support for democratic and human rights values in China and may not be politically palatable.

Europe has several formats for consultation and engagement with Asia—in particular the Asia-Europe meeting of fifty-three partners across Europe and Asia, the EU-ASEAN format, and the EU-India strategic partnership—that it can strengthen and utilize to promote a liberal order in Asia with like-minded partners. The open question is whether there will be sufficient interest in both Europe and Asia to organize collective action on issues that support the liberal order. It is, of course, difficult to galvanize and unite political interests among many countries, which are inevitably diffuse, on issues of general interest and that may have long-term shared benefit but incur short-term costs.

Finally, apart from France and the United Kingdom, Europe has limited military assets in Asia. However, the EU could explore launching civilian missions or military operations, pursuant to its Common Security and Defence Policy (CSDP), to help advise on rule of law, security-sector reform, the national security process, or military training, as it does in sixteen such missions and operations across Africa, Eastern Europe, and the Middle East. This kind of assistance could be a valuable contribution to regional security in states such as Sri Lanka or Myanmar.

The EU Global Strategy aims for "an appropriate level of ambition . . . to promote peace and security within and beyond its borders."[27] This applies with special force to Europe's strategies in Asia, which span multiple layers of abstraction, encompass numerous decisionmakers and political entities, and require balancing a range of diverse and potentially conflicting interests. Europe's economic scale, internal resilience, and institutional stability give it a vast range of tools and policy options to design sophisticated and successful strategies for the future.

———

Neither the internal nor external challenges to the liberal order can be confronted by Europe or the United States alone. However, if both can agree on the sharing of burdens and the division of benefits, together, they can hope to muster a strategy that preserves the liberal order.

5

Toward a New Atlantic Charter

Europe is the cornerstone of our engagement with the world, and Europe is . . . our catalyst for global cooperation. . . . Europe remains America's indispensable partner of first resort. And, if you forgive some presumptuousness, I believe we remain your indispensable partner.

—*Vice President Joseph Biden,*
Munich Security Conference (2013)

Over the last eight years, we have reinforced our transatlantic alliances as the cornerstone of our engagement in the world. . . . Amid transformational challenges . . . we remain overwhelmingly confident in the future of our partners of first resort and as committed as ever to supporting both a strong United Kingdom and a strong European Union.

—*John Kerry, Exit Memo to President Obama (2017)*

Perhaps counterintuitively, this era of transatlantic uncertainty and anxiety can be cathartic in surfacing and resolving long-accumulated tensions. At least there is hope to do so with the new Biden administration. In the past, NATO was viewed in Europe "as the primary place where consultations on important international events, in particular crises, should be consulted and where the fundamental decisions should be taken."[1] Yet, apart from the 2011 intervention in Libya and the 2001 intervention in Afghanistan, this has not been true for other foreign policy issues over the past two decades.

Even in the case of terrorist attacks in Europe in 2015 and 2016, instead of turning to NATO's Article 5 (as was the case after September 11), France invoked Article 42.7 of the EU treaties, the so-called mutual defense clause whereby EU member states have an obligation to provide "aid and assistance" to each other in case of armed aggression. France's decision, arguably, reflected a certain preference for relying on European partners rather than its transatlantic allies and could signal Europe's increasing tendency to turn inward.

Indeed, the litany of common global challenges—the rise of China, Russia's aggression, instability in the Middle East and Africa, counterterrorism, economic growth, climate change, cyberspace, trade, technology, and public health—are beyond NATO's purview and cannot be adequately addressed in U.S.-EU summits, which are limited in duration, tend to elicit only general strategic thinking, and usually produce nonspecific promises to work together.[2] Partly because of these institutional constraints, the uneasy truth about the transatlantic alliance is that it had stagnated even before Trump, as leaders met in good faith but with few concrete accomplishments (in contrast to significant deliverables from summits at the G20, in Asia, or even the initial two years of the reset with Russia). As President Obama noted after one meeting with EU leaders, the "summit was not as exciting as other summits because we basically agree on everything."[3] However, much has changed during President Trump's time in office: European leaders preferred not to meet with the U.S. president, and if they had to, they limited discussions with him to symbolic photo opportunities. But crises continued to arise that demand the attention of leaders on both sides of the Atlantic.

Although it seems hard to imagine in the aftermath of Trump, the United States and Europe should, nevertheless, use this historic moment to design a new Atlantic Charter, akin to what Henry Kissinger called for explicitly first in New York in April 1973.[4] Two generations later, at the World Economic Forum in Davos in 2017, Kissinger returned to the theme of the "Atlantic partnership," declaring that it "needs to be reconstructed but with the attitude that it is the key element of both American and European policy."[5] Yet, he advised in his book *World Order,* "because repetition of the familiar leads to stagnation, no little daring is required."[6]

To build on prior achievements rather than simply repeating past practices, Western leaders can reinvigorate the alliance through innovative efforts, culminating in a new Transatlantic Strategic Partnership Agreement (TSPA) and the creation of a Transatlantic Council. A new TSPA could set out key areas of foreign policy and economic coordination and establish a Transatlantic Council to facilitate intergovernmental cooperation at head-of-state, ministerial, and staff levels.

Both sides should establish structured dialogues on regions of common interest, such as Asia, Africa, and Latin America, where transatlantic coordination has been sporadic, usually only at the highest levels, and too often without the prerequisite staff-level preparatory work. For instance, the U.S. assistant secretary of state for East Asian and Pacific Affairs and her staff are currently unlikely to meet their European counterparts to consult on joint strategies related to the rise of China or other issues of mutual interest. This was apparent in 2015, when the transatlantic reaction to the Asian Infrastructure Investment Bank (AIIB) was visibly chaotic. The United States eventually dropped its opposition to European countries joining the AIIB board if certain standards were met, but better communication before a crisis emerges would enable both sides to respond more effectively. Transatlantic summits could be layered on top of NATO summits, where the first day would focus on NATO's core mission of collective defense, feeding into a second day of wider discussion of foreign policy challenges (with presence from all NATO and EU member states).

A new TSPA could also create a powerful alliance on fighting climate change. Since President Trump announced the withdrawal of the United States from the Paris Agreement on climate change, European leaders have asserted themselves by announcing the EU's first package of climate and energy measures, including a 20 percent reduction in greenhouse gas emissions, a 20 percent increase in the share of renewable energy, and a 20 percent improvement in energy efficiency. China, notwithstanding its attempt to be viewed as a global leader on limiting the effects of climate change, continues to outpace the United States and Europe combined in terms of total energy consumption and emissions. Despite President Trump's failure to lead on climate issues, the United States—through state and local governments—continued to pursue policies to limit the effects of global warming. But it isn't enough. As the largest and most innovative economy in the world, and the second-largest emitter of greenhouse gases, the United States, under committed leadership, could join forces with Europe to tap into what is undeniably a multibillion-dollar economic opportunity, providing greater environmental security and healthier living conditions for the entire world.

The TSPA could also facilitate common assessments of global trends, akin to *Global Governance 2025*, the 2010 joint publication by the U.S. National Intelligence Council and the EU Institute for Security Studies. It could lead to joint regional or thematic strategies; for example, on Russia, China, development, or cyberspace. None of these steps would limit the freedom to maneuver by either side but would help facilitate joint decision-making when interests align, as they often do, and create synergies between common positions. Indeed, U.S. and EU strategies toward Russia are largely the same, but without joint communications to that effect, Russia seeks to exploit perceptions of transatlantic divisions and to sow confusion. Likewise, there is currently significant overlap between EU and U.S. strategic approaches toward China, but lack of coordination often means disparate and conflicting moves and statements. The Trump administration sent a large policy team of Asia experts to Paris and Brussels to consult on China, and the U.S. ambassador to the EU urged Europe in February 2019 to "link arms" against China. But these efforts were complicated by President Trump's description of the EU as "almost as bad as China, just smaller," and by U.S. and EU strategies that developed separately rather than jointly. A disciplined review and discussion of all the relevant issues by the United States and Europe working together would be enormously powerful.

Finally, the TSPA could reaffirm the fundamental values of democracy, human rights, rule of law, and market capitalism that serve as the bedrock for the West. Whereas the U.S. National Security Strategies and the EU Global Strategy tend to speak in more neutral terms about a "rules-based international order," it is important to remember that liberal values are rooted in a historical context and provide the foundation for understanding why certain rules remain essential to the West. After all, China may very well subscribe to a rules-based order as well, but one comprised of illiberal rules designed to promote authoritarianism, state capitalism, or spheres of influence. Since the EU has already concluded several strategic partnership agreements with Japan and Canada, and has included them in trade negotiations with Australia and New Zealand, the baseline text is readily available for the two sides to utilize, though it would require some modification.

Doubling down on liberal values as foundational to the Western alliance does not necessarily imply the universalist aspirations of the 1990s, when

U.S. national security strategy envisioned a long-term goal of "a world in which each of the major powers [including Russia and China] is democratic."[7] Notwithstanding the difficulty in building liberal institutions and spreading Western liberalism around the globe, the transatlantic community can and should expand support for local democratic movements. In Ukraine, for instance, transatlantic unity is essential to consolidating the gains made in pursuit of liberal values.

The TSPA also could facilitate continued U.S.-UK-EU coordination on foreign policy post-Brexit. In particular, the post-Brexit negotiations on the UK's new relationship with the EU-27 could result in a privileged British position in terms of coordinating foreign, defense, and security policy with the EU-27, potentially through a European Security Council as proposed by Chancellor Angela Merkel or within a smaller format (with France and Germany) as suggested recently by President Emmanuel Macron.[8] If this were to happen, the United States might be able to associate with the EU-27 (or its subset) in a similar manner as the UK.

Likewise, a TSPA could address the issue of burden-sharing within the alliance. For example, NATO's pledge of 2 percent of GDP on defense spending could be expanded to include a greater percentage of GDP across a broader range of security spending, such as counterterrorism, law enforcement, and intelligence. In the same vein, there should be serious discussion about linking increased defense spending in Europe with increased development aid by the United States, given that both are part and parcel of resources allocated in support of the liberal order and transatlantic strategic interests.

SOLIDARITY IN BURDEN-SHARING

During President Obama's first term, Secretary of Defense Robert Gates noted the general downward trend in European defense spending since 1990 and advocated for greater equilibrium in the relationship. President Trump seized on the issue, as he could use it for political advantage. To divert public discontent over domestic income inequality, Trump focused, instead, on burden-sharing among allies in defense spending. He also used the issue as a rhetorical cudgel against European and other allies.

Indeed, aggregate levels of defense spending in Europe have declined over a period of decades. In 2017, defense spending was nearly 10 percent below 1991 levels and stood in stark contrast to the steady increase of over 100 percent during the Cold War, as shown in figure 5-1. Among the top six spenders in Europe, the biggest decreases between 1990 and 2016 occurred in Germany (minus 33 percent) and the United Kingdom (minus 20 percent), with the biggest increase in Poland (60 percent). And some European countries have been able to drastically increase their defense spending within a single year: for instance, Lithuania (33 percent in 2015), Latvia (44 percent in 2016), and Romania (50 percent in 2017). Thus, the conventional wisdom around wholesale European free-riding on U.S. defense spending and security provision is inaccurate across time and across Europe. It does not acknowledge the significant aggregate increases in European spending throughout the Cold War. Nor does it account for the variation of spending growth across the EU. Notably, Germany's spending in 2016 was lower than in each of the years between 1969 and 2000—a period of *Ostpolitik*, détente, reunification, and globalization. On the other hand, some of the spikes in U.S. defense spending resulted from wars of choice, later deemed to be mistakes, such as the Vietnam War or the 2003 Iraq War.

In fact, since Russia's illegal annexation of Crimea, European defense spending has increased steadily over the past five years, adding the near-equivalent of Italy's entire defense budget to its arsenal. Moreover, European countries have still managed to deploy their troops on numerous missions

FIGURE 5-1. Military Spending in the World

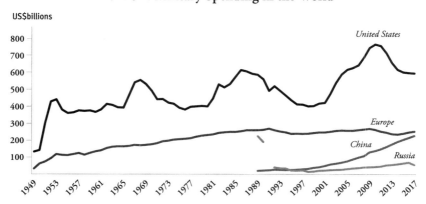

Notes: Europe consists of Western European countries before 1990 and includes Central European countries after 1990; Russia includes USSR data for 1989–1990 for sake of comparison.

Source: SIPRI (2020).

and operations, and in significant numbers, throughout the Middle East and Africa. Collectively, Europe fielded around 34,000 troops in more than twenty countries in 2017, including on missions with high degrees of risk in combat zones such as Iraq, Afghanistan, and the Sahel. Although the disparity in defense capabilities and power projections between Europe and America is significant, the main point is that Europe already has a significant core base of resources and battle experience that it can expand and build on. There may be a logical division of labor between Europe and America in projecting stability based on comparative advantage, historical linkages, and regional proximity.

The burden-sharing debate has focused thus far on defense spending but has overlooked a widening gap between the United States and Europe in terms of official development assistance. The European Union collectively spends $50 billion more than the United States on development, as shown in figure 5-2. While development assistance is not yet viewed as especially significant in public debates over defending the liberal order, it should be. Development aid is often a more effective way to spend money to prevent problems from arising in the first place, and deserves recognition as a key tool in the panoply of instruments to preserve the order.

Defense spending is only one of several imbalances, in addition to development aid and domestic income distribution, that have emerged over time within the transatlantic alliance. Defending the liberal order also en-

FIGURE 5-2. Official Development Assistance

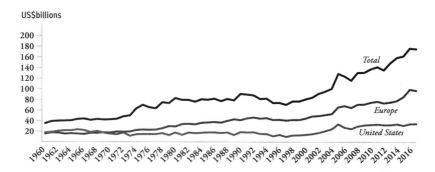

Notes: Europe consists of Development Assistance Committee EU Members + European Commission.

Source: OECD (2020).

compasses instruments of power, such as economic leverage, political influence, and development aid. Redressing the imbalances in both burdens
and benefits in each of these areas will be crucial toward restoring the sense
of solidarity and common destiny that serve as the foundation for the liberal order. Even if the United States increased development aid and Europe
spent more on defense, other grievances would, undoubtedly, surface. But
these steps, which are politically feasible over a sustained period of time,
would go a long way toward restoring transatlantic solidarity in defense of
the free world.

EU-NATO COOPERATION

In recent years, NATO and the EU, with over twenty member states in
common, have engaged systematically in closer cooperation at both the
strategic and operational levels. In 2002, the two institutions had already
established, through the so-called Berlin Plus agreement, a framework for
cooperation, including the EU's ability to utilize NATO's assets in peacekeeping operations. EU-NATO coordination has now reached an unprecedented degree, with initiatives ranging from joint declarations on strategic
partnership in 2016 and 2018 to mutual invitations to summits and other
high-level meetings and cooperation on numerous projects across several
policy areas. Yet, notwithstanding the already high level of coordination,
the EU and NATO should go even further, moving beyond complementar-
ity to synergies. In particular, the new "level of ambition" for EU-NATO
operational cooperation should include joint planning and joint action in
service of conflict prevention and crisis management.

In the area of Common Security and Defence Policy, the EU currently
has approximately 3,000 troops deployed across six military operations[9]
and approximately 2,000 officials working in ten civilian missions.[10] EU
member states also have deployed troops to various counterterrorism operations, such as Counter-ISIS in Iraq and Syria and Operation Barkhane in
the Sahel and to peacekeeping operations such as the UN missions in Mali
and the Central African Republic.

NATO has eight military operations and missions, including troop de-
ployments in Afghanistan (Resolute Support Mission, with about 13,000
personnel from thirty-nine allied and partner countries), Kosovo (KFOR,
with about 4,000 troops from twenty-eight countries), Iraq (NATO Mission

in Iraq [NMI], with several hundred personnel), and in the Mediterranean Sea with Operation Sea Guardian.[11] In addition, it has several thousand troops on its eastern and southeastern flanks as part of the Enhanced Forward Presence and Tailored Forward Presence deterrence measures against Russia. NATO also has active defense capacity-building projects in Georgia, Iraq, Jordan, the Republic of Moldova, and Tunisia.

Moving toward greater synergy between the EU and NATO will be neither automatic nor easy. The two organizations have overlapping membership and similar long-term interests, but, ironically, their similitude also provides a basis for competition. Given their broad institutional mandates, overlapping treaty obligations, and self-concepts, the EU and NATO need enlightened strategies to foster greater cooperation. For instance, both the EU and NATO have an interest in deterring Russian aggression, promoting peace and stability in the Balkans, and projecting stability in the Middle East and North Africa. While their power and resources can be pooled, ultimate responsibility lies with the member states; only they can determine how to utilize both institutions to accomplish their foreign policy objectives.[12]

First, competition arises from the EU and NATO wanting to act everywhere yet remain autonomous—at least in principle. Moreover, there is an inherent tendency for any institution to maximize its mandate, which can lead to confusion and lack of coordination when so many actors are involved. For instance, a country's ambassador to the EU might view an issue differently than that country's ambassador to NATO. Likewise, the ministries of foreign affairs and defense in member state capitals might have different agendas.

Second, NATO's Article 5 on collective defense and the EU's Article 42.7 on mutual defense present another source of potential friction. Those countries that are members of both the EU and NATO acknowledge that the text, history, and structure of Article 42.7 suggests that Article 5 takes precedence over Article 42.7. However, in recent years, there has been a growing debate over this interpretation. For instance, after the terrorist attacks in Paris in November 2015, France invoked the EU's solidarity clause but not NATO's.[13] Still others point out that the two clauses operate at different levels: Article 5 has to be collectively invoked, whereas Article 42.7 can be individually invoked.[14] This debate is unlikely to be resolved soon but is partly revisited in the context of the current momentum toward a stronger EU defense identity and the EU aspiration to strategic autonomy.

Third, problems also can arise from psychological dissonance between the EU and NATO about which organization can claim more credit for preserving peace in Europe. While it is difficult to parse this issue, and each institution positions itself from time to time as the primary security guarantor in Europe, both organizations have, undoubtedly, contributed to this success. However, recent crises with Russia have made clear the advantages of the EU and NATO working together to provide resilience and deterrence. This kind of pragmatism applied more broadly should help overcome obstacles to cooperation.

As a consequence of these factors, any quest for a full and equitable division of labor between the EU and NATO is going to be a Sisyphean task. Some overlap and duplication is inevitable—and may even be beneficial—in covering possible contingencies and providing greater security for all participants. The next-best alternative stems from what Jean Monnet called *solidarité de fait*—solidarity through action on the ground, or practice before principles—whereby operational cooperation occurs in practice even when all of the theoretical issues are not resolved.

To date, the EU and NATO have coordinated missions and operations largely through de-confliction (that is, not doing the same activities and avoiding duplication) rather than joint planning or joint action. The paradigmatic example has been Afghanistan, where both the EU and NATO operated police training missions, but differed in emphasis so as to maximize their impact: the EU focused on improving standards at the interior ministry, while NATO trained police officers.

Inter-institutional cooperation has, nevertheless, taken place at different levels. For example, in Bosnia-Herzegovina, the EU-led Operation Althea is the only so-called "Berlin Plus" operation under which the EU can access NATO assets, with the NATO Deputy Supreme Allied Commander Europe acting as the operation commander while the force itself is under EU command. This arrangement, in place since 2004, enables the EU to serve as the operational lead, with NATO providing a supporting role. In Kosovo, the EU and NATO have reinforced each other through the separate work of the EU mission on the rule of law (EULEX) and NATO's military mission (KFOR) in maintaining security. At the inception of EULEX in 2008, NATO foreign ministers welcomed its deployment as an "urgent priority."[15] The two missions currently work together in a layered security role, with the Kosovo police in the lead, EULEX as backup, and NATO as ultimate backstop.[16] A joint operational procedures document, signed in 2013, and full-time liaison officers at each organization's headquarters facilitate cooperation.

In 2016, in the Mediterranean Sea, NATO launched Operation Sea Guardian, which operated in parallel with the EU's Operation Sophia to counter human smuggling. The two sea operations have benefited from information sharing and logistical support, including refueling, between the EU and NATO.[17] In the Aegean Sea, NATO has also provided real-time information to Greek and Turkish coastguards, as well as to EU's Frontex, to locate smugglers.[18] Even though classified information cannot be formally exchanged between the two institutions, EU and NATO staff can advise each other and cooperate pragmatically. For example, one operation might intercept a smuggler boat based on information shared by the other but short of providing the supporting imagery.

NATO and the EU have convened several staff-level meetings on potential joint counterterrorism efforts, which could serve as a basis for future operational coordination. However, as long as the Cyprus-Turkey dispute continues to confine the formal relationship of the EU and NATO to the framework of the Berlin Plus agreement, operational cooperation will remain difficult. Currently, it is only in the Bosnian context that an EU-led military mission has recourse to NATO assets and capabilities. Informal cooperation can play a role, but it is inherently limited.

In this institutional context, coalitions of the willing, both within and across the EU and NATO (that is, member states and institutional staff) initiate action, which leads to greater trust, confidence, and solidarity. Senior officials and commanders have already developed ways to cooperate and are likely to build on these practices in the future. Response to crisis, as opposed to abstract discussion, will also reveal where duplication is beneficial; thus, there should be a healthy tolerance for trial and error, experimentation, and course corrections. According to current senior EU and NATO officials, many of the habits developed in this way will never be codified and, in fact, any attempt to do so might unduly restrict flexibility of action during crises and impede operational understandings. But cooperation in practice, when it works well, becomes part of the "muscle memory" and DNA of each institution, producing true synergies.

In light of these dynamics, where the EU and NATO have a separate presence in the same country (Iraq, Georgia, and the Republic of Moldova), they should look into what is feasible through common political messaging, policy coordination, and joint staff and resources.

Iraq may be one arena where true synergies can be achieved. Since October 2017, the EU has established a civilian advisory mission assisting the country's national security advisor and the interior ministry with security sector reform (SSR). The EU Advisory Mission in Iraq has around 100 authorized civilian personnel based in Baghdad. In parallel, NATO launched a defense capacity-building mission in 2018 to "train the trainers" of the Iraqi military while also working with the national security advisor and the defense ministry "to help Iraq develop its capacity to build more sustainable, transparent, inclusive and effective national security structures and professional military education institutions."[19] The NATO mission in Iraq has several hundred military trainers based in and around Baghdad.

The EU's and NATO's missions in Iraq clearly relate to each other, although they address different aspects of Iraq's national security process. EU and NATO planners have started to coordinate their efforts and, ideally, will be able to institutionalize their cooperation on the ground. Greater synergy will allow for greater capacity building due to a united message and swifter implementation due to time efficiencies. Increased exchange of information will also reveal remaining gaps that need to be addressed, ensuring future success.

Ukraine, where the EU has a rule-of-law mission and NATO has various security-related projects, could be another area where the two institutions could more usefully integrate their efforts. For instance, one project could be for the EU to support the various NATO Trust Funds in Ukraine, akin to its support for NATO's Building Integrity program to reduce corruption and promote good governance in the defense and security sector, to which the EU has contributed €2 million. Staffs from the EU Advisory Mission in Ukraine and from NATO already periodically meet jointly with Ukrainian counterparts to leverage their efforts. These practical, on-the-ground practices should be further institutionalized.

The EU and NATO should also explore the idea of establishing liaison teams in the European Commission, the European External Action Service (EEAS), and at NATO headquarters that could coordinate efforts across the two organizations. This proposal would build on the current respective cells that NATO and the EU have at each other's institutions: the

NATO Liaison Team with the European Union Military (EUMS) and the EU cell at SHAPE (Supreme Headquarters Allied Powers Europe). The EU and NATO are complex institutions, with distinct decisionmaking processes and cultures, and there are only a few individuals who have extensive knowledge and experience of both. In particular, such teams could facilitate simultaneous, coordinated, and parallel crisis-management exercises and, potentially, even joint exercises. They could also work with classified information that would not be directly exchanged but used in a timely way to advise and inform decisionmaking (for example, locating a smuggler boat without sharing the underlying imagery).

With regard to counterterrorism, stability projection through capacity building and SSR have been NATO's and the EU's most valuable (if underutilized) tool on their respective peripheries. Whether in Georgia, Iraq, Jordan, the Republic of Moldova, Tunisia, or elsewhere, increasing assistance packages on counterterrorism, defense, SSR, and institution building can facilitate governance, help prevent conflict, and preclude safe havens for terrorist groups. Particularly now that ISIS is likely to metastasize into disparate groups scattered throughout the Middle East and North Africa, it is imperative that NATO allies and like-minded partners deny terrorists the territory and capability to organize and plot further terrorist attacks in Europe and North America.

Of course, the EU and NATO will remain separate organizations, and they should continue to conduct separate missions without creating the perception that they are necessarily in competition, in conflict, or duplicating each other's efforts and functions. In some areas of the world, one institution might have a unique competitive advantage that may be better suited to a particular operation or mission. For instance, NATO has extensive battlefield experience in Afghanistan, while the EU has greater expertise in countering violent extremism, anti-radicalization programs, and law enforcement programs. In other instances (for example, in Bosnia), it may be better for one institution to be in the lead, with the other in a supporting role. Still, in other situations, each institution's objectives may be better served by working quietly behind the scenes with multilateral partners such as the United Nations (for example, in Libya) or the African Union (for example, in Somalia). In all cases, it is imperative that both organizations view one another as core partners—partners of first resort—thereby ensuring full consultation and transparency in decisionmaking.

Moreover, by engaging in strategic planning, the EU and NATO could move toward a new level of ambition and cooperation, serving both their own interests and those of their member states. Even in the absence of further institutionalization (in part due to the deadlock caused by the political dispute between Turkey and Cyprus), coordination between the two institutions is likely to grow organically. Similarly, staff can develop innovative policy ideas and proposals for institutional cooperation if they have previously worked in the other institution or are familiar with its specific decisionmaking processes.

The test case for true operational synergies may be in Iraq, where the EU Advisory Mission and the NATO Training Mission have sought to link efforts. The logic of common interests of EU and NATO member states will drive both institutions toward cooperation, but officials also should be cognizant of the underlying impediments deriving from broad institutional mandates, overlapping treaty obligations, and distinctive strategic cultures. Finally, both institutions should resist the siren calls for a clear division of labor, either by region or function. As noted, it is difficult to identify *ex ante* any clear lines of demarcation, and forcing agreement on all theoretical issues may impede practical cooperation in ongoing operations, which, in the end, is what matters most.

Even with greater solidarity in burden-sharing and synergies in EU-NATO cooperation, the necessity for new institutional arrangements, such as the TSPA and the Transatlantic Council, is evident in a range of global challenges, which often fall below the radar of high-level political attention but have long-range consequences for the West and the wider world: climate, cyber, technology, trade, and public health. The following overviews describe the challenges in each of these areas, identify the gaps in current policymaking, and suggest how greater consultation and coordination between the United States and Europe will have beneficial outcomes.

CLIMATE CHANGE

Climate change is arguably the most important global challenge of the twenty-first century. In 2015, government representatives from around the world met in Paris with the goal of preventing an existential crisis due to global warming. Recognizing that Earth's temperature could spike more than two degrees above the preindustrial era, negotiators in Paris, after extremely difficult talks, reached a broadly worded agreement to curb greenhouse gas emissions. Although the Paris Agreement represents a positive milestone, the negotiations also exposed the profoundly different perspectives of industrialized versus developing countries. The emerging economies, many of which have a low GDP, demanded more financial assistance from the high-income countries to meet the costs of mitigation and adaptation measures. For instance, China and India might be among the world's biggest polluters, but Europeans and Americans create far more emissions on a per capita basis. To bridge this divide, the Paris Agreement adopted an approach, first articulated at the Lima Climate Change Conference (COP), consistent with "common but differentiated responsibilities and capabilities in light of different national circumstances (CBDR)"—meaning that all states have a shared obligation to address climate change with their commitments nationally determined.[20]

While climate change was being negotiated in Paris, Republican candidates in the United States squared off in primaries for the 2016 presidential election. After winning his party's nomination, Donald Trump, who had never before held elective office, pledged to withdraw from the pact, claiming that the Agreement disadvantaged American businesses and workers. Trump stated that withdrawal would be in accordance with his "America First" policy.

After his victory in the 2016 election, President Trump continued to disparage the climate agreement, threatening to withdraw but simultaneously allowing that he would be open to renegotiating the accords. The European Union rejected Trump's offer to renegotiate the Paris Agreement and pledged, instead, to bypass Washington and work with U.S. business leaders and state governors to implement the historic accord's commitments.

Miguel Arias Cañete, the former European commissioner for climate action, declared that the global agreement would not be allowed to fall at the whim of a domestic election and stated, "The Paris Agreement is here to stay. The 29 articles of this Paris Agreement are not to be renegotiated. They are to be implemented. That's what the EU will do."[21]

However, President Trump remained undeterred and, on June 1, 2017, announced that the United States would cease all participation in the agreement. Echoing his statements during the 2016 presidential campaign, he affirmed, "The Paris accord will undermine [the U.S.] economy," and "puts [the United States] at a permanent disadvantage." While some members of the Republican Party celebrated the withdrawal, the decision received substantial criticism from religious organizations, businesses, environmentalists, scientists, and the American public.

Following Trump's announcement, several governors formed the United States Climate Alliance to continue to advance the objectives of the Paris Agreement at the state level despite federal withdrawal. By 2019, twenty-four states had joined the alliance.

Some of the strongest denunciations of Trump's decision came from European officials, including newly elected French President Emmanuel Macron. The French president urged U.S. scientists, engineers, and entrepreneurs frustrated by the decision to move to Europe and continue their work. Later, Macron met with Chinese President Xi Jinping in Beijing to sign a common text on climate and biodiversity. In Shanghai, he called the "cooperation between China and the European Union . . . decisive."[22]

Other European leaders echoed Macron, including President of the European Commission Jean-Claude Juncker, who declared Trump's decision "against what we stand for."[23] Donald Tusk, president of the European Council, described American withdrawal from the Paris pact as a big mistake, but said the fight against climate change would continue with or without the United States.

Like Macron, Tusk also called for stronger relations with China. At the end of a 2017 EU-China summit in Brussels, Tusk, standing next to Chinese Premier Li Kequaing, said, "China and Europe have demonstrated solidarity with future generations and responsibility for the whole planet." Tusk also referenced a joint EU-China statement that vowed to "step up" efforts on global warming, including raising $100 billion a year by 2020 to help poorer countries cut emissions.[24] When it was his turn to speak, Premier Li tweaked the United States, declaring, somewhat ironically, that China believed in abiding by international rules. He also made a pitch for greater cooperation with the European Union, "There have been changes in the international situation and there have been rising uncertainties and destabilizing factors and in such circumstances it is important for China-EU relations to become more stable."[25]

Not wishing to close the door on future U.S. support, Tusk noted that "strong transatlantic ties are far more important and far more durable than the latest unfortunate decisions of the new administration."[26] Tusk was clearly aware that, in accordance with Article 28 of the Paris Agreement, the United States could not give notice of withdrawal from the agreement until November 4, 2019. Indeed, on that date, the administration gave a formal notice of intention to withdraw, making the effective withdrawal date by the United States on November 4, 2020—one day after the 2020 U.S. presidential election.

Indeed, the White House later clarified that the United States would abide by the four-year exit process. During this time period, the United States may have been obligated to maintain its commitments under the Agreement, such as the requirement to continue reporting its emissions to the United Nations.

The United States move did not have an appreciable impact on recent negotiations to finalize the rules of the Paris Agreement at COP25 climate talks in Madrid except in so far as there proved to be a stunning lack of leadership and adherence to the accords. President-elect Joe Biden has committed that the United States will rejoin the Paris Agreement. The United States and the EU should begin now to explore cooperation around three important areas related to climate change: the circular economy, energy innovation, and green growth.

The "circular economy" is a term of art used to describe the fact that 90 percent of the world's resources—which include the metals, plastics, and all other materials in circulation—are used in a single product before becoming waste. Recycling and reusing waste products achieves greater sustainability, driving forward not just environmental but also economic progress. Given that Western levels of consumption are much greater than those in the rest of the world, the circular economy poses a considerable challenge for both the United States and the European Union.

Moreover, as a MacArthur Foundation study recently reported, "adopting a circular economy framework in these areas can achieve a reduction totaling 9.3 billion tonnes of greenhouse gases in 2050. This is equivalent to eliminating current emissions from all forms of transport globally. These examples provide a clear message to other industries—such as fashion, electronics, and packaging—of the value the circular economy can offer."[27]

The European Commission adopted a Circular Economy Plan in 2015, laying out fifty-four ways to "close the loop" of product lifecycles. The plan emphasized ways "to move away from a 'take-make-dispose' culture." The commission has committed over €10 billion in funding.

In contrast to Europe, the circular economy in the United States relies largely on corporate incentives and market forces. In February 2019, ING, the Dutch financial services firm, conducted a survey titled *"Opportunity and Disruption: How Circular Thinking Could Change U.S. Business Models."* Based on interviews with 300 U.S.-based executives in companies of various sizes, the report assessed whether U.S. companies included sustainability issues in their growth strategies. The research found that, in 2018, nearly 85 percent of the firms surveyed—twice as many as in 2017—had "considered" sustainability in their strategic decisionmaking. Of course, that means only that many corporations undertake a cost-benefit analysis related to sustainability; it does not mean they necessarily either have, or will, change the way they do business.

While the U.S. government does not provide financial assistance to support the circular economy, the Environmental Protection Agency (EPA) issued a five-year strategic plan in 2017 to encourage the private sector to: "1.) Decrease the disposal rate, which includes source reduction, reuse, recycling and prevention; 2.) Reduce the environmental impacts of materials across their life cycle; 3.) Increase socio-economic benefits; and 4.) Increase the capacity of state and local governments, communities and key stakeholders to adopt and implement SMM (sustainable materials management) policies, practices and incentives."[28]

The circular economy is, of course, merely a subset of the global economy. The United States, the largest economy in the world, and the European Union, whose members together comprise the second largest economy in the world, should explore regulatory best practices and private sector partnerships that can drive faster adoption of circular economy measures.

Both the United States and Europe are strong supporters of energy innovation, directing public finance and using other tools to stimulate key industries that will deliver both near- and long-term solutions to address climate change. A more coordinated transatlantic approach could help bring key climate solutions to market more rapidly.

Already, Europe is moving ahead with measures to incentivize energy innovations by announcing in February 2019 a €10 billion "innovation" investment fund in new "clean" technologies. According to the European Commission website, the fund will be used to stimulate "energy storage and energy intensive industries," by offering grants to cover up to 60 percent of the additional capital and operational costs linked to innovation for the selected projects, disbursing the money in a flexible way based on the needs of individual projects.[29]

However, the Trump administration had a somewhat mixed record in this area. In 2019, Trump proposed an 86 percent cut in funding to the Office of Energy Efficiency and Renewable Energy (EERE) and called for elimination of impactful programs such as the Advanced Research Projects Agency-Energy (ARPA-E) and the Weatherization Assistance program. Congress rejected the administration's proposed cuts, and significantly increased funding for clean energy innovation programs at the U.S. Department of Energy (DOE) through September 2020.

EERE received a 17 percent increase in funding, instead of the president's proposed 86 percent cut, while Congress raised ARPA-E's budget by 16 percent. According to the EPA, "ARPA-E invests in potentially transformational clean energy projects that are not supported by the agency's other programs. Since 2009, ARPA-E has provided greater than $1.8 billion in R&D funding to more than 660 projects that have led to the formation of 71 new companies and have raised more than $2.6 billion in private-sector follow-on funding." These companies are commercializing the next generation of clean energy technologies that will reduce pollution.

There were, however, some positive signals from the Trump administration in the area of energy innovation. For instance, the administration kicked off new funding for energy storage technologies, carbon capture, and energy efficiency.

Green growth in the United States has been most boldly encapsulated in legislation known as the Green New Deal. Introduced by Democrats in the U.S. Congress to transition the American economy to 100 percent renewable, zero-emission energy sources, the plan also includes investment in high-speed rail systems and electric cars. However, the Green New Deal is more of an aspirational document than a serious legislative initiative. Besides its focus on climate, the legislation also aims to address poverty issues, universal healthcare, increased minimum wages, and the elimination of monopolistic enterprises. As currently written, the legislation has virtually no chance of ever being passed into law—no matter what the makeup of Congress or who the occupant of the White House. Nonetheless, the Green New Deal appears to have inspired the EU's green-growth strategy.

In December 2019, the EC presented a climate plan billed as the European Green Deal. The document outlined a roadmap for the EU's economic transition, meant to transform Europe into the world's first climate-neutral continent by 2050 by applying climate-friendly and sustainable solutions that also create economic development and job opportunities. The European Green Deal raises the 2030 target of the Paris Agreement to 50 percent reductions and set the 2050 target at 100 percent. The goals represent a drastic increase in climate-change ambition from the bloc.

Ursula von der Leyen, the new president of the European Commission, told a press conference that the "European Green Deal is our new growth strategy—for a growth that gives back more than it takes away."[30] Von der Leyen stressed that climate protection is at the heart of her political program, and the new commission's number one priority is to present a European climate law designed to anchor the 2050 climate neutrality target and make progress toward it irreversible in law. In addition to creating national climate and energy plans for each EU member state, the Green Deal calls for strategies to decarbonize sectors like industry and agriculture, as well as strategies to protect biodiversity.

The European Green Deal sets the bar for climate action in every economic sector. According to current commission estimates, €260 billion ($288.5 billion) of additional annual investment is needed to meet the plan's 2030 climate and energy targets, or about 1.5 percent of the bloc's 2018 GDP. The mechanism would mobilize €100 billion "precisely targeted to the most vulnerable regions and sectors" during the transition. It also calls for subsidies to address "energy poverty" and to reduce energy bills for the EU's poorest.

It seems incontrovertible that climate is an issue on which both the United States and the European Union have intersecting interests and on which they can work together. Not only is the science compelling, but the United States and Europe both confront a security threat coming from many angles. The prospect of more arid climate change in the Middle East, Africa, Asia, and Latin America will increase the strain on the most precious natural resource: fresh water. Tensions are rising already, creating unrest, instability, and weak governance—the ingredients for violent extremism. Climate change is a driving force in mass migration from places where farmland is disappearing, water is drying up, and political instability is rising. But climate change endangers far more than national security. Countless economic studies on both sides of the Atlantic demonstrate that it is cheaper to invest now in alternative energy sources and prevent further damage than it is to wait for worse to come.

In Europe, climate has proved to be the rare unifying issue, not only for individual member states in the EU but also for Europe's various institutions. In particular, the European Commission has provided strong leadership, vision, and even an allocation of funding that offers a promising start in the fight against climate change.

The private sector, both in the United States and Europe, recognizes the public's increasing concern about climate change. Though there is clearly excitement about alternative energy—and tens of thousands of new jobs are being created in new carbon-neutral industries—most multinational corporations seem content to continue to operate in the fossil fuel economy.

Unfortunately, the Trump administration appeared to have little interest in providing leadership on this issue. One critical question for both the EU and the United States is how they will pay for such an ambitious agenda. It is currently not only unclear how much each plan will cost and how much each side is willing to invest, but given the current massive deficit spending required to combat COVID-19, it is unclear how spending goals will be realized.

Notwithstanding these challenges, in many important respects, the United States and Europe are already aligned in terms of having laid out the essential components of an agenda to mitigate climate change. Perhaps more than any other issue, climate change is an area where more transatlantic leadership, coordination, and cooperation will not only advance transatlantic interests, but global ones as well.

CYBER

Since the advent of the internet in 1990s, the number of networked people in the world has grown from a few million to billions. Social media has proven to be an extremely powerful tool affecting society in a variety of ways, ranging from economics to culture, from social interaction to politics.

Early in this century, activists around the world used the internet as an increasingly powerful tool for political organizing. For example, in the early 2010s, social media facilitated the removal from power of four long-ruling despots in the Middle East—in Egypt, Libya, Tunisia, and Yemen.[31] But as citizens, governments, and corporations have become more reliant on social media for messaging and communication, and more dependent on technology in general, the internet and cyber have evolved. Digitally savvy authoritarian regimes now use the internet to control their populations. Terrorist organizations like ISIS are more likely to use digital operations than to control physical ground; global disrupters such as China, North Korea, Iran, and Russia use cyber to disorder adversaries.[32]

During the Obama-Biden administration, the United States committed to an open, interoperable, reliable, and secure internet resting on the four pillars of protection, innovation, deterrence, and influence. Only a little more than a decade ago, U.S. intelligence agencies did not include cyber-attacks in their annual report to Congress on global "threat assessment."[33] However, more recently, former CIA Director Leon Panetta expressed concern about potential attacks on America's infrastructure, claiming that a sophisticated and powerful cyber strike could "paralyze, and shock the nation, and create a profound sense of vulnerability."[34] The U.S. military began to quietly adopt cyber warfare as a tool for economic, military, and social disruption—one that could be used covertly, with precision, and without putting American soldiers in the line of fire. As David Sanger has written, cyber weapons are "cheap to acquire, easy to deny, and effective for a variety of effective purposes," and they have become "the weapons of choice for dictators, democracies and terrorists." He adds, "The weapons remain invisible, the attacks deniable, the results uncertain."[35]

The United States was one of the first countries to authorize its military to engage in cyber warfare. In 2010, it successfully deployed malware in an operation code-named "Olympic Games," commonly referred to as "Stuxnet," designed to disable Iran's nuclear facilities.[36] Likewise, it used cyber to sabotage Kim Jung Un's missile program in North Korea. In both instances, the cyberattacks were successful—not in permanently eliminating the programs but certainly in delaying their progress.

Notwithstanding efforts by the U.S. government to maintain total secrecy about its cyber warfare capabilities, other foreign intelligence agencies—and even investigative journalists—eventually discovered U.S. involvement in efforts to stymie the Iranian and North Korean development of nuclear weapons. This led to a number of countries seeking to advance their own cyber warfare capabilities.

As Michael Hayden, former director of National Intelligence, explained, when the United States introduces a new form of warfare, "the rest of the world now feels that this is the new standard, and it's something that they now feel legitimized to do as well."[37] Indeed, that was the case when the North Koreans used malware in 2014 to disrupt Sony Corporation after it released a movie that spoofed the Supreme Leader.

While no foreign adversary has yet launched a cyberattack against the United States designed to inflict death and destruction, during the Obama-Biden administration, then CIA Director Panetta warned of a potential "Cyber Pearl Harbor."[38] Perhaps with this in mind, the Trump administration's cyber policy placed far greater emphasis on preemptive action against adversaries. Its policy was laid out in three documents: the "National Cyber Strategy," the "Department of Defense Cyber Strategy," and the "National Security Presidential Memorandum 13."

The "National Cyber Strategy," published in 2018, articulated a strategy resting on four pillars: protecting networks; promoting American prosperity through a thriving and innovative digital economy; deterring and punishing adversaries; and globally expanding American influence to maintain the internet as an open engine of economic growth, innovation, and efficiency. The strategy discounted the Obama-Biden administration's "law enforcement approach" in favor of one emphasizing competition, deterrence, and technological superiority.[39]

The "Department of Defense Cyber Strategy," also published in 2018, addressed United States' ability to confront threats in cyber space, particularly those from China, Russia, North Korea, and Iran. It emphasized the need to collect intelligence, "defend forward" by disrupting cyber threats at their source, and strengthen the resiliency and security of the network. Trump's policy implemented the aggressive stance of the "National Cyber Strategy" by seeking "to preempt, defeat, or deter malicious cyber activity targeting US critical infrastructure" and promised "swift, costly and transparent consequences" to online attackers.[40]

At the request of senior DOD officials, "National Security Presidential Memorandum 13," published in September 2018, shortened the Obama-Biden administration's approval process, allowing the Pentagon to launch offensive cyber operations in a more timely fashion.[41] CYBERCOM commander Admiral Mike Rogers testified before Congress that U.S. cyber capabilities were "not optimized for speed and agility," and CENTCOM Commander Joseph Votel stated publicly that the previous process was so "cumbersome" that U.S. cyber capabilities were "narrowly irrelevant."[42]

Europe faces an even more daunting challenge than the United States. David Sanger refers to Europe as "Putin's petri dish."[43] Indeed, according to the NATO Communication and Information Agency, communication and computer networks at NATO headquarters in Belgium face hundreds of significant hacking attempts every month. Russia, North Korea, and China constantly deploy sophisticated computer-hacking weapons and surveillance software. In the fall of 2019, NATO accused hackers working for China's ministry of state security of breaking into the networks of eight of the world's biggest technology service providers to steal intellectual property. Finland accused Russia of blocking GPS signals in October 2019, when Finnish forces took part in NATO military exercises in Norway. Dutch military intelligence accused the Kremlin of trying to launch a cyberattack on the headquarters of the international chemical weapons watchdog. The Dutch ultimately foiled the attack.

Russian cyberattacks are especially acute against Ukraine. Ukraine's top cyber cop concedes, "there is a digital war, every day, in Kiev,"[44] and Russian General Valery Gerisamov has described his country's approach as merging conventional warfare with "economic coercion, propaganda, and, most recently, cyber."[45] Since Ukraine is a member of neither EU nor NATO, there are no immediate and direct consequences for Russia's aggressive behavior. Even if Ukraine were a member of either organization, the two are not synced up, and there is a gap between their ambitions and capabilities in both cybersecurity and cyber warfare.

There are three problem areas for Europe when dealing with cyber warfare. First, though cyberattacks are on the rise worldwide, the EU and NATO have only recently focused on the threat. According to Sanger, in 2014 former NATO Supreme Allied Commander General Philip Breedlove, NATO "had no cyber counter attack unit, nor any information in 'information warfare.' "[46] Until recently, NATO's main focus in cyber defense has been to protect its own networks (including operations and missions) and to enhance resilience across the alliance. In fact, NATO's computer security center protected only its own networks, and until a few years ago, only during working days. As one senior official put it, the "only thing [NATO] forgot to do was send a postcard to the Kremlin was that they could save themselves a lot of trouble if they just attacked NATO on nights and weekends."[47]

Second, NATO lacks resources to plan for a cyber war. However, at the June 2016 Defense Ministers Meeting, NATO defense ministers agreed to recognize cyberspace as an operational domain. Their decision was endorsed and reaffirmed at the NATO summit in Warsaw in July 2016. As part of this effort, NATO directed the development of an implementation roadmap for review in the February 2017 Defense Ministers Meeting, and it was subsequently approved. NATO has established cyber rapid reaction teams, who are on standby to assist allies twenty-four hours a day, if requested and approved. At the Brussels summit in 2018, allies agreed to set up a new Cyberspace Operations Centre as part of NATO's strengthened Command Structure. They also agreed that NATO can draw on national cyber capabilities for its missions and operations. A new NATO military command center to deter computer hackers should be fully staffed in 2023 and able to mount its own cyberattacks, but the alliance is still grappling with ground rules for doing so. When fully operational, the cyber center aims to coordinate NATO's cyber deterrent through a seventy-strong team of experts fed with military intelligence and real-time information about hackers ranging from Islamist militants to organized crime groups operating on behalf of hostile governments.

Third, NATO, the EU, and the United States are still trying to agree on a strategy to respond to cyberattacks when they can be considered an "act of war." There is no agreement on whether collective defense should be permissible against nonstate actors. Western countries also struggle to agree on ground rules to respond to state-sponsored cyberattacks. NATO and the European Union signed a Technical Arrangement on Cyber Defense in February 2016, and they are strengthening their cooperation on cyber defense, notably in the areas of information exchange, training, research, and exercises.

"This is an emerging domain and the threat is growing," said Major General Wolfgang Renner, a German air force commander who oversees the new cyber operations center in Mons. "We have to be prepared, to be able to execute operations in cyberspace. We have already gone beyond protection and prevention," he observed during a NATO cyber conference. While NATO does not have its own cyber weapons, the U.S.-led alliance established an operations center at its military hub in Belgium. The United States, Britain, Estonia, and other allies have since offered their cyber capabilities.[48]

"Our ultimate aim is to be completely aware of our cyberspace, to understand minute-by-minute the state of our networks so that commanders can rely on them," said Ian West, chief of cybersecurity at NATO. The center could potentially use cyber weapons that can knock out enemy missiles or air defenses, or destroy foes' computer networks if commanders judge such a cyberattack is less harmful to human life than a traditional offensive with live weaponry.

To more effectively prevent and counter cyber warfare measures, member states of both NATO and the EU need to devote more resources. In NATO's case, this could be counted in terms of meeting their 2 percent contribution. In 2018, the EU's leaders committed to "a coordinated response to hybrid and cyber-threats" and asked the European Commission and member states to "work on measures to enhance the resilience and improve the security culture" of the bloc.[49]

Although there is general agreement among alliance members within NATO that cyber will be an integral part of future warfare, there is debate and disagreement among those NATO members as to what would trigger NATO's Article 5 (collective defense) clause. If NATO can agree on cyber warfare principles, the alliance hopes to integrate individual nations' cyber capabilities into alliance operations, coordinated through the Mons cyber operations center and under the command of NATO's top general, the Supreme Allied Commander Europe. That could allow the top general to take quick decisions on whether to use cyber weapons, similar to existing agreements for NATO's air defenses and its ballistic missile shield, where a commander has only minutes to decide what action to take.

Gregory Edwards, former director of infrastructure services at NATO's communication and information agency, stated in 2015 that it could be possible to "make a case-by-case decision" about responding to attacks. He argued: "You need to have a policy that says, 'if our operation is disturbed, we will take a specific action.' The action will be listed. It will be listed what things the commander is allowed to do in that regard. It will be a specific action."[50]

There is no panacea for Europe and the United States to meet cyber challenges in the twenty-first century. But there are steps that the EU, NATO, and the United States should take to innovate in the area of cyber, to improve coordination of cybersecurity, and to both preempt and defend against cyberattacks.

The "National Cyber Strategy" correctly asserts that the "United States influence in cyberspace is linked to its technological leadership."[51] However, as the director of National Intelligence testified in January 2019, the United States is already losing its technological edge relative to its adversaries.[52] The United States and the EU should work together with technology companies on both sides of the Atlantic to maintain that leadership.

Under the Trump administration, the United States adopted a hard line against malicious actors. While it may not be possible to always coordinate with the EU in every instance, the United States needs be cognizant of how its actions impact Europe, and work to avoid unnecessary escalation that will harm the EU. EU member states should also devote greater resources to cybersecurity and coordinate their response to major cyberattacks; for example, by establishing guidelines to help determine under what circumstances economic sanctions are warranted. There also needs to be coordination in the implementation of sanctions.

The United States and Europe should also work to improve a competitive edge by resourcing internet and cybersecurity capability development in developing countries, where the Chinese currently lead. However, the United States and Europe should also engage in internet governance bodies that include cyber adversaries such as Russia and China. Doing so will allow the transatlantic alliance to address competing visions of the internet and to forcefully advocate for the rule of law in the use of cyber and the internet in general.

The EU should also facilitate the sharing of electronic evidence both within and outside the EU. Because vast amounts of European data sit outside the EU, making it extremely difficult to obtain digital evidence in cross-border disputes, the European Commission's recent decision to allow member states to ask companies directly for evidence is unlikely to solve the problem of transatlantic data exchange. The EU should replace current EU-U.S. agreements with a more explicit treaty on digital evidence.

Brussels should also step up its efforts to understand the cyber threats it is facing so it can better support member states in their attempts to counter them. For this, the European Commission could set up a task force from all the relevant departments of the commission, to advise it on cyber issues. Members of NATO could also be encouraged to adapt Article 4 to cyberattacks. Invoking Article 4 will not trigger military intervention, as in the case of Article 5, but rather consultation over military matters.

Finally, Europe and the United States should continue to work together to marginalize ISIS online. This has been something of a success story for the transatlantic partners, but it requires an even broader coalition to include not only governments but also companies, nonprofits, and international organizations. Human-run accounts on social networks need to be separated from automated ones. In 2015, Jared Cohen wrote of the need "to zero in on the Islamic states digital central command, identifying and suspending the specific accounts responsible for setting strategy and giving orders to the rest of its online army . . . The suspension of accounts needs to be targeted—more like kill-or-capture raids than strategic bombing campaigns."[53]

TECHNOLOGY

In many ways, cyberspace has been a precursor to the need for transatlantic cooperation in other areas of technology, particularly artificial intelligence (AI), 5G, and big data. Technology, or the application of knowledge for practical purposes, can transform the use of existing resources and amplify an actor's power. That principle applies especially to AI; according to Putin, "the one who becomes the leader in this sphere will be the ruler of the world."[54] Setting aside the veracity of this particular claim, leadership in technology—dating from the Industrial Revolution and the British Empire to nuclear weapons and the U.S.-led free world during the Cold War—has historically translated into political leadership. Given the inevitable expansion of knowledge and progress in technology, the main questions are: Who controls new technological developments and whose interests and values do they reflect?

Whereas, over the past seven decades, technological breakthroughs largely occurred in the West, China currently competes on the same level as the United States and Europe in many areas, and leads in some important technologies, such as 5G. China has been able to attain its prominence not only through original research in its universities and research laboratories, which deserve due credit, but also through its economies of scale and state subsidies. Since, according to one global ranking, China has only one university in the top twenty and six in the top fifty, with nearly all the other top universities concentrated in America and Europe, the two other factors— scale and subsidies—are likely responsible for China's current technological competitiveness, especially on AI, 5G, and big data. However, the United

States has also accused Chinese companies, individuals, and the government itself of stealing Western technology, with estimates that range from $225 billion to as much as $600 billion per year.[55] This was one of the Trump administration's most significant disputes with China and one of its rationales for imposing tariffs on China.

The next technology revolution will occur in the area of artificial intelligence. As Levi Tillemann and Colin McCormick have written, it "will have profound implications for safety, ethics, environment, and distribution of wealth," making it "desirable that countries establish standards that promote shared values, economic and social goals."[56] The truth is that neither the United States nor Europe alone can currently match China in terms of the scale necessary to compete. Because AI simulates human intelligence in machines, large data sets are required for computers to learn and improve their AI algorithms: from selecting images of cats on a screen to identifying individual human beings within a large crowd. The larger the network of data, the faster the algorithm can learn and the better its effectiveness will be. Given that the U.S. population is only 24 percent of China's, and that Europe's is only about 40 percent (including the EU-27 and the UK), the only way for either the United States or Europe to be able to compete with China is to join together and combine their efforts.

Unfortunately, the current policy intuition and approach on both sides of the Atlantic is exactly the opposite. The Trump administration rightly identified the U.S. "National Security Innovation Base" as a key strategic element, defining it as the "American network of knowledge, capabilities, and people—including academia, National Laboratories, and the private sector—that turns ideas into innovations, transforms discoveries into successful commercial products and companies, and protects and enhances the American way of life."[57] But its methods of attaining this objective were primarily domestic and protectionist, focused on screening foreign investment, prosecuting violations of intellectual property rights, and tightening visa restrictions on "foreign STEM students from designated countries."[58]

For its part, Europe has also turned inward in seeking "technological sovereignty."[59] In February 2020, the European Commission released a White Paper outlining an AI strategy that focused on human and ethical dimensions of the technology. It focuses on AI applications in "high-risk" sectors such as healthcare, transport, and energy, where certain mandatory requirements should apply regarding training data, recordkeeping, and human oversight. In contrast, other sectors would be subject to a voluntary labeling scheme, whereby AI operators could obtain a "quality label" for their AI applications.[60] Noting the centrality of data to AI development, the commission also released a separate strategy for data[61] as part of an overall approach on shaping Europe's digital future.[62]

The key element missing to fully develop these technologies is a joint transatlantic approach. Autonomous vehicles are but one area cited by Tillemann and McCormick, who recommend that the United States and Europe collaborate "on this and other AI-enabled robotics technologies." They note, for instance, that "Germany's 'Digital Testbed Autobahn,'" established by the German federal government, is a potential platform, using "the A9 autobahn as a testing ground for vehicles and other emerging technologies."[63]

Another important issue related to technology concerns whether European countries should allow China's Huawei to install 5G infrastructure, thereby transforming how society is connected through the so-called Internet of Things. The Trump administration argued that, notwithstanding Huawei's claims to be a private enterprise, the Chinese government ultimately controls it; countries that use Huawei's 5G technology could, thereby, be exposed to surveillance and other vulnerabilities. Some European states, even long-standing U.S. allies such as the United Kingdom, have welcomed Huawei's investment, arguing that it is the most competitive on the global market and that the security risks can be managed by restricting the 5G network to non-core functions.

It is difficult for nonexperts on 5G to resolve this specific debate, but we argue for a new approach to these types of problems that emphasizes the necessity for transatlantic cooperation. Whereas the United States may currently have an advantage in the market balance, with global tech companies such as Google, Amazon, Facebook, and Apple, Europe has a long-term advantage in the data generated by its larger population. Moreover, greater administrative scope and bureaucratic centralization in many European countries means that valuable data, for instance in the health sector, is more readily available and potentially useable. Finally, with respect to some technologies, such as 5G, European companies such as Ericsson and Nokia are more competitive relative to the United States; indeed, the Trump administration floated a proposal for the U.S. government to invest in those companies to develop 5G technology that could compete with China's.

Our approach would not necessarily require joint regulation—

determining what technologies are permissible and under what conditions—but, instead, could rely on joint efforts related to international standardization in determining alongside private sector actors what technical practices, protocols, and procedures should shape the new technologies. Likewise, the two sides could explore a coordinated approach to foreign investment screening to enable exchange of technical information related to investor identity and other relevant considerations. Moreover, they could support potential linkages among universities or research laboratories to facilitate joint development of technologies. The Transatlantic Council, involving the United States, UK, and all EU-27 member states, would be a particularly useful format in bringing together the relevant decisionmakers and forging joint action. As Google's CEO Sundar Pichai mentioned in a speech in Brussels, the necessary agreement on "core values" that the new technologies should reflect means that a partnership between Europe and the United States on tech policy is "critical."[64]

TRADE

Perhaps no area has been as riddled with missed opportunities and internal contradictions during the Trump administration as transatlantic trade. Based on a warped view of international economics, Trump came into office resolved to decrease U.S. trade deficits, which he viewed as international theft of the U.S. economy. He claimed:

> Years of unfair trade have hammered American families and plundered American wealth. It's been absolutely terrible for our country. We turned a blind eye while other nations targeted our industries and ransacked our factories. They took advantage of our country. They took advantage of our people. Over the last two decades, the United States racked up $12.5 trillion dollar [sic] trade deficits in goods, and watched nearly one-third of our manufacturing jobs disappear or go to other countries. We financed the rise of other countries at the expense of our own middle class people. Yet our leaders in Washington did absolutely nothing. They allowed other countries to cheat, to break the rules, and to steal our jobs with impunity.[65]

While Trump construed trade deficits as equivalent to corporate losses, reflecting underlying weakness in economic activity, basic principles of macroeconomics show that trade deficits are agnostic on whether or not the economy is strong, as they merely reflect the difference between domestic savings (including government savings or deficit) and investment. Thus, budget deficits will translate into trade deficits unless they are compensated with extra domestic private savings. In turn, trade deficits also mean capital account surpluses, namely more capital investment into than out of a country. Foreign investors may finance a country's trade deficit because it is an attractive destination for investment or because the country is living beyond its means. Trump confused the two scenarios, arguing that either was disadvantageous for the U.S. economy.

Instead, the Trump administration proceeded to dismantle the international trading system by raising tariffs, first against China and more recently against the European Union. In February 2020, at a meeting in Washington with state governors, President Trump declared, "Europe has been treating us very badly. . . . They have barriers that are incredible."[66] The administration subsequently imposed tariffs on European aircraft and products such as steel nails and aluminum vehicle bumpers.[67] He has also threatened to impose tariffs on European automobiles.

Meanwhile, U.S. trade deficits kept increasing during the administration's first three years, largely due to expanding U.S. budget deficits. Trump also turned his ire against the World Trade Organization, which he claimed had "been very unfair to the United States for many, many years."[68] The WTO is a "catastrophe," he argued, that "makes it almost impossible for [the United States] to do good business."[69]

Part of the critique against the WTO is that its provisions do not sufficiently cover intellectual property (IP) protection, thereby allowing China to steal IP from the United States and Europe without economic consequences. Another issue, voiced less by Trump but more by U.S. trade representative Robert Lighthizer, is the WTO's dispute settlement mechanism, which provides for binding arbitration through a two-tiered level: an initial panel and an appellate body. In contrast to prior rules under the General Agreement on Tariffs and Trade, which required unanimous approval of arbitration decisions from all member states (including the losing party), the WTO adopted an arbitration structure that envisions a winning and losing party in a dispute—as in any other standard litigation or arbitration. Trump periodically claims that the United States loses "almost all of the lawsuits in the WTO,"[70] but the truth is that the U.S. both wins and loses many cases. The United States is a frequent litigant on both sides, and WTO members tend to bring only those cases in which they are likely to prevail (with nearly a 90 percent success rate); otherwise, cases get settled beforehand. Instead of recognizing this reality and the overall benefits that accrue to the United States from a system whose rules can be enforced, the Trump administration has blocked the appointment of judges to the WTO appellate body, effectively obstructing the functioning of the organization's dispute settlement mechanism.[71]

The United States and the EU can find ample common ground on trade. As European Commission President Ursula von der Leyen stated in her letter setting out the mandate for Trade Commissioner Phil Hogan, WTO reform is a "top priority" for the EU, "notably on the issues of subsidies, forced transfer of technologies and dispute settlement."[72] The EU had submitted an extensive concept paper on these and other topics of reform at the WTO that can serve as the basis for further discussion and transatlantic cooperation.[73]

Beyond WTO reform, the two sides should restart their negotiations on a new transatlantic trade agreement that would help shape global standards on environment, labor, and intellectual property. T-TIP talks started too late in the Obama-Biden administration to be successfully concluded, so a new U.S. administration should prioritize this issue with the EU.

Finally, the United States and the EU should address growing domestic income inequalities as part of the international agenda. The theory of international economics is that countries gain overall through trade liberalization and that those gains are sufficient to compensate specific parts of the economy (displaced industries and workers) that may lose from free trade. In practice, however, those compensation measures—unemployment benefits and job retraining—depend on domestic policies that are separate from international trade negotiations and often are never enacted. The perceived unfairness of globalization to various groups on both sides of the Atlantic— who were promised that new trade agreements would be beneficial to everyone but, instead, saw only lost jobs and wages—needs to be redressed. The two issues of income inequality and international trade should be linked in future U.S.-EU talks as a way of ensuring continued public support for further economic liberalization and of shaping international practice.

PUBLIC HEALTH

Perhaps no single issue has highlighted both the current fissures between the United States and Europe and the need for greater transatlantic unity than the response to the coronavirus, also known as COVID-19. The virus, which originated in China, is highly contagious, infecting the human respiratory system and leading to death in approximately 1 to 5 percent of cases. There are currently two vaccines in mass production in the United States and Europe, but it will take months to conduct inoculations on a large scale.

In 2005, a Democratic freshman member of the U.S. Senate Foreign Relations Committee teamed up with the Republican chair to write an opinion piece for the *New York Times* about the avian flu, a killer disease that had originated in Asia and threatened to spread around the world. Senators Barack Obama and Richard Lugar declared that the avian flu had the potential "to cause millions of deaths, destabilize Southeast Asia, and threaten the security of governments around the world." They warned of a potential pandemic, noting that, "in an age when you can board a planes on Bangkok and Hong Kong and arrive in Chicago, Indianapolis or New York in hours, we must face the reality that these exotic killer diseases are not half a world away, but direct and immediate threats to security and prosperity here at home."[74]

In the end, though the avian flu, also known as H1N1, ravaged poultry throughout Asia, North Africa, and the Middle East, the overall human death was low—in the hundreds. Nevertheless, the senators' warning was eerily prescient, for today, fifteen years later, the world is facing a full-blown pandemic not seen since the Spanish flu early in the early twentieth century.

There was no vaccine to protect against the Spanish flu of 1918, which lasted for years, infected an estimated 500 million people worldwide, and claimed the lives of tens of millions of people. The tools to combat the disease were limited to isolation, quarantine, sound personal hygiene, use of disinfectants, and limitations of public gatherings.

COVID-19 is currently present in 190 countries and territories around the world. At this writing, there are more than 75 million confirmed cases worldwide and nearly 2 million people have died. Notwithstanding extraordinary advances in science, technology, and communication, the world is currently using many of the same tools it did 100 years ago.

Nowhere has the virus proved more lethal than in the United States, where there are now more than 18 million confirmed cases and more than 300,000 deaths. To put the fatality number in perspective, nearly twice as many Americans have died from COVID-19 over a twelve-week period as American soldiers died during the Vietnam War over a period of twenty years. In December 2020, the same number of Americans died on a daily basis as during the 9/11 attacks. The final death toll is too difficult to estimate.

The question facing leaders on both sides of the Atlantic is how we fight the disease given that it is a global scourge. Notwithstanding that the virus has spread to every continent, the governmental response has varied widely from country to country. For instance, in Sweden, the government decided to isolate its older and more vulnerable citizens but otherwise allow life to essentially continue as it did before the virus became present. In South Korea, the government decided early on to impose vigorous quarantine measures, and, most important, immediately began testing hundreds of thousands of asymptomatic people. South Korea also established drive-through centers and used a central tracking app, Corona 100m, to publicly inform citizens of known cases within a 100-meter radius. It remains to be seen which approach works best given that every country in the world must balance the economic and healthcare effects of the virus.

On a global basis, the World Health Organization is the institution responsible for responding to international health emergencies such as COVID-19. Founded in 1948, the WHO directs international health within the United Nations system. Over the years, it has received plaudits for expanding vaccination programs for tuberculosis, polio, and other infectious diseases, particularly in developing countries. Among its many roles, the WHO purports to "1.) Prepare for emergencies by identifying, mitigating and managing risks. 2.) Prevent emergencies and support development of tools necessary during outbreaks. 3.) Detect and respond to acute health emergencies. 4.) Support delivery of essential health services in fragile settings."[75] The WHO has no enforcement powers, so while it can urge countries to be transparent and to take precautions, it cannot issue fines for noncompliance. Indeed, the WHO failed early on to elicit information on the coronavirus that might have mitigated spread of the disease and saved lives.

It appears that the Chinese government was well aware that the virus had originated in the city of Wuhan and was spreading, but did not notify the WHO until December 3, 2019. Less than a week later, the WHO issued a statement saying that China had reported forty-four cases but noted that Chinese investigators found no evidence of human-to-human transmission. In the meantime, the virus spread unchecked. It was not until January 20, 2020, that Chinese officials acknowledged that the virus was spreading person-to-person. By that time, Wuhan was in crisis and cases were confirmed in multiple Chinese cities, as well as in Japan, Korea, Thailand, and the United States.

The WHO also bears responsibility for having made a number of mistakes. First, the organization amplified Chinese claims and figures without signaling that they could be inaccurate. The organization was slow to address the risk of human-to-human transmission, slow to declare a public health emergency, and slow to label the virus a "pandemic." The WHO had the authority to challenge Chinese officials and ascertain what steps they were taking to address the crisis, yet they continued to lend credibility to China's narrative.

The panel waited until January 30—a full month after Chinese doctors issued a warning—to make the declaration. Then, Tedros Adhanom Ghebreyesus, director general of the WHO, congratulated the Chinese government "for the extraordinary measures it has taken, "and its "commitment to transparency."[76] In February and early March, as evidence of China's misinformation intensified, Tedros and the WHO continued to praise Beijing. Finally, on March 11, the WHO declared that COVID-19, by then ravaging multiple continents, was a "pandemic."

Notwithstanding the failure of China to alert the world of the virus, and the failure of the WHO to ask more questions of China and sound the alarm earlier, they both remain important players in ending the pandemic. A number of political, scientific, and medical leaders have made the point that there will be plenty of opportunity in the future to assess blame and to seek reforms. For instance, Bill Gates tweeted: "Halting funding for the World Health Organization during a world health crisis is as dangerous as it sounds . . . their work is slowing the spread of COVID-19 and if that work is stopped no other organization can replace them. The world needs @ WHO now more than ever."[77]

Trump primarily sought to deflect from his own slow, incoherent, and ineffective response to the virus. President Obama's national security advisor, Susan Rice, noted that during the presidential transition in January 2017, the Obama team "provided briefing papers and conducted side-by-side exercises . . . focused on pandemic threats," but "the assistance was discarded." She also recounted how she established the office of Global Health Security and Biodefense at the National Security Council to monitor, "prepare for and prevent global health crises."[78] According to Rice, Trump dismantled the office. When asked about this at a press conference, he responded, "Some of the people we cut—they haven't been used for many, many years. If we ever need them, we can get them very quickly. And rather than spend the money—and I'm a business person. I don't like having thousands of people around when you don't need them."[79]

Trump waited until January 22 to made his first public comments about the virus. While attending the World Economic Forum in Davos, Switzerland, he noted that the virus had spread to four countries and the first American case had been announced the day before. Nonetheless, he claimed that he was "not at all" worried, declaring: "We have it totally under control. It's one person coming in from China, and we have it under control. It's going to be just fine."[80]

On January 30, after the WHO proclaimed the coronavirus to be a "public-health emergency of international concern" and announced 7,818 confirmed cases around the world, Trump declared, "We have it very well under control. We have very little problem in this country at this moment—five." Three weeks later, on February 23, the WHO announced that the virus had spread to thirty countries, with 78,811 confirmed cases. Four days later, Trump stated, "It's going to disappear. One day—it's like a miracle—it will disappear." Later that same month, he predicted a vaccine would be available "very quickly" and "very rapidly" and praised his administration's actions as "the most aggressive taken by any country." As *New York Times* columnist David Leonhardt wrote, "None of these claims were true."[81]

Trump's statements and actions in response to COVID-19 had significant international implications. On March 10, the WHO reported 113,702 cases of the virus in more than 100 countries. The following evening, without consulting or notifying European leaders, Trump delivered an address from the Oval Office in which he announced that he suspended travel from most of Europe. He also criticized Europe for not acting quickly enough to enact travel restrictions for China, claiming that the spread of the virus in the United States had been "seeded by travel from Europe."[82] But instead of working with Europe to mitigate the pandemic, he chose only to deflect responsibility from his administration's lack of preparedness.

Trump's remarks were met with a combination of surprise and disdain in Europe. In a joint statement, President of the European Commission Ursula von der Leyen and President of the European Council Charles Michel criticized the decision to impose the ban "unilaterally and without consultation." The European leaders noted, "The coronavirus is a global crisis, not limited to any continent, and it requires cooperation rather than unilateral action."[83]

There is no doubt that the coronavirus has tested the transatlantic alliance, but it has also tested the European alliance, where individual leaders relied on experts to react to the outbreak but took widely different approaches. There is clearly a need for ongoing close economic cooperation, given the resultant severe global recession. Cooperation between the U.S. Federal Reserve and the European Central Bank is also critical.[84] As of this writing, the United States and Europe—indeed, the rest of the world—are learning more about COVID-19 every day. Bill Gates recently wrote that, "All of humanity can work together to learn about the disease and develop the capacity to fight it."[85]

Lead developers of active COVID-19 vaccine candidates are distributed across nineteen countries, and there are now as many as 100 candidate vaccines in development, with two vaccines in mass production in Europe and the United States. Nearly half of COVID-19 vaccine development activity is in North America, with the rest equally divided between Europe, China, and the rest of Asia. As scientists study whether the epidemiology of COVID-19 differs according to geography, it is clear that effective control of the pandemic will demand significant international cooperation and coordination.

Of the COVID-19 vaccines in development, only a handful are currently in clinical trials, meaning they are being tested on humans. Clinical trials are designed to assess the safety and efficacy of a new drug, and typically consist of three phases, with each phase involving a larger number of patients. Now that two vaccines are being distributed on a large scale, there remain issues to decide on a global basis. As Gates noted:

> Even before there is a vaccine, government needs to work out how to distribute it. The countries that provide the funding, the countries where the trials are run, and the ones that are the hardest-hit will all have a good case that they should receive priority. Ideally, there would be global agreement about who should get the vaccine first, but given how many competing interests there are, this is unlikely to happen. Whoever solves this problem equitably will have made a major breakthrough.[86]

There are countless other issues related to the virus and its effects that are best answered on a multilateral basis, and the United States and Europe should be working together to begin the process. For instance, what will international travel look like in the future? Should the mandate of the WHO be changed, and what institutional reforms are needed so that there is a more rapid and transparent response to a future pandemic? What will be the effect of COVID-19 on international trade? And, are there lessons for other multilateral crises; for example, how should the world prepare to respond to a climate emergency and other urgent sustainability challenges as a result of this experience? It nearly goes without saying that none of these questions can be addressed, let alone answered adequately, through current institutional arrangements between the United States and Europe.

Barack Obama not only warned of a pandemic as a senator, as president, he cautioned that there needed to be a more comprehensive strategy in place. He observed: "There may and likely will come a time in which we have both an airborne disease that is deadly. And in order for us to deal with that effectively, we have to put in place an infrastructure . . . It is a smart investment for us to make . . . particularly in a globalized world, where you move from one side of the world to the other in a day."[87]

Obama understood that nations not only needed to have a national strategy in place but also had to work together to mitigate, and ideally avoid, a crisis. He knew the United States did not need to relinquish its sovereignty to cooperate with other nations. In the case of COVID-19, no nation can conquer this disease by itself. It will take sustained individual, institutional, and, most of all, international cooperation. And at each level, success will depend not only on science and fact but on truth and transparency as well.

The coronavirus has only reaffirmed the strategic necessity of transatlantic coordination. There is a critical need for much greater cooperation, not only related to the scientific and health issues of COVID-19. While the WHO remains the principal multilateral organization for combatting diseases on a global level, the transatlantic alliance could combine its expertise in cybersecurity and scientific research to meet the growing challenges of the digital biotech industry.

PLAYING THE LONG GAME

There should be no illusions that a TSPA and a Transatlantic Council will be easy to establish in the near-term future, given the extensive damage left by the Trump administration and the plethora of competing priorities faced by the new Biden administration. Ultimately, even more important than negotiating a new text or establishing novel structures will be the psychological impact of restoring the old ethos that characterized the West. The instinctive muscle memory of relying on each other as the partner of first (even if not only) resort has atrophied within the transatlantic community amid acrimony and mutual recriminations. For the sake of the United States and Europe, as well as the wider liberal order, a new, common strategic culture must emerge. The alternatives are bleak.

Conclusion

This is a time of mutual decisionmaking for the United States and Europe. Douglas Lute, former U.S. ambassador to NATO, believes the transatlantic relationship during the Trump administration descended to its "lowest point" in seven decades—worse even than in 1966 or 2003.[1] Yet, as former U.S. Deputy Secretary of State Bill Burns argues, "the transatlantic relationship matters today as much as it did during the Cold War."[2] Likewise, his predecessor in the George W. Bush administration, John Negroponte, stressed that "it is very important for the next administration to focus on Europe."[3]

With the election of Joe Biden and Kamala Harris, the observations of these three distinguished public servants, who served in both Republican and Democratic administrations, only reinforce the timeliness for undertaking a clear-eyed examination of both the history and the future of the transatlantic relationship.

Their views are echoed by Wolfgang Ischinger, former German ambassador to the United States and to the Court of St James, who recently said, "We are not going to return to the golden age of transatlantic relations. This relationship will require a lot more care and engagement than previously. It is not going to work if we believe we can put it on automatic pilot."[4] On the other hand, he noted that, "for most Europeans, there is no viable, credible alternative, in terms of security and defense, to a functioning NATO Alliance."[5]

In short, the fundamental question implicitly asked on both sides of the Atlantic is how we arrived at this point and where we go from here.

In answering the first part of this question, a number of European and American practitioners and scholars have blamed U.S. President Trump. Charles Kupchan, former senior director for European affairs at the National Security Council under President Obama, observed that this is an "existential moment for the United States and Europe, largely due to Trump."[6] Ambassador Lute notes, "Even when U.S. policies were previously called into question, the commitment of the United States to both NATO and to the EU was never in doubt. Today, however, President Trump has completely upended the transatlantic alliance because he has cast doubt on American commitment."[7]

Not surprising, many Europeans also blame Trump for the deterioration in transatlantic relations. David O'Sullivan, former EU ambassador to the United States, called Trump's foreign policy "upside down" and complained that the U.S. president "treats allies as enemies and potential enemies as allies."[8] However, in many ways, Trump only exacerbated a relationship that, as former Deputy Secretary of State William Burns argues, "had already atrophied due to bad habits on both sides of the Atlantic."[9]

While it is, undoubtedly, correct that for too long both the United States and Europe neglected to update, to reinvigorate, and to fundamentally rethink the transatlantic relationship, it is also true that the institutions created post–World War II have not only brought peace and prosperity to the European continent but have undergirded the liberal order for seven decades.

A new vision grounded in principled pragmatism is needed for the transatlantic community, one informed by a more complete understanding of the strategic geopolitical context and an analysis of respective U.S. and European strategic interests. An appreciation for transatlantic history enables better analysis for what interests Europe and America have in common as well as what role the United States should play in European politics in the future: whether merely as a power in Europe (akin to other great powers such as China or Russia) or as a European power (akin to France or Germany). For instance, the United States did not take any part in the Brexit negotiations over the UK's withdrawal from the EU, notwithstanding the significant consequences of this decision on U.S. interests, but perhaps it should involve itself in future talks on the UK's new relationship with the EU. Indeed, these negotiations provide a unique opportunity for U.S. reengagement in Europe. For any such engagements to be viable, the intellectual groundwork would need to be laid making the case, as was done decades earlier, why the United States should become more involved in European politics.

The 2015 National Security Strategy noted that the United States "has been and will remain a Pacific power." It is time to reassert that the United States is also an Atlantic power. The practical implications of such a commitment would include greater involvement in resolving European conflicts such as in Ukraine, as well as contributing the American perspective on issues such as democratic backsliding in Poland and Hungary.

For America and Europe to strengthen their bonds, they will need creative new institutional arrangements in combination with a pragmatic agenda. To paraphrase former U.S. Secretary of State Madeline Albright, they need to "see further than other countries into the future" to retain their competitive advantage.[10]

Political leadership is critical to the health and effectiveness of the transatlantic relationship—it is in short supply in Europe and was virtually absent in the United States under Trump. But in many ways, these gaps have only revealed the structural challenges facing Europe and, more important, how multilateral institutions created in the postwar period have either matured, become irrelevant, or require reimagining. However, as Charles Kupchan notes, the challenge goes beyond political leadership and political institutions: during prior periods of tension, the two sides were "pursuing the same ends even if they chose different means; now there is no longer agreement as to what are the ends."[11]

It is precisely for this reason that we believe broad-minded leaders from the United States and Europe should convene in 2021 to discuss, debate, and, ultimately, articulate a new Atlantic Charter. Just as Franklin D. Roosevelt and Winston Churchill laid out a set of principles—and a set of very specific issues to work on together—so, too, must European and American leaders evaluate the greatest challenges facing the globe today and then set out a vision for the future.

America and Europe are "each other's closest partners," as President Obama argued, and "neither Europe nor the United States can confront the challenges of our time without the other." Europeans flew the majority of airstrikes during NATO's intervention in Libya in 2011, contributed the majority of troops to the Counter-ISIL coalition in 2016, and provided the vast preponderance of funds and diplomacy in Ukraine. French and British special forces fought alongside American troops in Syria in equal measures. On the humanitarian front, Europe also welcomed over ten times more refugees than the United States, and provided three times more development aid. Yet, from this era of genuine partnership, Trump has brought the West to rock bottom.

As Vice President Joe Biden has argued powerfully, Europe should remain America's "indispensable partner of first resort" to confront common future challenges, such as public health, economic recovery, Russia, China, and illiberalism. Since first resort does not mean only resort, other partners, such as Australia, India, Japan, and South Korea, also will be integral for global collective action. The transatlantic partnership is merely the core engine for the wider machinery of the liberal order, akin to Franco-German leadership within the European Union.

The liberal order no longer has global aspirations, as during the twenty-year post–Cold War interlude, in that China and Russia are not expected to become liberal democracies in the foreseeable future. Nonetheless, it can continue to expand on the margins, whether in Ukraine or Tunisia and, above all, it needs to build up internal strength to defend the free world against illiberal great powers, particularly China. In this effort, there is no viable alternative for a vibrant transatlantic partnership leading the liberal order.

Institutional innovation is sometimes anathema in U.S. policy circles, surprisingly so given that many of the current international institutions, such as the UN and NATO, were American creations. Likewise, one does not have to search back to World War II for new institutions, as the G7 was a creature of the 1970s, the OSCE was founded in the 1990s, and the G20 was established at the leaders level in 2008. To be sure, some ambitious institutions, such as the Community of Democracies (reflecting aspirations of the 1990s), have floundered, but that should not prevent current policymakers from thinking imaginatively about future possibilities. Our institutional proposal of the Transatlantic Council, with a Transatlantic Strategic Partnership, seeks to layer on top of the existing architecture in a manner that mirrors the flexibility of the G7 while providing a more inclusive membership and agenda.

We hope to have convinced the reader, and future policymakers, on our core arguments. But we think we will have succeeded even if, as a first resort, we resurrect the not-so-distant memory of transatlantic partnership under the Obama-Biden administration as we experienced it firsthand, which can serve as a sound basis for future efforts at collective action.

The United States and Europe should restate that the liberal order, undergirded by democratic values, the rule of law, respect for human rights, and the dignity of work, remains an extraordinarily powerful organizing vision for people around the world. Basic principles should include a declaration that globalization is actually a byproduct of the Fourth Industrial Revolution, representing a fundamental change in the way we live, work, and relate to one another. Powered by extraordinary technological advances, this revolution, similar to ones before it, signifies a new chapter in human development and cannot be reversed. Harnessed correctly, it can create greater prosperity, greater health, and greater environmental sustainability.

With these basic principles in mind, a greater focus on the following areas of common interest can strengthen the transatlantic relationship:

- The United States and Europe should forge new institutional mechanisms to coordinate foreign policy, especially on economic sanctions.

- The United States should ally with Europe to address urgent global issues such as climate change, technology, and health pandemics.

- The United States and Europe should develop approaches to address the challenge posed by rising authoritarianism from states such as Russia and China.

- The alliance should protect U.S. and European sovereignty and electoral processes from foreign interference. These practical steps would go beyond the current stale arguments around defense spending and aim at a true partnership with fair burden-sharing across various policy areas.

- The United States should strengthen its economic partnership with Europe, by ending Trump's trade war. The United States and the European Union should revise the Transatlantic Trade and Investment Partnership and negotiate a new transatlantic trade agreement.

- The transatlantic community should prioritize and enhance counter-terrorism cooperation (including through greater sharing of intelligence and law-enforcement information).

- The United States should support the formation of robust European defense cooperation to complement NATO.

- The European Union should establish a baseline cyber capability for its members and develop a strategy for confronting cyberattacks. NATO needs to clarify whether Article 5 could be invoked in the case of a cyberattack and should adapt Article 4 to cyberattacks.

- The United States should rejoin the Iran nuclear deal. The United States and Europe should work to establish a common set of policy principles and policy goals to guide their presence and future efforts in the Middle East.

The year 2021 will mark the eightieth anniversary of the Atlantic Charter. Its central premise, first articulated by President Roosevelt and Prime Minister Churchill—that the United States and Europe, because of their common interests and values, should work together to build a better world—remains as true today as it was in 1941. There is no doubt that by working as partners we have achieved extraordinary success. We believe that by resurrecting the transatlantic ethos to defend and expand the liberal order amid new and complex challenges of the twenty-first century our progress will continue.

Appendix

Distribution of Power since 1945

The United States and Europe are not just a powerful political alliance; they have the potential to create an enormously powerful economic alliance, as well. Consider the material resources of the West in 1945.[1] As table A-1 demonstrates,[2] the G7 countries (as a reflection of the broader West) were collectively dominant in the world, with 84 percent of global GDP, 308 percent of the world's average GPD per capita, 89 percent of military spending, and 59 percent of military personnel.

However, these statistics, which show the United States in an especially predominant global role, are somewhat misleading, as the world had been engaged for six years in total war and not able to sustain the inflated levels of military deployment indefinitely. Moreover, GDP information for 1945 is unavailable for many countries, and the existing data are likely to be abnormally deflated in the case of some countries (for instance, France and the Soviet Union, which sustained much of the fighting on their territories). Thus, the Harry S. Truman and Dwight D. Eisenhower administrations, with vivid memories of the Great Depression, fully recognized the ephemeral nature of the U.S. global position and the continuing need to build alliances and institutions.

For purposes of comparison with the contemporary world, a more accurate picture of the post–World War II global distribution of power resources is 1950, when the world demobilized to Cold War levels and war-torn depressed economies resumed peacetime levels of output. Also, 1950 is the first year for which reliable statistics exist across the world. As table A-2 shows, the West was still collectively strong, with 49 percent of global GDP, 269 percent of the world's average GPD per capita, 42 percent of military spending, and 18 percent of military personnel.

In 2010, as depicted in table A-3, the respective levels for the G7 (the original West) were effectively the same in terms of share of global GDP (about 49 percent), and actually much better in terms of average income (448 percent) and share of military spending (60 percent). The declinist view of the West and its global position was simply inaccurate.

Over the past decade, the state of play has not changed drastically. In fact, the current overall picture for the West is even better than in 1950: wealthier and stronger militarily. The U.S. economic position has actually improved, contrary to prior predictions, and its military capabilities continue to be unparalleled even as its defense spending has decreased on a relative basis. The most notable change since 1945 is the rapid rise of China, which initially took sixty-five years to double its share of global GDP, but then nearly doubled it again over the following decade (table A-4).

These statistics illustrate potential economic power among Western allies if they can define common interests and identify ways to serve them. There is no one-to-one relation between material resources and the ability to achieve preferred objectives, as evidenced starkly by the disastrous U.S. experience in Iraq—purportedly at the peak of its superpower status. Translating resources into power requires political will, intellectual creativity, and diplomacy, which have not been in ample supply over the past four squandered years.

TABLE A-1. 1945

Share of Resources	GDP*	GDP Per Capita*	Military Spending**	Military Personnel**	Population*
United States	39.41	580.14	63.45	23.44	6.79
United Kingdom	8.31	349.53	11.99	9.84	2.38
Soviet Union	8.00	95.15	6.06	24.17	8.41
Germany	7.24	223.30	7.51	10.25	3.24
India (1947)	6.54	32.95	0.15	0.60	19.85
China (estimated)	4.79	18.60	0.16	9.23	25.76
Japan	2.47	66.94	2.82	11.79	3.69
France	2.44	127.28	0.87	1.12	1.92
Canada	2.11	355.36	1.88	1.55	0.59
Italy	2.08	94.85	0.22	0.53	2.20
World	100.00	100.00	100.00	100.00	100.00
West	64.06	307.83	88.74	58.52	20.81

Sources: *Angus Maddison, Historical Statistics of the World Economy (2020); **Correlates of War (2020).

TABLE A-2. 1950

Share of Resources	GDP*	GDP Per Capita*	Military Spending**	Military Personnel**	Population*
United States	27.32	438.46	31.29	8.34	6.23
Soviet Union	9.57	134.58	33.34	24.56	7.11
United Kingdom	6.53	328.67	5.11	3.94	1.99
Germany	4.98	183.81	N/A	N/A	2.71
China	4.50	20.78	5.50	22.85	21.66
India	4.17	29.32	0.79	1.95	14.22
France	4.14	249.67	3.20	3.40	1.66
Italy	3.10	165.86	1.21	1.34	1.87
Japan (1952)	3.02	90.97	0.62	0.68	3.32
Brazil	1.68	79.18	0.72	1.32	2.12
Canada	0.26	345.36	0.96	0.26	0.56
World	100.00	100.00	100.00	100.00	100.00
West (G7)	**49.35**	**269.08**	**42.39**	**17.96**	**18.34**

Sources: *Angus Maddison, Historical Statistics of the World Economy (2020); **Correlates of War (2020).

TABLE A-3. 2010.

Share of Resources ($)	GDP*	GDP Per Capita*	Military Spending**	Military Personnel**	Population*
United States	22.71	518.87	45.58	5.58	4.47
European Union	25.80	361.51	15.32	8.09	7.26
China	9.19	99.16	8.00	10.47	19.34
Japan	8.63	376.79	2.58	0.92	1.84
Brazil	3.34	154.14	1.70	2.53	2.81
India	2.59	47.42	3.01	9.33	17.32
Russia	2.47	241.80	2.99	5.08	2.06
Canada	2.45	428.00	1.00	0.02	0.49
World	100.00	100.00	100.00	100.00	100.00
U.S.-EU	48.51	435.18	60.90	13.67	11.73
West (U.S., EU, Japan, Canada)	59.59	381.24	64.47	14.82	15.63
G7	49.93	448.01	59.82	10.74	10.63

Sources: *IMF, World Economic Outlook Database (2020); **SIPRI (2020); ***IISS, The Military Balance (2017).

TABLE A-4. 2019

Share of Resources ($)	GDP*	GDP Per Capita*	Military Spending**	Military Personnel***	Population*
United States	24.46	499.12	35.59	4.96	4.28
European Union	21.43	342.68	14.77	7.54	6.67
China	16.29	150.43	13.44	9.83	18.18
Japan	5.93	351.14	2.55	0.95	1.64
Brazil	2.25	128.40	1.73	2.66	2.72
India	3.41	35.38	3.74	11.06	17.56
Russia	1.85	233.38	3.61	5.30	1.87
Canada	1.99	390.14	1.20	0.26	0.49
World	100.00	100.00	100.00	100.00	100.00
U.S.-EU	45.89	426.06	50.36	12.50	10.95
West (U.S., EU, Japan, Canada)	53.82	372.29	54.11	13.70	14.46
G7	45.66	421.84	49.38	9.75	9.98

Sources: *IMF, World Economic Outlook Database (2020); **SIPRI (2018 data); ***IISS, The Military Balance (2017 data).

Notes

Acknowledgments

1. President Barack Obama, Europe and America, Aligned for the Future, *New York Times*, November 19, 2010.

Epigraph

1. Barack Obama, "Remarks and a Question-and-Answer Session at a Young Leaders of the United Kingdom Town Hall Meeting in London, England," April 23, 2016.

Introduction

1. "Address to the United Nations General Assembly by President George H. W. Bush," September 23, 1991; see also, George Bush and Brent Scowcroft, *A World Transformed* (Random House, 1998).

2. Adam Tooze, *Crashed: How a Decade of Financial Crises Change the World* (Penguin Random House, 2018), p. 156.

3. Jeff D. Colgan and Robert O. Keohane, "The Liberal Order Is Rigged: Fix It Now or Watch It Wither," *Foreign Affairs* 96, no. 3 (May/June 2017), pp. 36–44.

4. Gunther Hellmann and Benjamin Herborth, *Uses of "the West": Security and the Politics of Order* (Cambridge University Press, 2016).

5. See, for example, Jonah Goldberg, *Suicide of the West: How the Rebirth of Tribalism, Populism, Nationalism, and Identity Politics is Destroying American Democracy* (Penguin Random House, 2018).

6. Francis Fukuyama, *The Origins of Political Order: From Prehuman Times to the French Revolution* (New York: Farrar, Straus and Giroux, 2011).

7. It is an open question to what extent the founders of the liberal order—FDR, Truman, Eisenhower, Acheson, Churchill, and others—viewed liberal values as universal or geographically delimited. The foundational statement of U.S. policy during the Cold War, NSC-68, articulated in 1950 a global perspective for the free world: the "assault on free institutions is world-wide now, and in the context of the present polarization of power a defeat of free institutions anywhere is a defeat everywhere." Moreover, the Universal Declaration of Human Rights, adopted in 1948, clearly has a worldwide perspective not linked to cultural underpinnings. On the other hand, some of the founding leaders at various times may have viewed the liberal order and the West as grounded in certain cultural or religious bases. In any event, by the time of the 1990s, when the liberal order was able to expand potentially across the world, there were no such perceived constraints to its possible scope.

8. See G. John Ikenberry, *A World Safe for Democracy: Liberal Internationalism and the Crises of Global Order* (Yale University Press, 2020).

9. G. John Ikenberry, *Liberal Leviathan: The Origins, Crisis, and Transformation of the American World Order* (Princeton University Press, 2013).

10. Michael Doyle, *Liberal Peace* (Routledge, 2011).

11. See, for example, Robert Kagan, *The Jungle Grows Back: America and Our Imperiled World* (Knopf, 2018); Robert Kagan, "The New German Question: What Happens When Europe Comes Apart?" *Foreign Affairs* 98, no. 3 (May/June 2019), pp. 108–20.

12. Interview with Bill Burns, January 13, 2020.

13. Zbigniew Brzezinski, *Strategic Vision: America and the Crisis of Global Power* (Basic Books, 2012). See also, Simon Serfaty, *The Vital Partnership: Power and Order, America and Europe Beyond Iraq* (Rowman & Littlefield, 2005), assuming the necessity of the West. For example, Bzezinski called for an enlarged West to include Russia and Turkey.

14. Timothy Garton Ash, *Free World: America, Europe, and the Surprising Future of the West* (Random House, 2004), calling for an enlarging Western liberal order to eventually span the globe.

15. But, see John J. Mearsheimer, *The Great Delusion: Liberal Dreams and International Realities* (Yale University Press, 2019); and Stephen M. Walt, *The Hell of Good Intentions* (Farrar, Straus and Giroux, 2018)

16. Roosevelt explained the rationale for the Lend-Lease program to support the British war effort in the following terms: "Suppose my neighbor's home catches fire, and I have a length of garden hose four or five hundred feet away. If he can take my garden hose and connect it up with his hydrant, I may help him to put out his fire . . . I don't say to him before that operation, 'Neighbor, my garden hose cost me $15; you have to pay me $15 for it.' . . . I don't want $15—I want my garden hose back after the fire is over."

17. Churchill Lecture by Prime Minister Mark Rutte, Europa Institut at the University of Zurich, February 13, 2019.

18. Martin Selmayr, "Europe, Multilateralism, and Great Power Competition," Brookings Institution, March 6, 2019.

19. See "Appendix: Distribution of Power since 1945," this volume, for a complete review of the military and economic potential of the transatlantic alliance.

20. U.S. discourse on European internal disputes—see, for example, Thomas Wright, *All Measures Short of War: The Contest for the 21st Century and the Future of American Power* (Yale University Press, 2017)—sometimes anachronistically treats Europe as a battleground for great-power contests and as a bystander to international challenges, but not as a pillar of the transatlantic community and a global player. But Europe—in its defense of the Iran nuclear deal, forceful stance toward Russia, and new trade deals with Canada, Japan, and others—has demonstrated global leadership on a range of issues and, for the duration of the Trump administration, can help sustain the spirit of the transatlantic community.

21. Opening Statement by Frank-Walter Steinmeier, Munich Security Conference, February 14, 2020.

22. "Chairman's Interview with Emmanuel Macron, Munich Security Conference," February 15, 2020.

23. "Emmanuel Macron in His Own Words," *The Economist*, November 7, 2019.

24. Victor Mallet, Michael Peel, and Tobias Buck, "Merkel Rejects Macron Warning over Nato 'Brain Death,'" *Financial Times*, November 7, 2019.

25. Alina Polyakova and Benjamin Haddad, "Europe Alone: What Comes After the Transatlantic Alliance," *Foreign Affairs* 98, no. 4 (July/August 2019), pp. 109–20.

26. Ivo H. Daalder and James M. Lindsay, "The Committee to Save the World Order: America's Allies Must Step Up as America Steps Down," *Foreign Affairs* 97, no. 6 (November/December 2018), pp. 72–83. See also, Ivo Daalder and James Lindsay, *The Empty Throne: America's Abdication of Global Leadership* (PublicAffairs, 2018).

27. Jennifer Lind and William Wohlforth, "The Future of the Liberal Order Is Conservative: A Strategy to Save the System," *Foreign Affairs* 98, no. 2 (March/April 2019), pp. 70–80.

28. Fareed Zakaria, *The Post-American World: Release 2.0* (W. W. Norton, 2011); and Fareed Zakaria, *The Future of Freedom: Illiberal Democracy at Home and Abroad* (W. W. Norton, 2007).

29. Charles A. Kupchan, *No One's World: The West, the Rising Rest, and the Coming Global Turn* (Oxford University Press, 2012).

30. Parag Khanna, *The Future Is Asian* (Simon & Schuster, 2019).

31. One notable example illustrating that material base is not determinative of global influence is Russia: on a paltry GDP of merely 2 percent of global income, it has been able to project an image of great power and shaper of destinies.

32. U.S. National Security Strategy, 2010.

33. Ibid.

34. U.S. National Security Strategy, 2015.

35. Ibid.

36. U.S. National Security Strategy, 2017.

37. See Michael Anton, "The Trump Doctrine," *Foreign Policy*, April 20, 2019.

38. Remarks to the United Nations General Assembly in New York City, September 20, 2016. See Matthew Kroenig, *The Return of Great Power Rivalry: Democracy versus Autocracy from the Ancient World to the U.S. and China* (Oxford University Press, 2020).

39. Barack Obama, "Message to the Nation on Serving as President," January 19, 2017.

40. See also, Kroenig, *The Return of Great Power Rivalry*.

41. See also, Stewart M. Patrick, "Atlantic Charter 2.0: A "Declaration of Principles for Freedom, Prosperity, and Peace,'" Council on Foreign Relations, February 16, 2019; and Richard Fontaine, "We Need an Atlantic Charter for the Post-Coronavirus Era," *The Atlantic*, April 16, 2020. For wider analysis of U.S. role in the world, see Rebecca Lissner and Mira Rapp-Hooper, *An Open World: How America Can Win the Contest for Twenty-First-Century Order* (Yale University Press, 2020); Mira Rapp-Hooper, *Shields of the Republic: The Triumph and Peril of America's Alliances* (Harvard University Press, 2020); Richard Haass, *The World: A Brief Introduction* (Penguin, 2020); Ian Bremmer, *Superpower: Three Choices for America's Role in the World* (Penguin, 2019); and Richard Haass, *A World in Disarray: American Foreign Policy and the Crisis of the Old Order* (Penguin, 2019).

42. Part of the manuscript has been published as an article: "The World Still Needs a United West," *Foreign Affairs* (September 2020); "Europe and the Liberal Order," *Survival* 61, no. 2 (April/May 2019), by GMF under the title "Europe's Strategies in Asia" in March 2019, and by the EU Institute for Security Studies and the NATO Defense College under the title "Operational Cooperation" in *The EU and NATO: The Essential Partners* (edited by Gustav Lindstrom and Thierry Tardy, 2019). Each respective publisher is the original source and copyright holder, and the text has been reproduced with its permission.

Chapter 1

1. Michael Beschloss, *Presidents at War*, p. 364.

2. Henry Kissinger, *World Order*, p. 273.

3. Douglas Brinkley and David R. Facey-Crowther, editors, *The Atlantic Charter* (New York: Palgrave-Macmillan, 1994).

4. Roosevelt, "Fireside Chat," January 6, 1945.

5. Ben Steil, *The Battle of Bretton Woods* (Princeton University Press, 1999).

6. Kershaw, p. 264

7. Robert L. Hutchings, "At the End of the American Century"; and Bowman W. Cutter, *A New International Economic Order?*, p. 134.

8. Kissinger, p. 277.

9. Ibid.

10. Weisbrode, *Atlantic Century*, p. 86

11. George Kennan, Memo to U.S. Secretary of State, February 22, 1946.

12. Winston Churchill, "The Sinews of Peace," Westminster College, Fulton, Missouri, March 5, 1946.

13. "X" (George F. Kennan), "The Sources of Soviet Conduct," *Foreign Affairs* (July 1947).

14. Kissinger, *World Order*, p. 282.

15. Dean Acheson, *Present at the Creation: My Years in the State Department* (W. W. Norton & Company, 1969).

16. Kershaw, p. 135.

17. Melyn Leffler, "Divide and Invest: Why the Marshall Plan Worked," *Foreign Affairs* (July/August 2018), p. 171.

18. Weisbrode, *Atlantic Century*, p. 100.

19. Derek Leebaert, *Grand Improvisation*, p. 157.

20. Ibid., p. 167

21. Helga Haftendorn, "Germany's Accession to NATO, 50 Years On," *NATO Review*, June 1, 2005.

22. John W. Holmes, The United States and Europe After the Cold War: A New Alliance, p. 1.

23. Quoted in Benn Steil, *Marshall Plan: Dawn of the Cold War* (Simon & Schuster, 2018).

24. BBC News November 27, 1976.

25. Kershaw, p. 139.

26. Kershaw, p. 40.

27. Kissinger, p. 277.

28. Under the Washington Treaty, NATO allies were restricted from withdrawing until 1969, twenty years after the treaty's adoption, after which they could exit the organization with one-year's notice.

29. The European Communities consisted of the European Coal and Steel Community (1952), the European Atomic Energy Community (1957), and the European Economic Community (1957). All three were merged into a single set of institutions in 1967.

30. Kershaw, p. 142.

31. See Guido Calabresi and Philip Bobbitt, *Tragic Choices* (New York: W. W. Norton, 1978).

32. NATO Declassified, "Origins, NATO Leaders: Lord Ismay, 1952–1957."

33. Kershaw, p. 165.

34. Kissinger, pp. 296–97.

35. Kershaw, p. 217.

36. Walter Laqueur, *Europe in Our Time*, p. 416.

37. Kershaw, p. 265.

38. Laqueur, p. 416.

39. Kershaw, p. 262.

40. Laqueur, p. xi.

41. See, generally, Philip Zelikow and Condoleezza Rice, *To Build a Better World: Choices to End the Cold War and Create a Global Commonwealth* (Basic Books, 2019).

42. See Mary Elise Sarotte, *1989: The Struggle to Create Post-Cold War Europe* (Princeton University Press, 2014).

43. Gideon Rose, "The Fourth Founding: The United States and the Liberal Order," *Foreign Affairs* (January/February 2019).

44. Transatlantic Declaration on EC-US Relations, 1990.

45. Zbigniew Brzezinski and Brent Scowcroft, *America and the World*, p. 10.

46. Robert L. Hutchings, editor, "At The End of the American Century: Hehir," *Strategy and Ethics in World Politics*, p. 115.

47. U.S. National Security Strategy, 1991, p. 1.

48. Ibid., p. 2.

49. Ibid., p. 4.

50. Anthony Lake, "From Containment to Enlargement," U.S. State Department Dispatch, September 27, 1993.

51. U.S. National Security Strategy, 1994, pp. 18–19.

52. Ibid., p. 20.

53. Quoted in Josip Glaurdić, *The Hour of Europe: Western Powers and the Breakup of Yugoslavia* (Yale University Press, 2011).

54. Henry Kissinger, *Diplomacy* (New York: Simon and Schuster, 1994), p. 806.

55. Richard Holbrooke, *To End a War: The Conflict in Yugoslavia—America's Inside Story—Negotiating with Milosevic* (New York: Modern Library, 1999); and Ivo H. Daalder, *Getting to Dayton: The Making of America's Bosnia Policy* (Brookings Institution Press, 1999).

56. Celeste A. Wallender, "Nato's Enemies Within," *Foreign Affairs* (July/August 2018), p. 70.

57. See Francis Fukuyama, *The End of History and the Last Man* (Free Press, 1992).

58. Brzezinski and Scowcroft, p. 15.

59. Steven Erlanger, "Poland Is Pressed to Choose Between Europe and U.S.," *New York Times*, June 4, 2000.

60. Ivan Krastev and Mark Leonard, "Europe's Shattered Dream of Order: How Putin Is Disrupting the Atlantic Alliance," *Foreign Affairs*, May/June 2015.

61. U.S. National Security Strategy, 2002, p. i.

62. Ibid.

63. Polyakova and Haddad, p. 111.

64. "Kate Connolly, I am Not Convinced, Fischer Tells Rumsfeld," *The Telegraph*, February 10, 2003.

65. Ian Black, "Furious Chirac Hits Out at 'Infantile' Easterners," *The Guardian*, February 18, 2003.

66. John L. Gaddis, *Surprise, Security and the American Experience*, p. 101. See also, Philip Gordon and Jeremy Shapiro, *Allies At War: America, Europe and the Split Over Iraq* (McGraw Hill, 2004).

67. European Security Strategy, 2003, p. 1.

68. Ibid., p. 9.

69. Ibid.

70. But, see Christopher Coker, *Twilight of the West* (Basic Books, 1997), arguing that modern challenges required a post-Western approach and that the West had outlived its utility as a concept.

71. Vladimir Putin, Speech and the Following Discussion at the Munich Conference on Security Policy, February 10, 2007.

72. NATO, "Bucharest Summit Declaration," April 3, 2008.

73. Nicu Popescu, "Interview with Jaap De Hoop Scheffer: The Bucharest Summit Revisited," *Georgia Today*, April 12, 2018.

74. Rebecca Frankel, "Putin Goes Gansta," *Foreign Policy*, November 13, 2008.

Chapter 2

1. United Nations General Assembly, 63rd sess., President Luiz Inácio Lula da Silva, September 23, 2008.

2. United Nations General Assembly, 63rd sess., Prime Minister Gordon Brown, September 23, 2008.

3. United Nations General Assembly, 63rd sess., President Nicolas Sarkozy, September 23, 2008.

4. The G20 countries formally consist of: Argentina, Australia, Brazil, Canada, China, the European Union, France, Germany, India, Indonesia, Italy, Japan, Mexico, Russia, Saudi Arabia, South Africa, South Korea, Turkey, the United Kingdom, and the United States. Moreover, additional invited participants have included the Netherlands, Singapore, Spain, Viet Nam, ASEAN, the African Union, the APEC president, the United Nations, the IMF, the World Bank, the WHO, the International Labor Organization, the Financial Stability Board, the OECD, and the Asian Development Bank. At the 2019 summit in Osaka, Japan, there were approximately forty leaders present.

5. President Barack Obama, G-20 Press Conference, April 2, 2009.

6. Ibid.

7. Adam Tooze, *Crashed: How a Decade of Financial Crises Changed the World* (Penguin Random House, 2018), p. 274.

8. President Barack Obama, "The President's News Conference with President Nicolas Sarkozy of France in Strasbourg, France," April 3, 2009.

9. Ibid.

10. President Barack Obama, "Remarks at a Town Hall Meeting and a Question-and-Answer Session in Strasbourg," April 3, 2009.

11. Ibid.

12. "Joint Statement by the United States and the European Council on the North Korean Launch," April 5, 2009.

13. One former official reported that Obama said he would fire any staff that would organize a similarly large summit in the future.

14. "Press Chat at the EU-USA Summit with US President Barack Obama," April 4, 2009.

15. "Speech by Federal Chancellor Angela Merkel before the United States Congress," November 3, 2009.

16. Ibid.

17. Other recipients include Pope John Paul II, Helmut Kohl, and Nelson Mandela.

18. "Remarks at a Welcoming Ceremony for Chancellor Angela Merkel of Germany," June 7, 2011.

19. "Remarks on Missile Defense Systems in Europe,' September 17, 2009.

20. "2009 EU-U.S. Summit Declaration," November 3, 2009.

21. "Remarks following a Meeting with European Union Leaders," November 3, 2009.

22. NATO, "Strategic Concept."

23. "NATO-Russia Council Joint Statement," November 20, 2010.

24. "The President's News Conference in Lisbon, Portugal," November 20, 2010.

25. "Remarks following the European Union-United States Summit in Lisbon," November 20, 2010. See also "The President's News Conference with Prime Minister Donald Tusk of Poland in Warsaw," May 28, 2011: "In addition to reestablishing a wonderful conversation with strong friends and allies, I wanted to make sure that everybody in our country, but everybody around the world, understands that the transatlantic alliance remains a cornerstone, a foundation stone for American security."

26. "Remarks following the European Union-United States Summit in Lisbon," November 20, 2010.

27. European Commission Press Release, "EU-US Summit in Washington to Further Strengthen the Transatlantic Partnership," November 25, 2011.

28. "EU-US Summit Joint Statement," November 28, 2011.

29. "The President's News Conference with Chancellor Angela Merkel of Germany," May 2, 2014.

30. "The President's News Conference with Chancellor Angela Merkel of Germany in Hannover, Germany," April 24, 2016.

31. "Remarks following a Meeting with President Herman Van Rompuy of the European Union and President Jose Manual Durao Barroso of the European Commission," November 28, 2011.

32. President Barack Obama, "Remarks at a Town Hall Meeting and a Question-and-Answer Session in Strasbourg," April 3, 2009.

33. Thom Shanker, "Defense Secretary Warns NATO of 'Dim' Future," *New York Times*, June 10, 2011.

34. "Remarks by Vice President Biden at 45th Munich Conference on Security Policy," February 7, 2009.

35. It should have been "perezagruzka" rather than "peregruzka." "Clinton, Lavrov Push Wrong Reset Button on Ties," *Reuters*, March 6, 2009.

36. Public Papers of the Presidents of the United States: Barack Obama, "Remarks

following a Meeting with President Dmitry A. Medvedev of Russia in London," April 1, 2009.

37. "Joint Statement between the United States of America and Russia Regarding Negotiations on Further Reductions in Strategic Offensive Arms," April 1, 2009.

38. "Joint Statement between the United States of America and the Russian Federation on Afghanistan," July 6, 2009.

39. "Joint Statement between the United States of America and the Russian Federation on Missile Defense Issues," July 6, 2009.

40. "Joint Statement between the United States of America and the Russian Federation on Nuclear Cooperation," July 6, 2009.

41. "Remarks at the Parallel Business Summit in Moscow," July 7, 2009.

42. "Joint Understanding by President Barack H. Obama and President Dmitry A. Medvedev on the START Follow-On Treaty," July 6, 2009.

43. "The President's News Conference with President Dmitry A. Medvedev of Russia in Moscow," July 6, 2009.

44. "Remarks Prior to a Meeting with Prime Minister Vladimir V. Putin of Russia in Moscow," July 7, 2009.

45. "Joint Statement by President Barack Obama and President Dmitry A. Medvedev of Russia Commemorating the 65th Anniversary of the Meeting of Soviet and American Troops at the Elbe River," April 25, 2010.

46. "Remarks on Signing the Strategic Arms Reduction Treaty with President Dmitry A. Medvedev of Russia and an Exchange with Reporters in Prague, Czech Republic," April 8, 2010; "Joint Statement by President Barack Obama and President Dmitry A. Medvedev of Russia on Afghanistan," June 24, 2010 (citing "over 320 flights have been carried out, and over 41,000 personnel and over 9,000 rail containers of valuable cargo have been transported in support of operations in Afghanistan").

47. "Statement on the Progress in Russia's World Trade Organization Accession Talks," November 10, 2011.

48. Of course, it is possible that Putin had always intended to resume the presidency and, in any event, had been ruling behind the scenes as prime minister in the meantime to avoid violating or changing the term limits set by the Russian constitution.

49. "Clinton Cites 'Serious Concerns' about Russian Election," CNN, December 7, 2011.

50. "Vladimir Putin Accuses Hillary Clinton of Inciting Post-Election Protests," PRI, December 8, 2011.

51. "Remarks following a Meeting with President Dmitry Anatolyevich Medvedev of Russia in Seoul," March 26, 2012; "Remarks following a Meeting with President Vladimir Vladimirovich Putin of Russia in Los Cabos," June 18, 2012; and "Remarks following a Meeting with President Vladimir Vladimirovich Putin of Russia in Lough Erne, Northern Ireland," June 17, 2013.

52. "The President's News Conference," August 9, 2013.

53. "Remarks at a Reception Honoring World Ambassadors," July 27, 2009.

54. Ibid.

55. "Remarks to the United Nations General Assembly in New York City," September 23, 2009.

56. "Remarks at the United Nations Security Council Summit on Nonproliferation and Nuclear Disarmament in New York City," September 24, 2009. This led to the 2010 Nuclear Security summit in Washington, DC, involving forty-seven countries, and the 2012 summit in South Korea. See "Remarks at the Opening Session of the Nuclear Security Summit," April 13, 2010; and "Remarks at the Opening Plenary Session of the Nuclear Security Summit in Seoul, South Korea," March 26, 2012.

57. "Remarks at the Millennium Development Goals Summit in New York City," September 22, 2010.

58. "Remarks at the Opening of an Open Government Partnership Event in New York City," September 20, 2011.

59. "Remarks in Cairo," June 4, 2009.

60. Ibid.

61. "The President's News Conference in Toronto, Canada," June 27, 2010.

62. "Remarks at the United States-China Strategic and Economic Dialogue," July 27, 2009.

63. "Remarks in Tokyo, Japan," November 14, 2009.

64. ASEAN consists of Indonesia, Thailand, Singapore, Malaysia, the Philippines, Vietnam, Brunei, Cambodia, Myanmar, and Laos.

65. "Remarks Following a Meeting With the Association of Southeast Asian Nations in Singapore," US-ASEAN Summit, November 15, 2009; see also, "Remarks at a United States-Association of Southeast Asian Nations Leaders Meeting in New York City," September 24, 2010.

66. Four ASEAN countries plus Australia, Japan, Canada, Chile, New Zealand, Mexico, and Peru.

67. "Remarks in Tokyo, Japan," November 14, 2009.

68. "ASEAN and East Asia Summits," November 18, 2011. Obama also attended the Asia-Pacific Economic Cooperation summit, involving twenty-one leaders (East Asia format, except for Cambodia and Myanmar, plus Canada, Mexico, Peru, Chile, and Papua New Guinea).

69. Hillary Clinton, "America's Pacific Century," *Foreign Policy*, October 11, 2011.

70. Hillary Clinton, "Europe Is and Remains America's Partner of First Resort," Munich Security Conference, February 4, 2012.

71. Elisabeth Bumiller and Steven Erlanger, "Panetta and Clinton Seek to Reassure Europe on Defense," *New York Times*, February 4, 2012.

72. "Presidential Address Before a Joint Session of Congress," January 25, 2012.

73. Hillary Clinton, "America's Pacific Century," *Foreign Policy*, October 11, 2011.

74. Interview with David O'Sullivan, October 28, 2019.

75. Interview with Anthony Gardner, November 18, 2019.

76. "Remarks at a Young Southeast Asian Leaders Initiative Town Hall and a Question-and-Answer Session at the University of Malaya in Kuala Lumpur, Malay-

sia," April 27, 2014 ("The crisis still confronts us in other parts of the world, from the Middle East to Ukraine. But I want to be very clear. Let me be clear about this, because some people have wondered whether, because of what happens in Ukraine or what happens in the Middle East, whether this will sideline our strategy. It has not. We are focused, and we're going to follow through, on our interest in promoting a strong U.S.-Asia relationship."). Indeed, Obama's final foreign trip to the APEC summit stressed the importance of "the rebalance of [U.S.] foreign policy to the Asia Pacific." See also, "The President's News Conference in Lima, Peru," November 20, 2016.

77. "Remarks at the Department of State," May 19, 2011.

78. SC Res. 1970 (February 26, 2011).

79. Quoted in Dan Bilesky and Mark Landler, "Military Action against Qaddafi is Backed by U.N.," *New York Times*, March 18, 2011, p. A1.

80. See Dan Bilesky, "Security Council Uncertain about Intervening in Libya," *New York Times*, March 18, 2011 ("Lebanon, the [Security C]ouncil's only current Arab member, presented the Arab League's request to the council to authorize a no-flight zone to protect Libyan civilians. Lebanese diplomats said that authorizing the no-flight zone had become urgent as Col. Qaddafi's forces continued to advance.").

81. SC Res. 1973 (March 17, 2011), paras. 4 (superseding the arms embargo imposed by paragraph 9 of Resolution 1970) and 6 (authorizing a no-fly zone).

82. Scott Wilson and Joby Warrick, "Obama's Shift toward Military Action," *Washington Post*, March 19, 2011, p. A1; and Jeff Zeleny, "Airstrikes in Libya; Questions Back Home," *New York Times*, March 21, 2011, p. A12 ("The president's national security adviser, Thomas Donilon, told reporters on Sunday that Libya was different from Bahrain and other countries where uprisings have taken place in the Middle East, particularly because the Arab League asked for intervention in Libya.").

83. Michael Slackman, "Dislike for Qaddafi Gives Arabs a Point of Unity," *Washington Post*, March 22, 2011, p. A12.

84. "Remarks on the Situation in Libya," March 18, 2011 ("Here's why this matters to us. Left unchecked, we have every reason to believe that Qadhafi would commit atrocities against his people. Many thousands could die. A humanitarian crisis would ensue. The entire region could be destabilized, endangering many of our allies and partners. The calls of the Libyan people for help would go unanswered. The democratic values that we stand for would be overrun. Moreover, the words of the international community would be rendered hollow."). See also, "Statement on the Situation in Libya," August 21, 2011 ("The surest way for the bloodshed to end is simple: Muammar Qadhafi and his regime need to recognize that their rule has come to an end.").

85. "Remarks on the Situation in Libya From Brasilia," March 19, 2011.

86. Ryan Lizza, "Leading From Behind," *New Yorker*, April 26, 2011.

87. "Address to the Nation on the Situation in Libya," March 28, 2011.

88. "Remarks following a Meeting with King Abdullah II of Jordan," May 17, 2011.

89. "Remarks at Cannes City Hall in Cannes," November 4, 2011 ("In fact, American pilots even flew French fighter jets off a French aircraft carrier in the Mediterranean. Allies don't get any closer than that.").

90. "CNN Fact Check: Comparing Costs of Iraq, Libya Missions," October 23, 2012.

91. "Remarks on the Death of Al Qaida Terrorist Organization Leader Usama bin Laden," May 1, 2011.

92. "Declaration of the G8 on the Arab Springs," May 26–27, 2011.

93. "G8 Declaration: Renewed Commitment for Freedom and Democracy," May 26–27, 2011.

94. "The President's News Conference with Chancellor Angela Merkel of Germany," June 7, 2011.

95. "Remarks on the Attack on the United States Mission in Benghazi, Libya," September 12, 2012.

96. The father, Hafez al-Assad, ruled Syria from 1971 to 2000, when his son, Bashar, took over. See "Statement on the Situation in Syria," April 8, 2011; and "Statement on the Situation in Syria," April 22, 2011.

97. "Statement on the Situation in Syria," August 18, 2011.

98. "Statement on the Arab League's Actions Regarding Syria," November 12, 2011.

99. "Statement on the Situation in Syria," February 4, 2012.

100. "Remarks at the Department of State," May 19, 2011.

101. "The President's News Conference," August 20, 2012.

102. "Remarks on the Situation in Syria," August 31, 2013.

103. "The President's News Conference with Prime Minister John Fredrik Reinfeldt of Sweden in Stockholm, Sweden," September 4, 2013.

104. "Remarks with United Kingdom Foreign Secretary Hague," September 9, 2013.

105. "Address to the Nation on the Situation in Syria," September 10, 2013.

106. "Statement on the Framework Agreement between Russia and the United States on the Elimination of Chemical Weapons in Syria," September 14, 2013.

107. "Chairman's Interview with Emmanuel Macron," Munich Security Conference, February 15, 2020.

108. "Remarks by President Obama in Address to the United Nations General Assembly," September 24, 2013.

109. Ibid.

110. Mark Mazzetti, Adam Goldman, and Michael S. Schmidt, "Behind the Sudden Death of a $1 Billion Secret C.I.A. War in Syria," *New York Times*, August 2, 2017.

111. "The President's News Conference with Chancellor Angela Merkel of Germany in Berlin, Germany," June 19, 2013.

112. David Remnick, "Going the Distance: On and Off the Road with Barack Obama," *New Yorker*, January 19, 2014.

113. "Remarks by the President at the United States Military Academy Commencement Ceremony," May 28, 2014.

114. Ibid.

115. "Address to the Nation on United States Strategy to Combat the Islamic State of Iraq and the Levant (ISIL) Terrorist Organization," September 10, 2014.

116. "Remarks Following a Meeting with Prime Minister Haider al-Abadi of Iraq in New York City," September 24, 2014.

117. "Remarks to the United Nations General Assembly in New York City," September 24, 2014.

118. "Remarks on the Situation in Syria," September 23, 2014.

119. "The President's News Conference in Krün, Germany," June 8, 2015.

120. "Remarks on United States Efforts to Combat the Islamic State of Iraq and the Levant (ISIL) Terrorist Organization and an Exchange with Reporters," July 6, 2015. Until then, there had been no ISIL-directed attacks against the United States, although there was one ISIL-inspired lone wolf attack in Garland, Texas, where two perpetrators injured a police officer. As Obama noted, "the threat of lone wolves or small cells of terrorists is complex" and "one of the most difficult challenges" to address, requiring a "larger battle for hearts and minds [in] a generational struggle. In the United States, ISIL-inspired attacks occurred in December 2015 in San Bernardino, California, killing fourteen and in June 2016, in Orlando, Florida, killing forty-nine.

121. Both the attacks in Paris and Brussels were planned by ISIL in Syria.

122. "Remarks on United States Strategy to Counter the Islamic State of Iraq and the Levant (ISIL) Terrorist Organization at the Pentagon in Arlington, Virginia," December 14, 2015; U.S. Army, "Operation Inherent Resolve Reached Turning Point at Ramadi, Commander Says," August 12, 2016.

123. "The President's News Conference," October 2, 2015.

124. "Statement by the President as Chair of the United Nations Leaders' Summit on Countering ISIL and Violent Extremism," September 29, 2015.

125. "Remarks to the United Nations General Assembly in New York City," September 28, 2015.

126. "The President's News Conference," October 2, 2015.

127. Ibid.

128. Ibid.

129. "The President's News Conference with President François Hollande of France," November 24, 2015.

130. "The President's News Conference," December 18, 2015.

131. "Letter to Congressional Leaders on the Global Deployment of United States Combat-Equipped Armed Forces," June 13, 2016.

132. Kathleen J. McInnis, "Coalition Contributions to Countering the Islamic State," Congressional Research Service, August 24, 2016.

133. "Letter to the Nation on Cabinet Member Exit Memorandums," January 4, 2017.

134. "Joint Statement by President Obama and President Viktor Yanukovych of Ukraine," April 12, 2010 (recognizing the "countries' common interests and shared

values mirrored in the Charter: democracy, economic freedom and prosperity, security and territorial integrity, energy security, cooperation in the defense arena, the rule of law and people-to-people contacts").

135. "EU Rejects Russia 'Veto' on Ukraine Agreement," BBC, November 29, 2013.

136. "Address before a Joint Session of the Congress on the State of the Union," January 28, 2014.

137. "Remarks on the Situation in Ukraine," February 28, 2014.

138. "Joint Statement by Group of Seven Leaders on the Situation in Ukraine," March 2, 2014; "Executive Order 13660—Blocking Property of Certain Persons Contributing to the Situation in Ukraine, March 6, 2014"; and "Executive Order 13661—Blocking Property of Additional Persons Contributing to the Situation in Ukraine," March 16, 2014.

139. "Address by President of the Russian Federation," March 18, 2014.

140. Ibid.

141. Ibid.

142. See "Remarks following a Meeting with Prime Minister Arseniy Yatsenyuk of Ukraine and an Exchange with Reporters," March 12, 2014; and "Remarks on the Situation in Ukraine," March 17, 2014.

143. "The President's News Conference with Prime Minister Mark Rutte of the Netherlands in The Hague," Netherlands, March 25, 2014.

144. "The President's News Conference," August 9, 2013. One senior EU official argued that this view was "probably correct," but "needlessly offensive to the Russian mind." Interview with senior EU official, November 8, 2019.

145. "Remarks on the Situation in Ukraine," March 20, 2014.

146. "The President's News Conference with President Herman Van Rompuy of the European Council and President José Manuel Durão Barroso of the European Commission in Brussels, Belgium," March 26, 2014.

147. "Remarks to European Youth in Brussels, Belgium," March 26, 2014.

148. Ibid.

149. Ibid.

150. Ibid.

151. "Joint Geneva Statement on Ukraine from April 17."

152. "Joint Statement by Group of Seven Leaders on the Situation in Ukraine," April 26, 2014.

153. "Statement on the European Reassurance Initiative," February 2, 2016.

154. "Remarks on the 25th Anniversary of Freedom Day in Warsaw, Poland," June 4, 2014.

155. "Remarks at Nordea Concert Hall in Tallinn, Estonia," September 3, 2014.

156. "The President's News Conference in Newport, Wales," September 5, 2014.

157. "Remarks to the United Nations General Assembly in New York City," September 24, 2014.

158. "Remarks in Hannover, Germany," April 25, 2016.

159. "Remarks on the Situation in Ukraine and an Exchange With Reporters," July 29, 2014.

160. "Joint Statement—Group of Seven Leaders' Declaration," June 8, 2015.

161. Ibid.

162. But even President George H. W. Bush—during the implosion of the communist bloc and only three months before the collapse of the Soviet Union—spoke at the Verkhovna Rada, Ukraine's parliament, with an affirmative non-escalatory and cautionary message.

163. "Remarks with Prime Minister David Cameron of the United Kingdom, President José Manuel Durão Barroso of the European Commission, and President Herman Van Rompuy of the European Council in Lough Erne, Northern Ireland," June 17, 2013.

164. "Joint Statement by President Obama, President Herman Van Rompuy of the European Council, and President José Manuel Durão Barroso of the European Commission," February 13, 2013.

165. "The President's News Conference with Chancellor Angela Merkel of Germany in Berlin, Germany," June 19, 2013.

166. "Remarks at the Brandenburg Gate in Berlin, Germany," June 19, 2013.

167. Ben Rhodes, "How Trump Designed His White House to Fail," *Atlantic*, March 13, 2020.

168. "Joint Statement by Group of Seven Leaders: The Brussels G-7 Summit Declaration," June 5, 2014.

169. "The President's News Conference," August 6, 2014.

170. Ibid.

171. "Remarks on the Ebola Outbreak in West Africa at the Centers for Disease Control and Prevention in Atlanta, Georgia," September 16, 2014.

172. "UN Announces Mission to Combat Ebola, Declares Outbreak 'Threat to Peace and Security,'" September 18, 2014.

173. "Remarks at a United Nations Meeting on the Ebola Outbreak in West Africa in New York City," September 25, 2014.

174. "Remarks at the Global Health Security Agenda Summit," September 26, 2014.

175. "Remarks and a Question-and-Answer Session at a Young Leaders of the United Kingdom Town Hall Meeting in London, England," April 23, 2016.

176. "Address before a Joint Session of the Congress on the State of the Union," January 12, 2016.

177. "EU Council Decision Amending Decision 2010/413/CFSP Concerning Restrictive Measures against Iran," January 23, 2012

178. See William Burns, *The Back Channel: A Memoir of American Diplomacy and the Case for Its Renewal* (Random House, 2019).

179. "The President's News Conference in Issy-les-Moulineaux, France," December 1, 2015.

180. "Remarks to the United Nations General Assembly in New York City," September 28, 2015.

181. "The President's News Conference with Prime Minister David W. D. Cameron of the United Kingdom in London, England," April 22, 2016.

182. "Remarks following a Meeting with President Donald Franciszek Tusk of the European Council and President Jean-Claude Juncker of the European Commission in Warsaw, Poland," July 8, 2016.

183. Ibid. ("Given our shared interests, Europe will remain a cornerstone of America's engagement with the world. European countries are and will remain among our closest allies and friends, and Europe is an indispensable partner around the globe.").

184. "Remarks in Hannover, Germany," April 25, 2016.

185. Ibid. See also "Remarks Following a Meeting With President Donald Franciszek Tusk of the European Council and President Jean-Claude Juncker of the European Commission in Warsaw, Poland," July 8, 2016 ("Given our shared interests, Europe will remain a cornerstone of America's engagement with the world. European countries are and will remain among our closest allies and friends, and Europe is an indispensable partner around the globe.").

186. "Remarks to the United Nations General Assembly in New York City," September 20, 2016.

187. "The Inaugural Address," January 20, 2017.

Chapter 3

1. "Remarks at the Democratic National Convention in Philadelphia, Pennsylvania," July 27, 2016 ("I can say with confidence there has never been a man or a woman—not me, not Bill, nobody—more qualified than Hillary Clinton to serve as President of the United States of America.").

2. "The Inaugural Address," January 20, 2017.

3. See Robert Jervis, Francis J. Gavin, Joshua Rovner, and Diane Labrosse, editors, *Chaos in the Liberal Order: The Trump Presidency and International Politics in the Twenty-First Century* (Columbia University Press, 2018); Hanns W. Maull, *The Rise and Decline of the Post-Cold War International Order* (Oxford University Press, 2018); and Edward Luce, *The Retreat of Western Liberalism* (Atlantic Monthly Press, 2018).

4. See, for example, Jon Finer, "Trump Has No Foreign Policy," *Politico*, February 19, 2017; Bart M. J. Szewczyk, Less is More? The US at the UN, EUISS Brief, October 11, 2017; and European Political Strategy Centre, "Geopolitical Outlook for Europe: Confrontation vs Cooperation," June 8, 2018. But, also see Michael Anton, "The Trump Doctrine," *Foreign Policy*, April 20, 2019; Hal Brands, *American Grand Strategy in the Age of Trump* (Brookings, 2018); and Brendan Simms and Charlie Laderman, *Donald Trump: The Making of a World View* (Lume Books, 2017).

5. Ryan Lizza, "Waiting for Obama," *Politico*, November 26, 2019.

6. Compare "Remarks at a Working Lunch on North Atlantic Treaty Organization Burden-Sharing and an Exchange with Reporters in Chandler's Cross, United Kingdom," December 4, 2019 with "Remarks Prior to a Meeting with Prime Minister Giuseppe Conte of Italy and an Exchange with Reporters in Chandler's Cross, United Kingdom," December 4, 2019.

7. "President Trump Clarifies Comment about Iran Protests: We Support Them, But Not Financially," December 3, 2019.

8. Glenn Kessler, Salvador Rizzo, and Meg Kelly, "President Trump Made 16,241 False or Misleading Claims in His First Three Years," *Washington Post*, January 20, 2020.

9. "Remarks by President Trump and Prime Minister May of the United Kingdom in Joint Press Conference," July 13, 2018.

10. European Political Strategy Centre, "Geopolitical Outlook for Europe: Confrontation vs Cooperation," June 8, 2018.

11. Fareed Zakaria, "Here's the Problem with Trump's Foreign Policy, CNN, Global Public Square, January 12, 2017.

12. See, for example, "Remarks by A/S Wess Mitchell: Anchoring the Western Alliance," Heritage Foundation, Washington, DC, June 5, 2018.

13. "Trump Worries NATO with 'Obsolete' Comment," BBC, January 16, 2017.

14. For instance, his campaign manager, later convicted for tax and bank fraud, removed from the Republic Party platform references to assisting Ukraine in its conflict with Russia.

15. U.S. Intelligence Community Assessment, "Assessing Russian Activities and Intentions in Recent US Elections," January 6, 2017.

16. Michael J. Morell, "I Ran the C.I.A. Now I'm Endorsing Hillary Clinton," *New York Times*, August 5, 2016.

17. "Russians Rejoice in Trump's Win, but America's Allies Are Anxious," CBS, November 9, 2016.

18. Andrew Kaczynski, Chris Massie, and Nathan McDermott, "80 Times Trump Talked about Putin," CNN, March 2017.

19. Peter Bergen, *Trump and His Generals: The Cost of Chaos* (Penguin Random House, 2019). See also, David Choi, "'What the Hell Were You Thinking?': Trump Berated White House Staff For Not Telling Him Putin Was Trying to Call Him," *Business Insider*, January 2, 2020 ("'Are you kidding me? Vladimir Putin tried to call me, and you didn't put him through? What the hell were you thinking?' Trump said.").

20. "The President's News Conference with Prime Minister Theresa May of the United Kingdom," January 27, 2017; "Trump Speaks with Putin in Saturday Phone Call," NPR, January 29, 2017.

21. K. K. Rebecca Lai, "Every Time Trump Has Talked to Putin," *New York Times*, January 15, 2019.

22. "Remarks in an Exchange with Reporters Aboard Air Force One En Route to Hanoi, Vietnam," November 11, 2017 ("Q: How did you bring up the issue of election meddling? Did you ask him a question? The President: He just—every time he sees me, he says, 'I didn't do that.' And I believe—I really believe that when he tells me that, he means it. . . . And then, you hear it's 17 agencies. Well, it's three. And one is Brennan, and one is whatever. I mean, give me a break. They're political hacks.").

23. "The President's News Conference with President Tran Dai Quang of Vietnam in Hanoi, Vietnam," November 12, 2017 ("What I said there is that I believe he be-

lieves that, and that's very important for somebody to believe. I believe that he feels that he and Russia did not meddle in the election. . . . As to whether I believe it or not, I'm with our agencies, especially as currently constituted with their leadership.").

24. "Remarks by President Trump and President Putin of the Russian Federation in Joint Press Conference," July 16, 2018 ("Q: President Putin, did you want President Trump to win the election? And did you direct any of your officials to help him do that? PRESIDENT PUTIN: [As interpreted] Yes, I did. Yes, I did. Because he talked about bringing the U.S.-Russia relationship back to normal.").

25. "Remarks by President Trump and President Putin of the Russian Federation in Joint Press Conference," July 16, 2018 ("My people came to me—Dan Coats came to me and some others—they said they think it's Russia. I have President Putin; he just said it's not Russia. I will say this: I don't see any reason why it would be, but I really do want to see the server. But I have—I have confidence in both parties. . . . So I have great confidence in my intelligence people, but I will tell you that President Putin was extremely strong and powerful in his denial today.").

26. "The President's News Conference with President Emmanuel Macron of France in Biarritz, France," August 26, 2019.

27. "Remarks and an Exchange with Reporters Prior to Departure for Atlanta, Georgia," November 8, 2019.

28. The Churchill Society, "The Russian Enigma," October 1, 1939.

29. The Moscow Project, "Trump's Russia Cover-Up by the Numbers—272 Contacts with Russia-Linked Operatives," April 30, 2019.

30. John Bolton, *The Room Where It Happened* (Simon & Schuster, 2020).

31. "Sen. Kay Bailey Hutchinson's Confirmation Hearing for U.S. Ambassador to NATO," January 3, 2017.

32. "President Trump and Prime Minister May's Opening Remarks," January 27, 2017; "Remarks at a Welcoming Ceremony for President Emmanuel Macron of France," April 24, 2018.

33. "Remarks by the Vice President at the Munich Security Conference," February 18, 2017

34. "Remarks at the Arab Islamic American Summit in Riyadh, Saudi Arabia," May 21, 2017.

35. "Remarks by the Vice President and European Council President Tusk," February 20, 2017.

36. "Remarks by the Vice President and NATO Secretary General Stoltenberg at a JPA," February 20, 2017.

37. "Xi Jinping's Keynote Speech at the World Economic Forum," April 6, 2017.

38. "Russia's Foreign Minister Wants a 'Post-West World Order,'" February 17, 2017.

39. Nicholas Vinocur, "Trump Handed Merkel 'Outrageous' NATO Bill: Report," *Politico*, March 26, 2017. See also, "Joint Press Conference with President Trump and German Chancellor Merkel," March 17, 2017.

40. Peter Müller, "The Germans Are Bad, Very Bad," *Der Spiegel*, May 26, 2017.

41. Susan B. Glasser, "Trump National Security Team Blindsided by NATO Speech," *Politico*, June 5, 2017.

42. "Remarks by President Trump at NATO Unveiling of the Article 5 and Berlin Wall Memorials—Brussels, Belgium," May 25, 2017.

43. "Statement by President Trump on the Paris Climate Accord," June 1, 2017.

44. "Readout of President Donald J. Trump's Meeting with European Union Leaders," May 25, 2017.

45. "The President's News Conference with President Klaus Iohannis of Romania," June 9, 2017.

46. "The President's News Conference with Secretary General Jens Stoltenberg of the North Atlantic Treaty Organization," April 12, 2017.

47. Josh Rogin, "Trump Is Trying to Destabilize the European Union," *Washington Post*, June 29, 2018; "Remarks by President Trump and Prime Minister May of the United Kingdom in Joint Press Conference," July 13, 2018 ("Are you still threatening to potentially pull the United States out of NATO for any reason? And do you believe you can do that without Congress's explicit support and approval? THE PRESIDENT: I think I probably can, but that's unnecessary.")

48. Robbie Gramer, "Trump Discovers Article 5 after Disastrous NATO Visit," *Foreign Policy*, June 9, 2017.

49. Interview with Rose Gottemoeller, January 21, 2020.

50. Giulia Paravicini, "Angela Merkel: Europe Must Take 'Our Fate' Into Own Hands," May 28, 2017.

51. "Speech by Federal Chancellor Dr Angela Merkel at the Ceremony Awarding the International Charlemagne Prize to French President Emmanuel Macron in Aachen on 10 May 2018."

52. "Statement by President Trump on Syria," April 13, 2018. Antony J. Blinken, "After the Missiles, We Need Smart Diplomacy on Syria," *New York Times*, April 7, 2018.

53. "Remarks by President Trump and President Macron of France at Arrival Ceremony," April 24, 2018.

54. Hanne Cokelaere, "Macron-Trump 'Friendship' Tree Dies," *Politico*, June 10, 2019.

55. "The President's News Conference with Prime Minister Stefan Löfven of Sweden," March 6, 2018.

56. "Remarks by President Trump and President Macron of France before Restricted Bilateral Meeting," April 24, 2018.

57. Rogin, "Trump Is Trying to Destabilize the European Union"; and Andrew Gray, "Macron on Trump Suggestion to Leave EU: 'You Can Imagine My Response,'" *Politico*, June 29, 2018.

58. "Remarks by President Trump and President Macron of France Before Restricted Bilateral Meeting," April 24, 2018.

59. "Remarks by President Trump and Secretary General Stoltenberg of NATO before Bilateral Meeting," May 17, 2018.

60. "I Think the European Union Is a Foe," Trump Says Ahead of Putin Meeting in Helsinki," CBS News, July 15, 2018.

61. "Remarks by President Trump on the Joint Comprehensive Plan of Action," May 8, 2018.

62. "Remarks by President Donald Tusk Ahead of the EU-Western Balkans Summit and the Leaders' Agenda Dinner," May 16, 2018.

63. Ibid.

64. Ibid.

65. Michael D. Shear and Catherine Porter, "Trump Refuses to Sign G-7 Statement and Calls Trudeau 'Weak,'" *New York Times*, June 9, 2018.

66. "Remarks by President Trump and NATO Secretary General Jens Stoltenberg at Bilateral Breakfast," July 11, 2018

67. "Remarks by President Trump and Prime Minister May of the United Kingdom in Joint Press Conference," July 13, 2018.

68. "Joint EU-U.S. Statement following President Juncker's visit to the White House," July 25, 2018.

69. "Remarks by President Trump and President Juncker of the European Commission in Joint Press Statements," July 25, 2018.

70. "Remarks by President Trump and Prime Minister Conte of Italy in Joint Press Conference," July 30, 2018.

71. "Remarks by President Trump and President Mattarella of the Italian Republic before Bilateral Meeting," October 16, 2019.

72. "Remarks by Secretary Pompeo at the German Marshall Fund," December 4, 2018.

73. Sharon LaFraniere, Michael Crowley, and Michael S. Schmidt, "Gordon Sondland Elbowed His Way Into Ukraine Policy. It Could Cost Him," *New York Times*, October 16, 2019.

74. "Audrey Wilson, "Trump Gives Erdogan Green Light for Syria Incursion," *Foreign Policy*, October 7, 2019.

75. Interview with Rose Gottemoeller, January 21, 2020.

76. John F. Harris, Florian Eder, and Ryan Heath, "Trump Roars, and Davos Shrugs," *Politico*, January 23, 2020.

77. "Remarks by President Trump to the 73rd Session of the United Nations General Assembly," September 25, 2018.

78. Interview with German foreign policy expert, January 9, 2020.

79. Ibid.

80. Interview with Rose Gottemoeller, January 21, 2020.

81. Interview with Wolfgang Ischinger, January 9, 2020.

82. Interview with senior German government official, February 21, 2020.

83. Interview with senior EU official, March 10, 2020.

84. "Remarks by President Trump to the People of Poland," July 6, 2017.

85. "Remarks by President Trump to the 72nd Session of the United Nations General Assembly," September 19, 2017.

86. "Remarks by President Trump to the World Economic Forum," January 26, 2018.

87. "Emmanuel Macron's Speech at the United States Congress," April 25, 2018.

88. "Emmanuel Macron's Speech at Paris Peace Forum," November 11, 2018.

89. "Speech by Federal Chancellor Angela Merkel to the European Parliament, Strasbourg," November 13, 2018.

90. "Remarks by President Trump to the 74th Session of the United Nations General Assembly," September 24, 2019.

91. Michael Anton, "The Trump Doctrine," *Foreign Policy*, April 20, 2019.

92. Ibid.

93. Edward Luce, "Henry Kissinger: 'We are In a Very, Very Grave Period,'" *Financial Times*, July 20, 2018.

94. Somini Sengupta, "Nikki Haley Puts U.N. on Notice: U.S. Is 'Taking Names,'" *New York Times*, January 27, 2017.

95. The Trump administration's limited diplomatic achievements in the Middle East in brokering new relations between Israel and several regional countries, such as Bahrain and the United Arab Emirates, were valuable but have been largely overshadowed by the administration's incoherent strategy in the region.

96. "A Conversation With Nikki Haley," Council on Foreign Relations, March 29, 2017.

97. "Remarks at a UN Security Council Thematic Briefing on UN Peacekeeping Operations," April 6, 2017.

98. "Remarks by President Trump at a Working Lunch with U.N. Security Council Ambassadors," April 24, 2017.

99. António Guterres, "Remarks to the Security Council Open Debate on 'Maintenance of International Peace and Security: Conflict Prevention and Sustaining Peace,'" January 10, 2017.

100. "Conversation with Dr. Subrahmanyam Jaishankar," Munich Security Conference, February 14, 2020.

101. Interview with David O'Sullivan, October 28, 2019.

102. Interview with senior EU official, March 10, 2020.

103. Ibid.

104. Ibid.

105. Ibid.

106. Interview with senior EU official, November 8, 2019.

107. Ibid.

108. Ibid.

109. See "Remarks by Vice President Pence at the Frederic V. Malek Memorial Lecture," October 24, 2019 ("President Xi himself, I'm told, said in a once-secret speech

shortly after his rise as Party General Secretary that China must 'conscientiously prepare for all aspects of long-term cooperation and struggle between the two social systems.' He also told his colleagues at that time not to underestimate the resilience of the West. And there was wisdom in those words."); "Remarks by National Security Advisor Ambassador Robert O'Brien at 2019 Atlantic Future Forum," November 25, 2019 (arguing that U.S. "allies such as the United Kingdom, who are fairly sharing the burden of the defense of the West by commissioning ships [whose] deployment will send an important message to China that the West retains the capability and will to protect Indo-Pacific sea lanes.").

110. Quoted in "NATO Secretary General Addresses Historic Joint Meeting of the United States Congress," April 3, 2019.

Chapter 4

1. See Michael A. Cohen and Micah Zenko, *Clear and Present Safety: The World Has Never Been Better and Why That Matters to Americans* (Yale University Press, 2019).

2. See, for example, Ian Bremmer, *Us vs. Them: The Failure of Globalism* (Penguin, 2019).

3. See also, Congressional Research Service, *Real Wage Trends, 1979 to 2017,* March 15, 2018; European Commission, "European Semester Thematic Factsheet: Addressing Inequalities."

4. Jeff D. Colgan and Robert O. Keohane, "The Liberal Order Is Rigged: Fix It Now or Watch It Wither," *Foreign Affairs* 96, no. 3 (May/June 2017), pp. 36–44.

5. See Congressional Research Service, *Real Wage Trends, 1979 to 2017,* March 15, 2018; European Commission, "European Semester Thematic Factsheet: Addressing Inequalities."

6. Amy Chua, *Political Tribes: Group Instincts and the Fate of Nations* (Penguin, 2019).

7. See, for example, Graham Allison, *Destined for War: Can America and China Escape Thucydides's Trap?* (Houghton Mifflin Harcourt, 2017); and Gilbert Rozman, *The Sino-Russian Challenge to the World Order: National Identities, Bilateral Relations, and East versus West in the 2010s* (Stanford University Press, 2014).

8. See Parag Khanna, *The Future Is Asian* (Simon & Schuster, 2019); Bruno Maçães, *Belt and Road: A Chinese World Order* (Kurst, 2019); Sulmaan Wasif Khan, *Haunted by Chaos: China's Grand Strategy from Mao Zedong to Xi Jinping* (Harvard University Press, 2018); Bruno Maçães, *Dawn of Eurasia: On the Trail of the New World Order* (Yale University Press, 2018).

9. See, generally, Angela Stent, *Putin's World: Russia Against the West and with the Rest* (Basic Books, 2019); Robert Legvold, *Return to Cold War* (Polity, 2016); Angela Stent, *The Limits of Partnership: U.S.-Russian Relations in the Twenty-First Century* (Princeton University Press, 2015); Andrei P. Tsygankov, *Russia and the West from Alexander to Putin: Honor in International Relations* (Cambridge University Press, 2012); and Robert Legvold, editor, *Russian Foreign Policy in the Twenty-First Century and the Shadow of the Past* (Columbia University Press, 2007).

10. See Dmitri Trenin, "The World Through Moscow's Eyes: A Classic Russian Perspective," Carnegie Moscow Center, March 3, 2020.

11. One former senior EU official argued that Russia is inherently a great power due to its sheer territorial size, nearly twice the size of the United States or China.

12. Remarks by Celeste Wallander, "Special Assistant to the President and Senior Director for Russia and Central Asia on U.S. Policy on Russia," June 26, 2015.

13. "Speech by President Donald Tusk at the Ukrainian Parliament in Kyiv," February 19, 2019 ("There can be no just Europe without an independent Ukraine. That there can be no safe Europe without a safe Ukraine. To put it simply: there can be no Europe without Ukraine!").

14. "The European Union's Global Strategy: Three Years On, Moving Forward," June 13, 2019 ("Politically, we have seen the emergence of different political narratives, some of which openly contest the values underpinning liberal democracies worldwide, and those of the EU itself. Greater contestation is playing out both globally and regionally, particularly in areas already experiencing fragilities, conflicts and rivalries. Nowhere is this clearer than in the EU's surrounding regions, both east and south. The EU itself has not been immune to the effects of greater contestation worldwide: the resilience and security of the Union are at stake. All this is equally harming the rules-based global order—an existential interest of our Union—precisely when multilateralism is most acutely needed. . . . The rules-based international order, centered on International Law, including Human Rights and International Humanitarian Law, is an existential interest of the Union.").

15. See John Bolton, *The Room Where It Happened* (Simon & Schuster, 2020).

16. See, generally, David C. Kang, *American Grand Strategy and East Asian Security in the Twenty-First Century* (Cambridge University Press, 2017); Michael R. Auslin, *The End of the Asian Century: War, Stagnation, and the Risks to the World's Most Dynamic Region* (Yale University Press, 2017); Parag Khanna, *Connectography: Mapping the Future of Global Civilization* (Simon & Schuster, 2016); Thomas Christensen, *The China Challenge: Shaping the Choices of a Rising Power* (W. W. Norton, 2016); Noah Feldman, *Cool War: The Future of Global Competition* (Random House, 2013); Henry Kissinger, *On China* (Allen Lane Penguin, 2011); and Joshua Kurlantzick, *Charm Offensive: How China's Soft Power Is Transforming the World* (Yale University Press, 2008).

17. Hillary Clinton, "America's Pacific Century," *Foreign Policy*, October 11, 2011.

18. Interview with David O'Sullivan, October 28, 2019.

19. "A Global Strategy for the European Union," 2016.

20. "Joint Communication, Connecting Europe and Asia—Building Blocks for an EU Strategy," 2018) (hereinafter "EU-Asia Connectivity Strategy").

21. "EU-Asia Connectivity Strategy," p. 1.

22. Data from World Bank Open Data.

23. With the exception of France and Great Britain, most of Europe has shown only limited interest in security in the Asia-Pacific region.

24. European External Action Service, "A Global Strategy for the European Union," 2016.

25. See, for example, Philippe Le Corre, "China's Rise as a Geoeconomic Influencer: Four European Case Studies," Carnegie Endowment for International Peace, October 2018.

26. See, generally, European Parliament, "Research for TRAN Committee: The New Silk Route—Opportunities and Challenges for EU Transport," 2018.

27. European External Action Service, "A Global Strategy for the European Union," 2016.

Chapter 5

1. Interview with Wolfgang Ischinger, January 9, 2020.

2. Admittedly, our interviewees were split on this issue. For instance, Doug Lute, former U.S. ambassador to NATO, saw the need for a "superstructure" overseeing both NATO and the EU in the future. On the other hand, Anthony Gardner, former U.S. ambassador to the EU, was "skeptical" of new institutional arrangements, requiring a high burden of proof for their utility.

3. "Remarks Following the European Union-United States Summit in Lisbon," November 20, 2010.

4. "Text of Kissinger's Speech at A. P. Meeting Here on U.S. Relations with Europe," April 24, 1973.

5. "Davos 2017—A Conversation with Henry Kissinger on the World in 2017," January 20, 2017. See also, Henry A. Kissinger and Lawrence H. Summers, Renewing the Atlantic Partnership, Report of an Independent Task Force, Sponsored by the Council on Foreign Relations (March 2004).

6. Henry Kissinger, *World Order* (Penguin, 2014).

7. National Security Strategy Archive, "A National Security Strategy of Engagement and Enlargement," July 1, 1994.

8. "Chairman's Interview with Emmanuel Macron," Munich Security Conference, February 15, 2020.

9. EUNAVFOR MED, EU NAVFOR Atalanta, EUFOR Althea, EUTM Mali, EUTM Somalia, and EUTM RCA.

10. EULEX Kosovo, EUMM Georgia, EUAM Ukraine, EUBAM Moldova and Ukraine, EUCAP Sahel Niger, EUPOL COPPS/Palestinian Territories, EUBAM Rafah, EUCAP Sahel Mali, EUAM Iraq, EUCAP Somalia, and EUBAM Libya.

11. The other missions include NATO Mission Iraq (NMI) (including several hundred trainers and starting in autumn 2018); Operation Althea (operational command headed by NATO Deputy Supreme Allied Commander Europe); Iceland's "Peacetime Preparedness Needs," Operation Sea Guardian (OSG), NATO Patriot Mission in Turkey, and NATO Air Policing.

12. Samantha Power, citing Richard Holbrooke, once quipped in the context of the United Nations that blaming the Security Council for its failures was akin to blaming

Madison Square Garden for the way the basketball team the New York Knicks play. The same principle applies to the EU and NATO.

13. See Carmen-Cristina Cîrlig, The EU's Mutual Assistance Clause: First Ever Activation of Article 42(7) TEU, Briefing, European Parliamentary Research Service, November 2015.

14. See European Council on Foreign Relations (ECFR), "Article 42.7: An Explainer," November 2015.

15. See NATO, KFOR, History.

16. See EULEX, "EULEX Head Met with KFOR Commander," December 18, 2018.

17. The EU and NATO, "Third Progress Report on the Implementation of the Common Set of Proposals Endorsed by NATO and EU Councils on 6 December 2016 and 5 December 2017," May 2018.

18. See Margriet Drent, "Militarising Migration? EU and NATO Involvement at the European Border," *Clingendael Spectator* 72, no. 4 (2018).

19. See NATO, "NATO Mission in Iraq (NMI)," Factsheet, December 2018.

20. CBDR is a principle from the 1992 UN Framework Convention on Climate Change (UNFCCC). By making emission targets nationally determined and public, the Paris Agreement, for the first time, made all parties accountable. Paris also included in the Agreement the clause "in light of different national circumstances." This clause was originally proposed at the Conference of the Parties before Paris in 2014 in Lima, so the concept was not new.

21. Daniel Boffey, Kate Connolly, and Anushka Asthana, "EU to Bypass Trump Administration after Paris Climate Agreement Pullout," *The Guardian*, June 2, 2017.

22. Marine Pennetier, "Macron Says Europe-China Climate Cooperation 'Decisive,'" Reuters, November 5, 2019.

23. "From Left to Right, European Leaders Bash Donald Trump," *Politico*, June 2, 2017.

24. "Remarks by President Donald Tusk after the EU-China Summit in Brussels," June 2, 2017.

25. "EU to Bypass Trump Administration after Paris Climate Agreement Pullout," *The Guardian*, June 2, 2017.

26. "Remarks by President Donald Trump after the EU-China Summit in Brussels," June 2, 2017.

27. Ellen MacArthur Foundation website, https://www.ellenmacarthurfoundation.org.

28. Environmental Protection Agency website, "EPA Sustainable Materials Management Program Strategic Plan for Fiscal Years 2017–2022."

29. European Commission website, "Energy, Climate Change, Environment," February 26, 2019.

30. "Press Remarks by President Von Der Leyen on the Occasion of the Adoption of the European Green Deal Communication," December 11, 2019.

31. Andrea Kendall-Taylor, Erica Frantz, and Joseph Wright, "The Digital Dictators," *Foreign Affairs* (March/April 2020), p. 104.

32. Ibid., p. 106.

33. David Sanger, *The Perfect Weapon: War, Sabotage, and Fear in the Cyber Age* (New York: Crown, 2018) p. xii.

34. Ibid., p. xiv.

35. Ibid., p. 8.

36. Ibid., p. 8.

37. Ibid., p. 11.

38. Ibid., p. 162.

39. "National Cyber Strategy of the United States of America" (US Government Printing Office, 2018).

40. "Summary: Department of Defense Cyber Strategy, 2018" (U.S. Government, 2018).

41. Dustin Volz, "White House Confirms It Has Relaxed Rules on U.S. Use of Cyberweapons," *Wall Street Journal*, September 20, 2018.

42. Annie Fixler and David Maxwell, "Midterm Assessment: Cyber" (Foundation for Defense of Democracies, 2019).

43. Ibid., p. 152.

44. Ibid., p. 153.

45. Ibid., p. 157.

46. Ibid., p. 181.

47. Ibid., p. 182.

48. Robert Emmott, "NATO's Cyber Command to be Fully Operational in 2023," Reuters, October 16, 2018.

49. Daniel Boffey, "EU to Run War Games to Prepare for Chinese and Russian Cyber Attacks," *The Guardian*, June 27, 2019.

50. Patrick Tucker, "NATO Getting More Aggressive on Offensive Cyber," *DefenseOne*, May 24, 2019.

51. "National Cyber Strategy of the United States of America" (U.S. Government Printing Office, 2018).

52. Amy Zegart, "America's Misbegotten Cyber Strategy," *The Atlantic*, February 2, 2019.

53. Jared Cohen, "Digital Counterinsurgency," *Foreign Affairs*, November/December 2015, p. 55.

54. "Putin: Leader in Artificial Intelligence Will Rule World," CNBC, September 4, 2017.

55. Keith Bradsher, "How China Obtains American Trade Secrets," *New York Times*, January 15, 2020.

56. Levi Tillemann and Colin McCormick, "Roadmapping a U.S.-German Agenda for Artificial Intelligence Policy," *New America Foundation* (2017), p. 5.

57. National Security Strategy of the United States, December 2017.

58. Ibid.

59. Ursula von der Leyen, "A Union That Strives For More: Political Guidelines for the Next Commission 2019–2024."

60. European Commission, "White Paper on Artificial Intelligence: A European Approach to Excellence and Trust," February 19, 2020.

61. European Commission, "A European Strategy for Data," February 19, 2020.

62. European Commission, "Shaping Europe's Digital Future," February 19, 2020.

63. Tillemann and McCormick, p. 4.

64. Bruegel, "Partnering with Europe on Responsible AI: A Conversation with Sundar Pichai," CEO Google and Alphabet, January 20, 2020.

65. "The President's Weekly Address," April 13, 2018.

66. "Remarks by President Trump at the White House Business Session with Our Nation's Governors," February 10, 2020.

67. David J. Lynch, "Trump's Adversarial Approach on Trade is Far from Over," *Washington Post*, February 19, 2020.

68. "The President's News Conference in Davos," Switzerland, January 22, 2020.

69. "Remarks at a Meeting with Members of the National Governors Association," February 26, 2018.

70. Robert Farley, "Trump Wrong About WTO Record," FactCheck.Org, October 27, 2017.

71. Keith Johnson, "How Trump May Finally Kill the WTO," *Foreign Policy*, December 9, 2019.

72. Mission letter, "Phil Hogan—Commissioner for Trade," December 1, 2019.

73. European Commission, "WTO Modernization," September 18, 2018.

74. Richard Lugar and Barack Obama, "Grounding a Pandemic," *New York Times*, June 6, 2005.

75. WHO, "What We Do," www.who.int/about/what-we-do.

76. WHO, "WHO Emergencies Coronavirus Emergency Committee Second Meeting," January 30, 2020.

77. Bill Gates, "Here Are the Innovations We Need to Reopen the Economy," *Washington Post*, April 23, 2020.

78. Susan Rice, "The Government Has Failed on the Pandemic Threat, but There Is Still Time," *New York Times*, March 13, 2020.

79. Carl Freidersdorf, "Trump Defended Cuts to Public Health Agencies," *The Atlantic*, March 17, 2020.

80. Matthew J. Belvedere, "Trump Says He Trusts China's Xi on Coronavirus and the U.S. Has It 'Totally Under Control,'" CNBC, January 22, 2020.

81. David Leonhardt, "A Complete List of Trump's Attempt's to Play Down Coronavirus," *New York Times*, March 15, 2020.

82. William Wan, Josh Dawsey, and Lori Aranti, "White House Suspends Travel from Most of Europe to The United States," *Washington Post*, March 11, 2020.

83. "Joint Statement by President von der Leyen and President Michel on the U.S. Travel Ban," March 12, 2020.

84. Eleonore Pauwels and Apratim Vidyarhirt, "How Our Unhealthy Cybersecu-

rity Infrastructure Is Hurting Biotechnology, The Wilson Center, March, 2016, p. 4.

85. Gates, "Here are the Innovation We Need to Reopen the Economy."

86. Ibid.

87. Richard Lugar and Barack Obama, "Grounding a Pandemic," *New York Times*, June 6, 2005.

Conclusion

1. Interview with Doug Lute, February 12, 2020.

2. Interview with Bill Burns, January 13, 2020.

3. Interview with John Negroponte, December 17, 2019.

4. Interview with Wolfgang Ischinger, January 9, 2020.

5. Ibid.

6. Interview with Charles Kupchan, January 31, 2020.

7. Interview with Doug Lute, February 12, 2020.

8. Interview with David O'Sullivan, October 28, 2019.

9. Interview with Bill Burns, January 13, 2020.

10. Quoted in Ivo Daalder and James Lindsay, *The Empty Throne: America's Abdication of Global Leadership* (PublicAffairs, 2018).

11. Interview with Charles Kupchan, January 31, 2020.

Appendix

1. Although power also depends on context and the intensity of interests, comparisons of the distribution of power across countries and over time are restricted by necessity to measurable statistics such as material resources.

2. While there is no reliable GDP data for China in 1945, $200 billion is a reasonable estimate given that China's GDP was $288 billion in 1938 and $240 billion in 1950. See Angus Maddison, "Historical Statistics of the World Economy," The Groningen Growth and Development Centre.

Bibliography

Dean Acheson, *Present at the Creation: My Years in the State Department* (New York: W. W. Norton & Company, 1969).

Graham Allison, *Destined for War: Can America and China Escape Thucydides's Trap?* (New York: Houghton Mifflin Harcourt, 2017).

Michael Anton, "The Trump Doctrine," *Foreign Policy*, April 20, 2019, https://for eignpolicy.com/2019/04/20/the-trump-doctrine-big-think-america-first-nation alism/.

Timothy Garton Ash, *Free World: America, Europe, and the Surprising Future of the West* (New York: Random House, 2004).

Michael R. Auslin, *The End of the Asian Century: War, Stagnation, and the Risks to the World's Most Dynamic Region* (Yale University Press, 2017).

Peter Bergen, *Trump and His Generals: The Cost of Chaos* (New York: Penguin Random House, 2019).

Michael R. Beschloss, *Presidents of War: The Epic Story, from 1807 to Modern Times* (New York: Penguin, 2018).

John Bolton, *The Room Where It Happened* (New York: Simon & Schuster, 2020).

Hal Brands, *American Grand Strategy in the Age of Trump* (Brookings, 2018).

Ian Bremmer, *Superpower: Three Choices for America's Role in the World* (New York: Penguin, 2019).

Ian Bremmer, *Us vs. Them: The Failure of Globalism* (New York: Penguin, 2019).

Douglas Brinkley and David R. Facey-Crowther, editors, *The Atlantic Charter* (New York: Palgrave Macmillan, 1994).

Zsolt Darvas and Bruegel, "Income Inequality Has Been Falling in the EU," Bruegel

(blog post), November 23, 2016, www.bruegel.org/2016/11/income-inequality-has
-been-falling-in-the-eu.

Zbigniew Brzezinski, *Strategic Vision: America and the Crisis of Global Power* (New York: Basic Books, 2012).

William Burns, *The Back Channel: A Memoir of American Diplomacy and the Case for Its Renewal* (New York: Random House, 2019).

George Bush and Brent Scowcroft, *A World Transformed* (New York: Random House, 1998).

Thomas Christensen, *The China Challenge: Shaping the Choices of a Rising Power* (New York: W. W. Norton, 2016).

Amy Chua, *Political Tribes: Group Instincts and the Fate of Nations* (New York: Penguin, 2019).

Carmen-Cristina Cîrlig, "The EU's Mutual Assistance Clause: First Ever Activation of Article 42(7) TEU," European Parliamentary Research Service, November 2015, www.europarl.europa.eu/RegData/etudes/BRIE/2015/572799/EPRS_BRI(2015) 572799_EN.pdf.

Jared Cohen, "Digital Counterinsurgency," *Foreign Affairs*, November/December 2015.

Jeff D. Colgan and Robert O. Keohane, "The Liberal Order is Rigged: Fix It Now or Watch It Wither," *Foreign Affairs*, May/June 2017.

Michael A. Cohen and Micah Zenko, *Clear and Present Safety: The World Has Never Been Better and Why that Matters to Americans* (Yale University Press, 2019).

Christopher Coker, *Twilight of the West* (New York: Basic Books, 1997).

Congressional Research Service, *Real Wage Trends, 1979 to 2017*, March 15, 2018.

Correlates of War, Data Sets (2020), https://correlatesofwar.org/data-sets.

Ivo H. Daalder and James M. Lindsay, "The Committee to Save the World Order: America's Allies Must Step Up as America Steps Down," *Foreign Affairs*, November /December 2018.

Ivo Daalder and James Lindsay, *The Empty Throne: America's Abdication of Global Leadership* (New York: PublicAffairs, 2018).

Michael Doyle, *Liberal Peace* (New York: Routledge, 2011).

Margriet Drent, "Militarising Migration? EU and NATO Involvement at the European Border," *Clingendael Spectator* 4, no. 72 (2018), https://spectator.clingendael.org/ pub/2018/4/_/pdf/CS-2018-4-drent.pdf.

European Council on Foreign Relations, "Article 42.7: An Explainer," November 2015, www.ecfr.eu/article/commentary_article_427_an_explainer5019.

European Political Strategy Centre, "Geopolitical Outlook for Europe: Confrontation vs. Cooperation," June 8, 2018, https://euagenda.eu/publications/geopolitical-out look-for-europe-confrontation-vs-cooperation.

Noah Feldman, *Cool War: The Future of Global Competition* (New York: Random House, 2013).

Jon Finer, "Trump has No Foreign Policy," *Politico*, February 19, 2017, www.politico. eu/article/donald-trump-has-no-foreign-policy.

Annie Fixler and David Maxwell, "Midterm Assessment: Cyber," Foundation for

Defense of Democracies, 2019, www.fdd.org/analysis/2019/01/31/midterm-assess
ment-cyber.

Richard Fontaine, "We Need an Atlantic Charter for the Post-Coronavirus Era," *The
Atlantic*, April 16, 2020, www.theatlantic.com/ideas/archive/2020/04/we-need
-new-atlantic-charter/610069.

Rebecca Frankel, "Putin Goes Gansta," *Foreign Policy*, November 13, 2008, https://
foreignpolicy.com/2008/11/13/putin-goes-gangsta/.

Francis Fukuyama, *The Origins of Political Order: From Prehuman Times to the French
Revolution* (New York: Farrar, Straus and Giroux, 2011).

Jonah Goldberg, *Suicide of the West: How the Rebirth of Tribalism, Populism, Nationalism, and Identity Politics is Destroying American Democracy* (New York: Penguin
Random House, 2018).

Philip Gordon and Jeremy Shapiro, *Allies At War: America, Europe and the Split Over
Iraq* (New York: McGraw Hill, 2004).

Robbie Gramer, "Trump Discovers Article 5 after Disastrous NATO Visit," *Foreign
Policy*, June 9, 2017, https://foreignpolicy.com/2017/06/09/trump-discovers-article
-5-after-disastrous-nato-visit-brussels-visit-transatlantic-relationship-europe.

Richard Haass, *A World in Disarray: American Foreign Policy and the Crisis of the Old
Order* (New York: Penguin, 2019).

Richard Haass, *The World: A Brief Introduction* (New York: Penguin, 2020).

Helga Haftendorn, "Germany's Accession to NATO: 50 Years On," *NATO Review*,
June 1, 2005, www.nato.int/docu/review/articles/2005/06/01/germanys-accession
-to-nato-50-years-on/index.html.

Gunther Hellmann and Benjamin Herborth, *Uses of "the West": Security and the Politics
of Order* (Cambridge University Press, 2016).

John W. Holmes, *The United States and Europe after the Cold War: A New Alliance*
(University of South Carolina Press, 1997).

Robert L. Hutchings, editor, *At the End of the American Century: America's Role in the
Post-Cold War World* (Johns Hopkins University Press, 1998).

G. John Ikenberry, *Liberal Leviathan: The Origins, Crisis, and Transformation of the
American World Order* (Princeton University Press, 2013).

G. John Ikenberry, *A World Safe for Democracy: Liberal Internationalism and the Crises
of Global Order* (Yale University Press, 2020).

International Institute for Security Studies (IISS), The Military Balance (2017), www
.iiss.org/publications/the-military-balance/the-military-balance-2017.

International Monetary Fund (IMF), World Economic Outlook Database (2020),
www.imf.org/.

Robert Jervis, Francis J. Gavin, Joshua Rovner, and Diane Labrosse, editors, *Chaos in
the Liberal Order: The Trump Presidency and International Politics in the Twenty-
First Century* (Columbia University Press, 2018).

Keith Johnson, "How Trump May Finally Kill the WTO," *Foreign Policy*, December 9,
2019, https://foreignpolicy.com/2019/12/09/trump-may-kill-wto-finally-appellate
-body-world-trade-organization.

John L. Gaddis, *Surprise, Security and the American Experience* (Harvard University Press, 2005).

Robert Kagan, *The Jungle Grows Back: America and Our Imperiled World* (New York: Knopf, 2018).

Robert Kagan, "The New German Question: What Happens When Europe Comes Apart?" *Foreign Affairs,* May/June 2019.

David C. Kang, *American Grand Strategy and East Asian Security in the Twenty-First Century* (Cambridge University Press, 2017).

Andrea Kendall-Taylor, Erica Frantz, and Joseph Wright, "The Digital Dictators," *Foreign Affairs*, March/April 2020.

George F. Kennan, "The Sources of Soviet Conduct," *Foreign Affairs*, July 1947.

Ian Kershaw, *The Global Age: Europe 1950–2017* (New York: Penguin, 2019).

Sulmaan Wasif Khan, *Haunted by Chaos: China's Grand Strategy from Mao Zedong to Xi Jinping* (Harvard University Press, 2018).

Parag Khanna, *Connectography: Mapping the Future of Global Civilization* (New York: Simon & Schuster, 2016).

Parag Khanna, *The Future Is Asian* (New York: Simon & Schuster, 2019).

Henry A. Kissinger and Lawrence H. Summers, "Renewing the Atlantic Partnership," Report of an Independent Task Force Sponsored by the Council on Foreign Relations, March 2004, www.cfr.org/report/renewing-atlantic-partnership.

Henry Kissinger, *On China* (New York: Penguin, 2011).

Henry Kissinger, *World Order* (New York: Penguin, 2014).

Matthew Kroenig, *The Return of Great Power Rivalry: Democracy versus Autocracy from the Ancient World to the U.S. and China* (Oxford University Press, 2020).

Charles A. Kupchan, *No One's World: The West, the Rising Rest, and the Coming Global Turn* (Oxford University Press, 2012).

Joshua Kurlantzick, *Charm Offensive: How China's Soft Power Is Transforming the World* (Yale University Press, 2008).

Philippe Le Corre, "China's Rise as a Geoeconomic Influencer: Four European Case Studies," Carnegie Endowment for International Peace, October 2018, https://carnegieendowment.org/2018/10/15/china-s-rise-as-geoeconomic-influencer-four-european-case-studies-pub-77462.

Derek Leebaert, *Grand Improvisation: America Confronts the British Superpower, 1945–1957* (New York: Farrar, Straus and Giroux, 2018).

Melyn Leffler, "Divide and Invest: Why the Marshall Plan Worked," *Foreign Affairs*, July/August 2018.

Robert Legvold, editor, *Russian Foreign Policy in the Twenty-First Century and the Shadow of the Past* (Columbia University Press, 2007).

Robert Legvold, *Return to Cold War* (New York: Polity, 2016).

Jennifer Lind and William Wohlforth, "The Future of the Liberal Order Is Conservative: A Strategy to Save the System," *Foreign Affairs*, March/April 2019.

Rebecca Lissner and Mira Rapp-Hooper, *An Open World: How America Can Win the Contest for Twenty-First-Century Order* (Yale University Press, 2020).

Ryan Lizza, "Leading from Behind," *New Yorker*, April 26, 2011, www.newyorker.com /news/news-desk/leading-from-behind.

Ryan Lizza, "Waiting for Obama," *Politico*, November 26, 2019, www.politico.com/ news/magazine/2019/11/26/barack-obama-2020-democrats-candidates-biden -073025.

Edward Luce, "The Retreat of Western Liberalism," *Atlantic Monthly*, June 2018.

Bruno Maçães, *Dawn of Eurasia: On the Trail of the New World Order* (Yale University Press, 2018).

Bruno Maçães, *Belt and Road: A Chinese World Order* (London: Hurst, 2019).

Angus Maddison, "Historical Statistics of the World Economy," The Groningen Growth and Development Centre, last accessed November 2, 2020, www.ggdc.net /maddison/Historical_Statistics/horizontal-file_03-2009.xls.

Hanns W. Maull, *The Rise and Decline of the Post-Cold War International Order* (Oxford University Press, 2018).

David McKean and Bart M. J. Szewczyk, "The World Still Needs a United West: How Europe and the United States Can Renew Their Alliance," *Foreign Affairs*, September 17, 2020.

John J. Mearsheimer, *The Great Delusion: Liberal Dreams and International Realities* (Yale University Press, 2019).

Kathleen J. McInnis, "Coalition Contributions to Countering the Islamic State," Congressional Research Service, August 24, 2016, https://fas.org/sgp/crs/natsec/ R44135.pdf.

The Moscow Project, "Trump's Russia Cover-Up by the Numbers—272 Contacts with Russia-Linked Operatives," April 30, 2019, https://themoscowproject.org/explain ers/trumps-russia-cover-up-by-the-numbers-70-contacts-with-russia-linked-opera tives.

Organisation for Economic Co-operation and Development (OECD), ODA Data (2020), https://data.oecd.org/oda/net-oda.htm.

Stewart M. Patrick, Atlantic Charter 2.0: A "Declaration of Principles for Freedom, Prosperity, and Peace," Council on Foreign Relations, February 16, 2019, www.cfr .org/blog/atlantic-charter-20-declaration-principles-freedom-prosperity-and-peace.

Sundar Pichai, "Partnering with Europe on Responsible AI: A Conversation with Sundar Pichai," *Bruegel*, January 20, 2020, www.bruegel.org/events/partnering -with-europe-on-responsible-ai-a-conversation-with-sundar-pichai-ceo-google-and -alphabet.

Eleonore Pauwels and Apratim Vidyarhirt, "How Our Unhealthy Cybersecurity Infrastructure Is Hurting Biotechnology," The Wilson Center, March 2016, www .wilsoncenter.org/publication/how-our-unhealthy-cybersecurity-infrastructure -hurting-biotechnology.

Alina Polyakova and Benjamin Haddad, "Europe Alone: What Comes After the Transatlantic Alliance," *Foreign Affairs*, July/August 2019.

Mira Rapp-Hooper, *Shields of the Republic: The Triumph and Peril of America's Alliances* (Harvard University Press, 2020).

David Remnick, "Going the Distance: On and Off the Road with Barack Obama," *New Yorker*, January 19, 2014, www.newyorker.com/magazine/2014/01/27/going -the-distance-david-remnick.

Ben Rhodes, "How Trump Designed His White House to Fail," *The Atlantic*, March 13, 2020, www.theatlantic.com/ideas/archive/2020/03/white-house-set-fail/60 7960.

Gilbert Rozman, *The Sino-Russian Challenge to the World Order: National Identities, Bilateral Relations, and East versus West in the 2010s* (Stanford University Press, 2014).

David Sanger, *The Perfect Weapon: War, Sabotage and Fear in the Cyber Age* (New York: Crown, 2018).

Martin Selmayr, "Europe, Multilateralism, and Great Power Competition," Brookings, March 6, 2019, www.brookings.edu/events/europe-multilateralism-and-great -power-competition.

Simon Serfaty, *The Vital Partnership: Power and Order, America and Europe Beyond Iraq* (Lanham, MD: Rowman & Littlefield, 2005).

Brendan Simms and Charlie Laderman, *Donald Trump: The Making of a World View* (New York: I.B. Tauris, 2017).

Benn Steil, *The Battle of Bretton Woods* (Princeton University Press, 1999).

Benn Steil, *Marshall Plan: Dawn of the Cold War* (New York: Simon & Schuster, 2018).

Angela Stent, *The Limits of Partnership: U.S.-Russian Relations in the Twenty-First Century* (Princeton University Press, 2015).

Angela Stent, *Putin's World: Russia Against the West and With the Rest* (New York: Basic Books, 2019).

Stockholm International Peace Research Institute (SIPRI), Military Expenditure Database (2020), www.sipri.org/databases/milex.

Bart M. J. Szewczyk, "Europe and the Liberal Order," *Survival* 61, no. 2 (April/May 2019), www.tandfonline.com/doi/abs/10.1080/00396338.2019.1589077.

Bart M. J. Szewczyk, "Europe's Strategies in Asia," German Marshall Fund (March 2019), www.gmfus.org/publications/transatlantic-security-cooperation-toward -2020.

Bart M. J. Szewczyk, "Operational Cooperation" in *The EU and NATO: The Essential Partners,* edited by Gustav Lindstrom and Thierry Tardy (Paris: EU Institute for Security Studies, 2019), www.iss.europa.eu/sites/default/files/EUISSFiles/EU%20 and%20NATO.pdf.

Bart M. J. Szewczyk, "Less Is More? The US at the UN," EUISS Brief, October 11, 2017, www.iss.europa.eu/content/less-more-us-un.

Adam Tooze, *Crashed: How a Decade of Financial Crises Change the World* (New York: Penguin Random House, 2018).

Dmitri Trenin, "The World Through Moscow's Eyes: A Classic Russian Perspective," Carnegie Moscow Center, March 3, 2020, https://carnegie.ru/2020/03/03/world -through-moscow-s-eyes-classic-russian-perspective-pub-81203.

Andrei P. Tsygankov, *Russia and the West from Alexander to Putin: Honor in International Relations* (Cambridge University Press, 2012).

U.S. Intelligence Community Assessment, "Assessing Russian Activities and Intentions in Recent US Elections," January 6, 2017, www.dni.gov/files/documents/ICA_2017_01.pdf.

Stephen M. Walt, *The Hell of Good Intentions* (New York: Farrar, Straus and Giroux, 2018).

Kenneth Weisbrode, *The Atlantic Century: Four Generations of Extraordinary Diplomats who Forged America's Vital Alliance with Europe* (New York: Da Capo, 2009).

Audrey Wilson, "Trump Gives Erdogan Green Light for Syria Incursion," *Foreign Policy*, October 7, 2019, https://foreignpolicy.com/2019/10/07/trump-erdogan-turkey-syria-pyd-kurds-incursion-baghdad-protests-security-north-korea-talks.

World Bank, GDP Data (2020), https://data.worldbank.org/.

Thomas Wright, *All Measures Short of War: The Contest for the 21st Century and the Future of American Power* (Yale University Press, 2017).

Amy Zegart, "America's Misbegotten Cyber Strategy," *The Atlantic,* February 2, 2019, www.theatlantic.com/ideas/archive/2019/02/trumps-national-cyber-strategy-overly-optimistic/581839.

Fareed Zakaria, *The Future of Freedom: Illiberal Democracy at Home and Abroad* (New York: W. W. Norton, 2007).

Fareed Zakaria, *The Post-American World: Release 2.0* (New York: W. W. Norton, 2011).

Index